SEXTING AND CYBERBULLYING
Defining the Line for Digitally Empowered Kids

Directed at policy makers, legislators, educators, parents, members of the legal community, and anyone concerned about current public policy responses to sexting and cyberbullying, this book examines the lines between unintentionally offensive online forms of expression such as jokes, sarcastic comments, and impulsive but non-consensual distribution of intimate images, and potential legal consequences. It offers an analysis of reactive versus preventive legal and educational responses to these issues using evidence-based research with digitally empowered kids.

Shaheen Shariff highlights the influence of popular and "rape culture" on the behavior of adolescents who establish sexual identities and social relationships through sexting. She argues that we need to move away from criminalizing children and toward engaging them in the policy-development process, and she observes that important lessons can be learned from constitutional and human rights frameworks. She also draws attention to the value of children's literature in helping the legal community better understand children's moral development. She highlights the need to understand assumptions about Digitally Empowered Kids (DE Kids) that can inform judicial decisions regarding children's culpability at various ages. She emphasizes the need to engage DE Kids and help them to define the line between jokes and harmful online postings that could land them in jail.

Shaheen Shariff is an Associate Professor at the Faculty of Education at McGill University, an Associate Member of the Law Faculty at McGill University, and an Affiliate Scholar at Stanford Law School's Center for Internet and Society. In 2012, she was awarded a Queen Elizabeth II Diamond Jubilee Medal for scholarship and service to Canada. Shariff is a frequent news media commentator, researcher, and policy advisor who has written extensively on the intersection of law and education, diversity, and pluralism. She has been an expert witness at the Canadian Standing Senate Committee on Human Rights and two House of Commons Committee hearings on legislative amendments involving cyberbullying. She is the author of *Confronting Cyberbullying: What Schools Need to Know to Control Misconduct and Avoid Legal Consequences* (2009) and *Cyberbullying: Issues and Solutions for the School, the Classroom, and the Home* (2008).

Sexting and Cyberbullying

DEFININ

EMPOW

Shaheen

McGill Univer

	DATE DUE		

CAM
UNIVE

CAMBRIDGE
UNIVERSITY PRESS

32 Avenue of the Americas, New York, NY 10013-2473, USA

Cambridge University Press is part of the University of Cambridge.

It furthers the University's mission by disseminating knowledge in the pursuit of education, learning, and research at the highest international levels of excellence.

www.cambridge.org
Information on this title: www.cambridge.org/9781107625174

© Shaheen Shariff 2015

First published 2015

Printed in the United States of America

A catalog record for this publication is available from the British Library.

Library of Congress Cataloging in Publication Data
Shariff, Shaheen.
Sexting and cyberbullying : defining the line for digitally empowered kids / Shaheen Shariff, McGill University.
    pages   cm
ISBN 978-1-107-01991-1 (Hardback) – ISBN 978-1-107-62517-4 (Paperback)
1. Sexting. 2. Cyberbullying. 3. Internet–Safety measures 4. Parent and teenager. I. Title.
HQ27.S5193 2015
302.34'302854678–dc23   2014026553

ISBN 978-1-107-01991-1 Hardback
ISBN 978-1-107-62517-4 Paperback

Cambridge University Press has no responsibility for the persistence or accuracy of URLs for external or third-party Internet websites referred to in this publication and does not guarantee that any content on such websites is, or will remain, accurate or appropriate.

I dedicate this book to my Define the Line *family at McGill University.*

Through your commitment, each of you models and defines the lines of leadership for future generations.

Mama Bear

Contents

Preface

This book was originally contracted to be the second edition of my earlier book with Cambridge University Press, *Confronting Cyberbullying: What Schools Need to Know to Control Misconduct and Avoid Legal Consequences*, published in 2009. It was certainly time for an update, given the continued media and public policy focus on cyberbullying. However, try as I might, I could not update the book because even though some of the issues remain the same, the modes of expression and digital media used to carry them out have evolved rapidly. That is not to say that the legal and educational dilemmas and challenges I addressed in *Confronting Cyberbullying* are not important, or that they have all been successfully resolved. In fact, the reactive responses I argued against in earlier publications continue, emerging as harsher and often misapplied laws to criminalize children's online behavior. This is a disturbing trend because in adopting reactive responses, we overlook young people's motivations and moral development, or the adult modeling and societal influences that bring out such behavior.

The face of what we broadly refer to as "cyberbullying" has also taken on a more sexually charged and insidious nature. Many news media reports and policy initiatives appear to confuse the actions of pedophiles and online child sexual predators with cyberbullying. Child pornography laws in the United States and Canada are being applied to arrest, charge, and jail adolescents who engage in sexting. However, as the research disclosed in this book illustrates, these kinds of behaviors demonstrated by adolescents are not the same thing as "child pornography." Although some forms of sexting among youth are seriously demeaning and offensive, and need to be prevented, my research finds that most young people are testing social boundaries online as their hormones rage and they attempt to establish social relationships. As one of my doctoral students, Ashley DeMartini, notes, many of these activities of sexual exploration have "moved from the back of a car [as in kissing in the back seat at a drive-in], to playing itself out over social media." The public policy spotlight has been on kids, as though they are the only ones engaging in online forms of harassment, teasing, and demeaning expressions. We should also be looking at what kinds of adult role models children have in popular culture, and the thriving rape culture that is increasingly perpetuated online among adults. Once again, I am concerned that we scapegoat kids for adult faults. The underpinnings of public policy are often grounded in assumptions that "kids are bad." But the fact of the matter is that we need to look at ourselves, and at the hostile, misogynist, homophobic, and racist social norms we model for our children. What can we possibly expect from future generations when they are growing up immersed in such a society? They see adult violence on the news and in movies; insulting and offensive put-downs and power plays on sitcoms, in stand-up comedy, and on reality shows; and they hear misogynist and power-driven words in music lyrics. Therefore, it is no wonder young people imitate the norms of modern society. In this book, I highlight examples and scholarship relating to some of these societal norms and their influences on children while also examining some studies on children's moral development.

In Chapter 3, I challenge the wisdom of criminalizing children using laws that are meant to protect them. I argue that we should spend more time finding and putting away pedophiles and online groups of "cappers" who are the real threat to children's safety. More so, umbrella terms, such as "cyberbullying," have resulted in shifting the blame away from the adult realm of rape culture to the turbulent, emotionally and impulsively driven attempts of young people trying to establish their social and sexual identities among peers. At their age, reputation and acceptance in a peer group are everything.

Scholars have always grappled with and debated the true definition of "cyberbullying." This is especially so because as soon as we understand one type of behavior, say, bullying on social media, there are a host of other online applications like Snapchat and Ask.fm that bring out other challenging forms of communication. I realized several years ago that trying to fit young people's online behaviors into an umbrella description, especially when they involve social exclusion, taunting, threats and harassments, and demeaning messages designed to humiliate peers or adults, is futile. Therefore I have also highlighted a range of legal responses that are grounded in constitutional, human rights, and tort law considerations that provide a better fit for these forms of expression, and that also contain an educational message.

I conclude the book with reference to ways in which children's literature can not only help us better understand how judges might apply the law in private civil actions involving defamation, but also how children's literature would be invaluable in helping children and teens define the lines between joking and teasing, especially when it concerns an act so harmful that it could result in legal or criminal liability. Children's literature would also help youths to develop empathy and their "moral underbellies" as they grapple with the challenges of growing up immersed in digital media. I have also emphasized the power of generations working together using social media that can be engaged to enhance socially responsible digital citizenship that is congruent with the substantive principles of constitutional and human rights frameworks.

Without being too legalist, I hope this book will be of interest to anyone who wants to better understand the complexities and nuances of children's online communication, and responses that show the greatest promise of balancing free expression and free press, safety, supervision, protection, and regulation in our digital society, while ensuring we avoid censorship, harsh punishment, and overregulation. The answers are clear – we simply need to recognize them. We need to critically question our own assumptions and those of adults who make decisions on how children's behavior ought to be addressed. This includes taking into consideration the norms, assumptions, and biases that might inform the police, prosecutors, and the judiciary – that analysis will follow in a second edition of this book. For now, I have focused on the need, once again, to concentrate our efforts on supporting, protecting, and educating children, instead of blaming and incarcerating them. With the onslaught of new laws and litigation directed at controlling children's online expression, such a focus will be essential if we want to develop future leaders, not criminals.

Acknowledgments

I would like to thank first and foremost my research assistants, Alyssa Wiseman, Ashley DeMartini, and Arzina Zaver, who have worked tirelessly to bring this book to fruition. Their teamwork, enthusiasm, and skill in attending to all the final details of referencing, formatting, and editing were exemplary, especially because they were in different parts of the world: Alyssa in Tokyo, Ashley in Winnipeg, and Arzina in Montreal. These researchers are part of my core Define the Line (DTL) team and have provided a significant amount of the research for this book, and also for my website. Alyssa, in particular, contributed to the legal research and analysis; Ashley brought her critical pedagogy and feminist perspectives to Chapter 2; Arzina, an efficient eye for detail; and all three brought superior and coordinated editing skills.

I would also like to thank the other members of my DTL team who contributed to this book directly or indirectly. In particular, I would like to thank Dr. Nelofar Sheikh who tackled the data coding, qualitative and quantitative analysis, and graphing using NVivo software. Dr. Sheikh is a master of data gathering, organization, and analysis, and a strong asset to DTL. Azrah Talib is a resourceful undergraduate student who is an exceptional researcher online. Azrah keeps us informed of media articles, cases and incidents of sexting and cyberbullying, emerging laws, policies, and journal articles on a daily basis. Similarly, our DTL website and social media page are managed by law student Laura Crestohl, who has also contributed to developing the tables of legal responses appended to this book. Nima Naimi, our DTL marketing manager, contributed to the legal research in Chapter 3; and Olivia Chow, who recently began to volunteer for our team, also deserves thanks for helping us retrieve court records for some of the criminal cases in the book. Yanick Touchette conducted research on provincial legislation discussed in the book.

The research reported in this book would not have been possible without consistent funding support from the Social Sciences and Humanities Research Council of Canada (SSHRC), which has funded my research for the last ten years, most recently with a five-year Insight Grant that will continue to support this work until 2017. The research was also funded in part by Facebook. In particular, I wish to thank Dave Steer and Meg Sinclair of Facebook and Elliott Schragg for awarding me with the inaugural Facebook Digital Citizenship Award.

I also wish to acknowledge the contributions of my McGill University colleagues and co-applicants under the SSHRC grant, especially Professor Shauna Van Praagh, whom I quote several times in this book because she brings such wisdom to her legal analysis as it applies to children; Professor Victoria Talwar, who has shared her expertise on children and their moral development; and Professor Jamshid Beheshti, who shared his wisdom on information systems organization to inform our compendium of legal responses. I also wish to acknowledge the benefits of being part of PREVNet, a Canadian National Center for Excellence organization that brings together researchers from multidisciplinary backgrounds. In that regard, I also wish to thank Professor Shelley Hymel of the University of British Columbia, who has shared her research on moral "disengagement" and Dean Faye Mishna of the University of Toronto's Faculty of Social Work.

On the legal aspects of the issues discussed in this book, I am forever grateful for the mentorship and shared knowledge of Professor A. Wayne MacKay of Dalhousie University, Professors Jane Bailey and Valerie Steeves of University of Ottawa Law School, and Canadian Senators Mobina Jaffer and Salma Attaulahjan for their support of our endeavors to contribute to the public policy debate, particularly to inform the legislative process as Ottawa deliberates legal responses.

Thank you also to John Berger, senior editor at Cambridge University Press, for his patience in waiting an extra year for this manuscript, and for his consistent support and encouragement of my work throughout.

Last but not least, I also want to thank past members of the DTL team, who – although they have moved on to fulfill their careers – made strong contributions to advancement of the research that informs this book. Stewart Lazarus was instrumental in recruiting a large number of participants for the focus groups in the United States and Canada. To Shazia Abji, Glenn Gear, Evan Dexter, Courtney Retter, Ann Pierkewski, Amelie Lemieux, Jay Lister, Jamie Sportun, Nika Naimi, and all the law and education students who have worked with me over the last few years, too numerous to name, to advance knowledge in this important education and public policy area, I thank you all for your dedicated commitment to improving our understanding of this important area of public policy.

Shaheen Shariff, Ph.D.
Associate Professor, McGill University

CHAPTER ONE

Confronting Cyberbullying:
Are We Any Wiser?

The notion of being "sage – good, wise, careful, in line with rules and expectations – is reflected in the picture of the reasonable person in the private law of civil wrongs. "Fun" is necessarily limited by "sagesse": self-fulfillment is necessarily shaped by the obligation not to hurt others. As children explore themselves and their surroundings, gradually becoming aware of others in their lives, they begin the move beyond the realm of "carefree" and into that of "caring." The obligation to care for others is slowly added throughout childhood to one's sense of self.

(Van Praagh, 2007, p.63)

INTRODUCTION

The opening quote by my colleague Shauna Van Praagh (2007) contains in a few sentences the essence of issues I grapple with in this book. It is about understanding the choices children make in being "good, wise, careful, in line with rules and expectations" (p.63). It is about how activities and expressions that children perceive as "fun" are often limited by "sagesse" – as defined by society's rules. And, it is about how children gain the self-fulfillment and awareness of others in their lives so as to move from being "carefree" to "caring." Furthermore, it considers how the obligation to care for others becomes integrated into children's agency and their own sense of self at various stages of moral development and in some cases, moral "disengagement."

This book is also about the "sagesse" (or lack thereof) applied by adults as children move from being carefree to becoming responsible citizens of society. How do we balance the laws and rules, not only in the private law of civil

I acknowledge the research, knowledge contributions and editing support of McGill University doctoral students, Ashley DeMartini and Arzina Zaver, and the legal research assistance, legal referencing, and analysis that has been contributed throughout this book by McGill Law and MBA candidate, Alyssa Wiseman.

wrongs as in Van Praagh's quote, but also under a range of legal frameworks? As I begin writing this book, I consider why we have not been successful in reducing online abuses that the Supreme Court of Canada (SCC) recently described as a "toxic phenomenon" (*A.B. [Litigation Guardian of] v. Bragg Communications, Inc.*, 2012). Although digital and social media have advanced by leaps and bounds, and despite the large body of research and numerous "anti-bullying experts" around the globe, we do not seem to have made significant progress in reducing the phenomenon we have come to define over the last decade as "cyberbullying."

I question the wisdom of applying criminal law (particularly child pornography laws) to charge young people when the original intent of those laws is to protect children. I draw attention to legal frameworks that are less often invoked, but ought to be, like constitutional and civil protections and international human rights conventions. The principles underlying these legal statutes recognize children's vulnerability to adult-made rules in society, and to the behavior of adults who never made the transition to become caring and who exploit and hurt children. I draw attention to the lack of public legal literacy of these constitutional and human rights protections, which could be invoked to protect the privacy and vulnerability of children. I also address the challenges that judges confront in a digital age, as they are bound by age-old doctrines like the "careful and prudent parent" and "reasonable person" tests under the private law of torts. As societal norms shift with increased globalization and online communication, making a judgment as to what is a "reasonable person" has become increasingly difficult. Moreover, peer pressure, impulsivity, and a sense of perceived anonymity in the virtual realm has complicated the circumstances under which children make the choices to be "good, wise, careful, in line with rules and expectations" (Van Praagh 2007, p. 63).

In *Confronting Cyberbullying* (Shariff, 2009), I compared the online environment and disappearing legal boundaries to William Golding's (1954) seminal work of fiction, *Lord of the Flies*, where the absence of adult supervision, laws, and rules resulted in bullying, anarchy, and breakdown of social norms among a group of children marooned on a deserted island. In making that analogy, I observed that Golding wanted us to realize certain ironies about humans as social beings. Without conventional laws, rules, or supervision, the children in *Lord of the Flies* reverted to subliminal and deep-rooted antisocial messages of hate, prejudice, and scapegoating, which they could only have seen or heard modeled by adults in their everyday lives. The children singled out and isolated peers who deviated from the norm, resulting in the tragic death of an overweight and nearly blind boy, Piggy, who did not fit in with his peers. Golding was talking about survival of the fittest. Readers were left to decide whether the breakdown of social norms was due to the lack of supervision and enforced rules, or whether in fact, as territorial beings, the fittest survived.

WHO IS THE FITTEST ONLINE?

In applying this analogy to the online world, we might ask who are the fittest members of society in an online world where laws and rules are difficult to define? Is it "cappers"[1] and "trolls"[2] who perpetrate specific types of online sexual violence and cyberbullying? Or, could the fittest members be individuals with the vision to secure the benefits of a global online world to make it a better place? Could the fittest be among those who lead the way to defining the lines between socially responsible digital citizenship and harm that cannot be considered legally, ethically, or socially acceptable?

It is difficult to categorize the participants of a digital world where norms of social communication have crept toward increased tolerance for sexism, misogyny, and homophobia and where popular culture, especially online marketing, comedy, and reality shows place physical appearance, social conformity, objectification of women, sarcasm, and demeaning humor on the highest pedestals of socially acceptable behavior. We might also ask whether this shift in acceptable norms of communication originates and resides only among young people growing up immersed in digital media. Or, is it simply a virtual extension of the antisocial physical world that adults have created? Children confront difficult challenges at both ends. They try to prove their strength in a digital and online social network where even friends can demean them publicly and excuse themselves with "jk" (just kidding) or "lol" (laugh out loud). When under peer pressure, they might impulsively react or post comments and photographs in response to things they might have ignored in different circumstances. Such reactions could get them into serious trouble with the law as, increasingly, law enforcement and governments grapple to find and develop appropriate laws and legal frameworks to deal with the range of possible online offenses.

SEEKING SUITABLE DEFINITIONS FOR DIGITAL GENERATIONS

Prensky (2001) defined young people who are growing up immersed in digital media as "digital natives." Although this term was commonly applied and taken up in academic and popular discussions over the past decade (e.g. Tapscott, 1998; 2009), it has also become highly polemic. So much so, that

---

[1] Cappers are pedophiles who coerce young people to take and share intimate and sexual photographs of themselves through webcams and videos. Morris, K. (November 13, 2012). The "Daily Capper" exposes alleged culprit in Amanda Todd Suicide. *The Daily Dot*. Retrieved from www.dailydot.com/news/daily-capper-amanda-todd-kody-viper/

[2] Trolls are a subculture of Internet users who wreak havoc on social media sites and online communities, posting offensive, violent, and cruel messages to invoke an emotional reaction from their targets. Schwartz, M. (August 3, 2008). The Trolls Among Us. *The New York Times*. Retrieved from www.nytimes.com/2008/08/03/magazine/03trolls-t.html?pagewanted=all

some academic conferences have asked people to remove the term from their papers to be considered for submission while other conferences continue to debate its definition as a category of new digital learners (Thomas, 2011). In the collected essays of *Deconstructing Digital Natives: Young People, Technology, and the New Literacies*, Thomas (2011) identifies three major themes that encapsulate existing discourses around the term, which include: 1) young people born after 1980 are homogenous; 2) they learn differently from previous generations; and 3) they require new ways of teaching and learning. My decision to move away from this term stems primarily from the first tenet; that is, the fact that "digital natives" tends to essentialize differences and similarities between generations (Buckingham, 2011). Rather than reinforce the divides between generations, I move in the direction of Thomas' suggestion; that is, research "should engage with the diversity rather than the conformity suggested by young peoples' use of digital technologies" (p. 9). Moreover, three major themes in the discourse that Thomas (2011) identifies are also reflected in news media reports, parent and teacher advocacy for harsher laws around cyberbullying, and the rhetoric used by politicians that single out these generations as troublesome in the ways that they use digital and social media. Popular narratives around this concept place digital technologies as something that can emancipate and empower young people to become anything they want to be. In certain cases this may be so, but these qualities of digital technologies are often exaggerated, tending to overlook the aspect of technological continuity between generations (Buckingham, 2011). One need only think about how many people over the age of fifty use and integrate digital technology every day: grandparents sending emails, texting, and Skyping; aging baby boomers buying the latest tablets or smart phones; or long-established small businesses integrating digital systems to shift to online appointment bookings to accommodate their clientele. All of this is to say there are differences and similarities among and between the generations, many of which correspond to socioeconomic status and the question of access.

Bennett and Maton (2011) discuss how even within affluent societies there are gaps in digital proficiency between young people. Moreover, the authors argue that most claims around digital natives lack strong empirical evidence. The authors cite a series of studies that offer evidence of the variation of digital proficiency and usage among young people. One such study examined young people's usage of digital technologies. The results revealed that a greater proportion of respondents used the technology for communication and consumption of information instead of creative or gaming-related activities. Bennett and Maton surmise that such empirical-based research reveals that a range of access, use, and skills exists even within the supposed generation of digital natives. To Prensky's credit, his terms ignited a decade-long debate around the merits and limitations of such a concept. Recently, Prensky (2011) wrote that the distinction between "digital natives" and "digital immigrants," those born before the advent of digital technology, was meant as metaphoric – it gave a "shorthand name to a phenomenon" that previously remained unclassified (p. 15).

My purpose in providing a brief snapshot of these current discussions is not to weigh in on either side, but rather, to position my work to move beyond these binary-like debates. The research and analysis contained in these chapters provides insights into the complex and nuanced relationships young people have with digital technologies and the legal challenges and dilemmas these relationships present for policy makers. Over the past decade, technologies have emerged that offer new ways to connect and express oneself. In spite of these opportunities, there remains a gap in societal understandings around legal frameworks, the application of law, and its intersections with youth culture in the twenty-first century. Disturbing trends in law have emerged that place these intersections in the adult realm and within the contexts of online harassment and rape culture. I argue that these adult crimes are much more complicated to assess when they involve youth. Therefore, they should not be addressed through blanket legal responses that tackle them under the umbrella of cyberbullying. As I argue in this book, the roots of these various forms of cyberbullying are deeply buried in systemic and hegemonic forms of discrimination, which are currently playing out through sexist and homophobic online expressions.

"GENERATION EMPOWERED" OR "GENERATION SCREWED"?

When we look to how youths are defining themselves, we also observe some pessimistic views about their futures. This is reflected in a cruder self-description that has recently been adopted by young people to depict their circumstances in life as a "Generation Screwed" (Seidman, 2014; Mansbridge, 2014). This self-proclaimed and self-defeating title speaks to the challenges youth confront in a world where economic and natural resources are depleting, the environment and climate are being destroyed, and traditional forms of employment and career options are reduced and uncertain. Moreover, educational systems catering to these digital generations are slow to keep up with technologies. Elementary and postsecondary curricula are often irrelevant and out of touch with young people's lived realities (Lankshear & Knobel, 2006; Gee 2004). "Digital technologies collapse social contexts," states boyd (2009, para. 8), which in turn, requires schools and teachers to consider how their roles extend beyond the institution's walls to support students in their online lives. boyd (2014) argues that overzealous applications of paternalism and protectionism impede young peoples' abilities to develop as thoughtful and knowledgeable citizens able to make informed decisions about how they conduct their lives. In addition, legal penalties that are being applied to "control" online communication among these youth reside in ancient laws – and the new laws are being applied without attention to unprecedented social and learning challenges. When we apply antiquated laws to youth behaviors that do not fit the offense, and create new laws that ignore the context in which youth are growing up, it could indeed be concluded crudely that the younger generation is a "generation screwed."

DIGITALLY EMPOWERED KIDS, YOUNG ADULTS, AND GENERATIONS

If we return to Golding's survival of the fittest analogy, it is partly true that digital expertise among all generations can better position and "empower" them to succeed in a future of evolving technologies. For youth, this may require several career changes and creative entrepreneurship, which they are in a stronger position to take advantage of than older generations who may be more generally established in traditional careers and ways of communicating. With this in mind, I have decided to give every generation a positive term of reference. To facilitate the discussion around research and specific issues that relate to youth and uses of digital and social media, I use the term Digitally Empowered Kids (DE Kids). When I specifically refer to young adults such as college and university students, I call them Digitally Empowered Young Adults (DE Young Adults). And when I discuss adults and youth as they engage in and are immersed in online forms of communication, I collectively refer to everyone as Digitally Empowered Generations (DE Generations).

I certainly acknowledge these descriptive terms might fall into the trap of overemphasizing the benefits of digital and social media. That being said, a positive connotation that allows for the benefit of doubt is especially important when discussing difficult topics like cyberbullying. There has been so much negative discourse around young people using this term, that it seems to me cyberbullying has become synonymous with kids and youth. In fact, so much so, that as I illustrate in upcoming chapters, sexually offensive online forms of communication and extortion by adults are all lumped together by news media, researchers, and politicians as cyberbullying. I want to emphasize the danger of this because it is this stereotype of children that fuels reactive measures to control, punish, and criminalize them. And I argue in this book that we must first look at adult forms of online and offline communication, in which are rooted the most intolerant forms of discrimination such as sexism and misogyny, homophobia, racism, ableism[3], and other forms of xenophobia. Consequently, I would argue that it is not younger generations who are a "generation screwed" but the boomer generations who are, to put it crudely, more "screwed" up. I discuss scholarly discourses that show how it is the older generations that influence kids through models in popular culture and rape culture, which is now increasingly prevalent in colleges and universities and filtering down to school children in the form of sexting. Interestingly, many kids are all too aware of the conflicting messages they receive from adults from early childhood. Consider the following anonymous quote posted on a young adult's Facebook page:

Me behave? Seriously? As a child, I saw Tarzan almost naked, Cinderella arrived home after midnight, Pinocchio told lies, Aladdin was a thief, Batman drove over 200 miles an hour and Snow White lived in a house with 7 men...The fault is not mine!

---

[3] Ableism refers to the discrimination of people with disabilities.

In this sense, one could argue that Prensky's (2001) "digital natives" are in fact "digital immigrants" because they are forced to live in a world that still runs under adult rules. As noted in the introduction, these rules may not reflect the realities of youth as they move from being carefree to responsible and caring. And DE Kids' notions of fun, as I establish in Chapter 2, are very different from fun in the minds of most adults who make and apply the rules. When DE Kids as a matter of course integrate their virtual and physical worlds without clearly differentiated boundaries, such as public or private, it is adults who raise the loudest objections, preferring to ban technologies from classrooms and lobby governments to clamp down on children's behaviors. Thus, it is important for my concept of digital empowerment to create a space for generative thinking – one that includes, rather than excludes, possibilities for each generation – children, teens, adults, and even grandparents.

The DE Kids and DE Young Adults definitions help us begin the conversation about youth from a positive and optimistic place. It gives youth the benefit of the doubt they deserve and recognizes their digital abilities and potential to succeed in a technologically driven world. It also reflects my position throughout the book that it is adult generations who created, sustain, and perpetuate a society and popular culture where misogyny, sexism, homophobia, racism, and other forms of discrimination thrive. Yet when youth imitate and reflect those attitudes and behaviors through digital and social media, we attempt to apply outdated or irrelevant sections of the law to control and punish those behaviors. Moreover, we have begun to develop new laws specifically to criminalize them.

Hence, I argue about the importance of gaining a better understanding of how DE Kids and DE Young Adults think about their engagement and social relationships on- and offline; what motivates them; how their social norms continue to evolve; and how we as adults can guide and facilitate (not control) their ethical judgments about where to define the lines with respect to online expression. I propose that if we decide to use existing legal frameworks and create new laws to address it, we need to ensure we understand the social contexts and levels of circumstances in which such communications occur.

In later chapters, I unpack the legal issues and examine several legal frameworks to address their relevancy and applicability to the types of offenses committed by some youth and the motivations behind them. I believe upcoming generations have enormous potential and the capacity to overcome the challenges the boomer generation leaves them. This is not to suggest that all adults are unsupportive of youth or that some adults are not equally proficient in using digital media. I strongly believe, however, that in general, DE Kids and DE Young Adults could use more collaborative support, guidance, and benefit of the doubt to enhance their leadership and promote more socially responsible on- and offline citizenship. Elsewhere (Shariff, 2008–2009), I have explained why this is especially true of their learning experiences in schools. Digital spaces give them the depth of perspective and creative lenses to spearhead boundless opportunities for connected, collaborative, and peaceful societies in the future. What they need most of all is guidance to realize the impact of their sometimes impulsive online postings. They also need legal literacy to recognize when such postings might result in legal liability and/or criminal convictions, landing them in jail.

In 2009, I initiated a discussion around the growing public policy vacuum and the rapid blurring of legal boundaries that exacerbate the difficulties of navigating free expression, safety, privacy, supervision, and regulation of negative and offensive online communication. Although there is significantly more public awareness about cyberbullying and online sexual abuse, the policy gaps remain. While new legislation has been introduced across North America, and numerous programs, websites, and publications attempt to guide parents and educators, young people still do not receive the help and support they need to stand up to perpetrators of cyberbullying.

Despite a robust body of research largely conducted and reported from behavioral psychology, criminology, and developmental perspectives on relational-aggression (Mishna, 2004; Werner & Crick, 2004; Beran & Wade, 2011; Cassidy, Faucher & Jackson, 2013), we are no further ahead in finding ways to guide, redirect, and support the increased number of teen suicides that are in some way connected to cyberbullying (Blanchard, 2014; Sonawane, 2014; Hinduja & Patchin, 2010). News media reports about teen suicides have become almost regular occurrences, especially in cases where young women such as Amanda Todd (Grenoble, 2012) and Jane Doe[4] (Huffington Post, April 9, 2013) have either been raped or coerced into sharing intimate photographs, which are then distributed online.

"CYBERBULLYING," CHILD PORNOGRAPHY, OR "FLIRTY FUN"?

Though we now have an improved understanding of the complexities and nuances involved in what has become widely recognized over the last decade as cyberbullying, clear definitions of this phenomenon continue to elude us, and the public policy dilemma persists. The word "bullying" has taken on such wide application, that despite hundreds of attempts by scholars to describe and define it, overuse has resulted in burnout and resistance to the word, especially in schools. Despite the proliferation of well-intentioned non-profit organizations, government agencies, and anti-bullying "consultants" and "experts" who provide schools with "toolkits" and "rubrics," a range of behaviors categorized as bullying continues. As explained in my earlier books (Shariff, 2008–2009), there is always a power imbalance that supports harassment, ostracism, threats, and embarrassment of targeted individuals.

---

[4] While I feel that the term "Jane Doe" is impersonal, I am restricted to its use due to a publication ban on this particular high profile child pornogaphy case. Jane Doe's father does not agree with the publication ban on her identity because he feels it protects the perpetrators and not his daughter. The interview can be found at: www.cbc.ca/day6/blog/2014/10/03/his-daughters-name-secre/; http://www.cbc.ca/day6/popupaudio.html?clipIds=2541120.

Though I have used the word "cyberbullying" in the title of this book to reach audiences with a vested interest in the issues raised here, I plan to reduce my use of the word bullying because generic use places it in a separate category from its discriminatory, misogynist, xenophobic, and intolerant roots. Instead, I refer to traditional, offline bullying as abuse, harassment, threats, physical beatings, physical or sexual assault, rape, and so on, indicating the legal frameworks under which they might be prosecuted and litigated.

Readers might wonder why for example, I substitute the word "rape" for an act of what the media might describe as "bullying." Unfortunately, rape prominently features in some teen sexual assaults that perpetrators film and distribute non-consensually. These violent acts have also been a common theme in a large number of the teen suicide cases described by the news media under the general umbrella term of cyberbullying.[5] This highlights the need to call an act what it is. In most cases, the rapists receive less attention than perpetrators who did not participate physically, but instead filmed and posted the attack online. The act of rape is illegal in most jurisdictions.[6] It is a violent sexual and physical assault. It is often used against women and children as a weapon of war. While there is definitely a power imbalance involved in acts of rape, as there is in bullying, the news media spotlight on the video-recorded distribution of this act as cyberbullying, directs the focus away from the extreme physical violation and emotional harm experienced by the victim. This is not to downplay the added humiliation experienced by the victim when she is re-victimized through the repeated online viewing of her rape. My point is that describing the videoing and distribution of images of rape as cyberbullying trivializes the act of rape. Although the taunting and public humiliation that follow such postings involves a power imbalance between perpetrators and victims, all the publicity around the online postings misdirects the public into thinking of those who post such videos as the primary perpetrators. While I do not argue that they too should not face consequences for their thoughtless actions, I want to emphasize the actual rapists as initiators of the crime and that they should also be the focus of public anger. Consequently, the definitions we give to people's actions can sometimes divert the focus from where it should be.

---

[5] For example, the video distribution of the rape of Jane Doe in Nova Scotia resulted in the Canadian government introducing Bill-13 known as the anti-cyberbullying law; the Steubenville rape case in the United States.; Amanda Todd's extortion by pedophilic "cappers." Morris, K. (November 13, 2012). The "Daily Capper" exposes alleged culprit in Amanda Todd Suicide. *The Daily Dot.* Retrieved from www.dailydot.com/news/daily-capper-amanda-todd-kody-viper/; Drimonis, T. (March 6, 2014). Steubenville Rape. *The Huffington Post Canada.* Retrieved from www.huffingtonpost.ca/news/steubenville-rape/

[6] As per section 271 of the *Criminal Code,* "everyone who commits a sexual assault is guilty of an indictable offense and is liable to imprisonment." In the United States, there is no national law for sexual assault in the United States – instead, each state has its own laws (e.g., Section 130 of the New York Penal Code and Section 261 of the California Penal Code both define "rape" or "sexual assault" and provide for the penalties for those who commit these offenses).

One of the reasons that I believe we have not made much progress in understanding cyberbullying is because the term is overbroad. I mentioned it has almost become synonymous with the sum of all online behaviors of children and youth. Even when adult pedophiles engage in it, as I will show later in my discussion of specific legal cases, the news media always manages to connect that behavior to the negative online behaviors of kids. In this book I want to emphasize repeatedly, at the risk of redundancy, that we cannot and must not mistake kids' online activities, especially when they include sexual content, for insidious and abusive forms of pedophilia and extortion driven by adults. Child pornography is not the same thing as kids experimenting with sexual and social relationships in their blended on- and offline worlds. Unfortunately, the word cyberbullying has become so generic that I have no choice but to use it in descriptions of the scholarly research, my own research, and the case law that refers to it. However, I am beginning to move away from its overuse in this book to define the online activities within the context of the legal rules and frameworks under which they are being considered. Thus, I call "sexual harassment" what it is; spreading of rumors, demeaning and malicious comments and gossip "libel, defamation or slander" as the case may be; and "criminal threats" what they are. The challenge for law enforcement, as I discuss in Chapter 3, is how to define children's sexting and "flirty fun" online activities when they are less serious than the distribution of images and videos that depict rape.

There is clearly a range of kids' online sexual communications – and most of them, with the exception of deliberate distribution of films depicting rape, can be categorized more accurately as "flirty fun." More often than not, the term cyberbullying is actually rooted in serious and offensive forms of sexist, misogynist, and/or homophobic harassment. These offensive forms include, but are not limited to the posting and distribution of physical sexual assaults and rapes as well as non-consensual online dissemination of intimate images by a trusted partner or friend. Moreover, these behaviors have also been linked in the media to tragic suicides of mostly female victims who felt trapped by the shame of their re-victimization while their sexual assaults were distributed publicly. In light of these unsettling trends, a new set of terms has also emerged to describe some online actions, including the term "selfie," which refers to a digital image taken of oneself and posted online. Perpetrator names such as "cappers" refer to those who extort and collaborate to distribute sexually offensive online material whereas "trolls" refer to those who are known to continue their online abuse of individuals even after they have committed suicide (Shariff, Wiseman & Crestohl, 2013).

The bulk of research in the field continues to place a significant amount of attention on statistics about relational-aggression and youth behavior, ignoring the discriminatory roots and attitudes that inform such behavior (Olweus, 2012; Cassidy, Faucher & Jackson, 2013; Sugarman & Willoughby, 2013). Although relational-aggression and behavioral studies are important in providing a foundational understanding of *how* and *how often* DE Kids and DE Young Adults engage in offensive, aggressive, and antisocial behaviors, there continues to be a widely overlooked knowledge gap in this field of multidisciplinary study. There is minimal attention in the bullying literature to broader societal influences, such as violence in popular culture, rape culture, misogyny, homophobia, and the gendered dynamics of power, albeit with some exceptions (Varjas, Meyers, Kiperma & Howard, 2013; MacKay, 2013; Bailey & Steeves, 2013; Wade & Beran, 2011; Ybarra *et al.*, 2008; Li, 2006; 2007). Yet, there is even less written on the evolving social norms among DE Kids and DE Young Adults and how news media frames and sensationalizes their reporting on these norms (Edwards 2005; Lankshear & Knobel, 2006). I have tried to somewhat fill this knowledge gap by including the literature in Chapter 2.

QUESTIONS ON THE ROLE OF LAW

These issues also bring to the forefront numerous emerging and unanswered questions about the role of law in regulating offensive online behavior. For example, it is important to consider the extent to which we need to develop new laws that come with harsher penalties for the range of online forms of communication that come under the broad umbrella of cyberbullying. A range of questions raised in this book address the role of law in deterring offensive online communication and ask whether the law alone can reduce or stop it. Throughout this book, readers will consider challenging questions that include the following:

- What existing legal frameworks might apply to the law and how fragile are the legal expectations given the context, complexities, and nuances of cyberbullying?
- How well are the social online norms and perspectives of young people understood by adults; particularly, prosecutors, judges, law enforcement, teachers, and school principals?
- Why are there more calls for legislation to control young people's online communication when adults are often the worst role models of abuse and online violence?
- What role does the news media play in enhanced pressure on governments to implement or amend legislation to contain cyberbullying?
- What impact will legislation have on the fundamental rights of children and teenagers? For example, how will them having a criminal record – if charged under new cyberbullying laws –impact their future acceptance to college and ultimately their earning capacity?
- Do we as a society know enough about the nuances of cyberbullying and are we reacting too soon?

Although a significant amount of research has been conducted globally on bullying over the last decade, North American researchers are just beginning to gain insight into how digital generations perceive and understand the difference between digital and face-to-face social interaction; public versus private spaces; and jokes versus criminal forms of expression. If we seek to clarify legal boundaries we need to ensure that cohesive and coordinated efforts are made to update *all* legal frameworks that apply, rather than making piecemeal amendments to specific legislation that is already applicable under certain circumstances. This raises additional questions mainly:

- To what extent are young North Americans legally literate? Do they have any concept of the point at which their joking and online pranks can be considered illegal or the online spaces wherein private conversations among friends can become public? Will criminal sanctions help them understand these boundaries?
- How can we best address the sexually based online forms of cyberbullying?
- Are law enforcement officers, lawyers, and judges sufficiently informed about existing research of communication norms and the way youth uses digital and social media? What assumptions inform judicial decisions about DE Kids?
- Are there sufficient resources provided by provincial/state governments to help teachers, school administrators, and staff understand the norms of communication among DE Kids and DE Young Adults?
- Will specific cyberbullying legislation exacerbate or reduce the problem?
- What is the guarantee that "big-stick sanctions" (Kift, Campbell & Butler 2010) will work to reduce cyberbullying?
- How will, and how is, *mens rea* or intent to harm addressed in new legislation? This is a concern because our research suggests a significant amount of cyberbullying among young people is unintentional.

GOAL, OBJECTIVES, AND CHAPTER ORGANIZATION

My ultimate objective in this book is to draw readers' attention to key social and legal issues that receive the least attention during public policy debates. When these considerations are brought to the forefront of the discussion, they will help us develop clear, non-arbitrary, and thoughtful legislation. It is hoped clarification of these issues will also help the legal community to implement existing legislation thoughtfully, by drawing on an informed set of principles grounded in constitutional and human rights, and balanced by educational responses that take precedence to big-stick sanctions. I maintain that for most children who engage in offensive online communications, legal literacy, empathy, and education on human rights and digital citizenship shows greater promise of reducing such forms of communication than threats of incarceration and criminal records.

As explained earlier, the word cyberbullying has become too generic. Moreover, in my view, since about 2010, the biggest thorn in the side of policy makers and law enforcement is how to deal with the sexualized aspects of this phenomenon among DE Generations. Accordingly, I have narrowed my focus in this book to address the public policy dilemma of preventing, reducing, and regulating an apparently increased tendency among DE Generations to engage in sexually driven and often demeaning and humiliating forms of online communication. I present my most recent empirical research data, which disturbingly show that these activities are taking place among DE Kids at even younger ages (8 to 12). To understand what drives DE Kids to engage in these risqué activities, I draw on scholarly literature from legal academics and psychologists as it relates to moral development. I then analyze these findings in the context of case law, emerging statutes, and empirical research with DE Kids who are growing up or have grown up immersed in varying modes of digital and social media.

Despite focused government and stakeholder attention to public policy, many teens and young adults like Amanda Todd, Jane Doe, and Tyler Clementi, all of whom committed suicide,[7] found no escape from incessant online taunts, threats, extortion, and insults accompanied by videos of physical and often sexual victimization. The vicious cycle continues as each young suicide or rape victim's plight is repeatedly aired in the media, unintentionally re-victimizing the targeted individual and providing public platforms that benefit perpetrators as their offensive postings are displayed over and over again on public television, radio, and online media outlets.[8] Parents and government officials express anger and once again, urgent calls for harsher legislation, stricter punishment, and increased regulation capture the attention of politicians, parents, and educators.

Many provincial and state laws across North America now also hold schools responsible for ensuring a safe school environment. The objectives of these laws are to encourage schools to pay attention and ensure they provide a sustainable learning environment that is free of bullying and sexually related online harassment.[9] Later, I present statutes that now hold parents accountable for their children's engagement in perpetrating these forms of abuse.

---

[7] Amanda Todd, 15, committed suicide after a "capper" blackmailed the teen into exposing her breasts via webcam online. The images were captured as screenshots and sent around to her family and peers. Prior to committing suicide, Todd posted a YouTube video describing her experience with bullying after the fact. Jane Doe, 17, attempted suicide after a video of her being gang raped was distributed online, leading to further bullying. The teen's suicide attempt left her in a coma, after which her family decided to eventually turn off life support. Tyler Clementi, 18, committed suicide after his roommate, Dharun Ravi, used his webcam to secretly film Clementi kissing another man. Ravi disclosed the content of the footage to his peers via Twitter.

[8] For example, consider how many times Tyler Clementi's suicide was discussed and aired on stations like CNN and Fox News; Amanda Todd's suicide note was shown repeatedly along with the comments of online "trolls" that demeaned her on social media after her death.

[9] See Appendix A. Examples include Bill 56, the Nova Scotia *Cyber-safety Act*, and the *Accepting Schools Act* of Ontario.

I repeatedly draw readers' attention to the need for *informed* public policy and educational responses that *engage* all DE Kids in contributing to thoughtful, non-arbitrary responses. It is essential that contemporary society, saturated by digital spaces, be instilled with at least a basic knowledge of the law ("public legal literacy"). The lived reality of DE Kids consists of fewer boundaries, which often blur the divide between physical and online spaces (Shariff, Wiseman & Crestohl, 2012; Retter & Shariff, 2012).

This does not mean that there should not be consequences for on- or offline abuses that carry devastating psychological and physical consequences for others. What this means is that disciplinary policies ought to have educational messages ingrained within them, and that preventative initiatives address the root of the issues, while also demonstrating an appreciation of how digital generations think about communication and relationships. This, however, is still not enough. I argue that we also need to address the assumptions and biases that inform the development of public policies and social rules by adults. It is essential to recognize and address assumptions and biases about DE Kids that might inform the implementation of new laws specifically designed to address cyberbullying by legislators. It is also important to understand similar assumptions and biases that might influence judges, police, and school officials who grew up without digital media when they think about how DE Kids ought to engage online. Here is an overview of what you will find in upcoming chapters.

Chapter 2: Sexism Defines the Lines between *Fun* and Power

Chapter 2 establishes context, providing a comprehensive platform from which to move on to my discussion of the legal dilemmas in Chapters 3 and 4. This background highlights the fact that there is an even wider gap in recognizing that many adults in society model intolerant and discriminatory attitudes through popular culture (Bailey & Steeves, 2013). A number of prominent scholars on digital and social media communications (Tapscott, 2009; boyd & Jenkins, 2006; Gee, 2009) provide useful insight into how differently most adults over forty think about on- and offline spaces and communication, reality shows, comedy, and boundaries of communication. When these perspectives and assumptions about on- and offline communications are compared with the conflicting perspectives that DE Kids bring to their thinking about "real" and "virtual spaces;" public versus private spaces; privacy rights versus privacy harm; the content of online postings and sharing rights and ownership of such content online (Shariff DTL Research, 2014), it is easy to see why we have so much difficulty filling the public policy vacuum on cyberbullying and why it can never be "controlled." It can however be reduced significantly with thoughtful, informed, and non-arbitrary approaches to the issues.

I also introduce known information on well-publicized cases involving sexting, extortion by adults, homophobic harassment, and video-recorded rapes that are then posted online perpetuating cyberbullying by peers. In some cases, such experiences were linked with, but may not have been the cause of, tragic suicides. I present Amanda Todd and Jane Doe's respective stories, as well as the Steubenville case within the backdrop of "rape culture" and popular culture in schools and universities. In universities, instances of online rape culture have been acknowledged as far back as the website, juicycampus.com. Ellen Kraft wrote about this controversial website in my book *Truths and Myths of Cyber-bullying* (Shariff & Churchill, 2010). In Chapter 2, I provide examples of rape culture as deeply ingrained not only in university and post-secondary institutions, but also as our Define the Line (DTL) research indicates, in high schools and even elementary schools. This is a disturbing trend and has its roots in popular culture that on the one hand, enables women and girls through role models that assert their sexuality, and on the other, promotes misogynist and sexist attitudes that continue to demean and objectify women and girls (Bailey & Steeves, 2013; SACOMSS Media Watch, 2013; Bailey & Hanna, 2011). I provide examples of frosh songs (St. Mary's and UBC), discussions of the desired rape of a student council female president by her male colleagues on social media (University of Ottawa), and hazing at universities and on college sports teams. An analysis of the St. Mary's incident is also presented in a report by Dalhousie Law Professor A. Wayne MacKay (MacKay, 2013), which is summarized.

Girls Receive Contradictory Messages from Society:
I also touch on discourses within feminist scholarship as it relates to concerns and debates about rape culture and popular culture. I discuss its impact on girls when they post or forward intimate and nude photographs online or send them to peers in confidence (Steeves & Bailey, 2013; Bailey, 2008; Ybarra, Mitchell, Wolak & Finkelhor, 2006). I explain the contradictions and influences teenage girls confront when they assert their sexuality like their celebrity idols, but who then end up being publicly humiliated through "slut-shaming." As the news media maintains its sensational spotlight on tragic teen suicides that are depicted as the results of cyberbullying, it is important to note that the posted content and forms of abuse both on- and offline have become more vitriolic, demeaning, power driven, and frequently rooted in sexism, misogyny, and homophobia.

Influence of Media:
Within the context of the literature on sexism and rape culture, I also highlight media framing of cyberbullying incidents and scholarly literature that speaks to the pros and cons of media reports (Edwards, 2005; Thomas, 2011; Thom *et al.*, 2011). Chapter 2 references a body of literature that suggests media reports of video-recorded suicide messages by cyberbullied victims, and post-ings to their social media pages after death, might glorify suicide. Such coverage might encourage other young people to seek their moment in the spotlight by committing suicide themselves (Hinduja & Patchin, 2010). Moreover, public broadcasting of social media pages that show offensive taunts, threats, and insults could provide perpetrators, especially "trolls," with the publicity they

crave. More importantly, repeated displays of this abuse serve to re-victimize targeted individuals every time the images are aired for public viewing. Images from the news media can also be saved, shared, and distributed and spread virally. In Chapter 2, I highlight factors often overlooked in the public policy debate, such as the role of media in causing moral panic or reactive legislation; the shifting norms of communication among DE Kids; and the modeling of similar attitudes and behaviors by adults.

Entertainment and "Fun" at All Costs:
To shed some light on what motivates this behavior, I present intriguing findings from our Define the Line Research (DTL Research). The data disclose confusion in the minds of two different age groups of elementary school participants (ages 8 to 12) and high school students (ages 13 to 18). It is disturbing to see the similarities and differences in the statistics obtained from these two groups that explained why they might engage in such forms of online harassment and peer embarrassment. Participants explained their motivations to participate in group postings of sexual assault or harassment. They also explained which participants are considered blameworthy when intimate images sent privately to a boyfriend are callously distributed without permission or warning.

The DTL Research findings in Chapter 2 draw attention to the perspectives of DE Kids. It illustrates how they define the lines between fun and harmful online interactions that have criminal repercussions or legal liability. It also discloses how youth think about culpability, accountability, and the consequences of their actions. The insightful and enlightening comments and responses were obtained by my Define the Line Project research team (www.definetheline.ca) at McGill University, from 1,083 North American participants between the ages of eight and twelve (pre-Facebook age) and thirteen and eighteen (Facebook age).

The research was funded with a combined Facebook Digital Citizenship Award and an Insight Grant from the Social Science and Humanities Research Council of Canada (SSHRC). With support from these two grants, my colleagues and I surveyed and engaged focus groups of children and youth in Canada (Montreal, Quebec and Vancouver, British Columbia) and the United States (Seattle, Washington and Palo Alto, California). We asked them to tell us how they "define the lines" between joking and teasing and harmful online postings that might break the law. We also asked them how they distinguished between public and private spaces, and between shared and personal online content. In later chapters, their responses are also considered in light of judicial assumptions regarding young people's legal culpability; due process; increased police powers; and the need for police sensitivity when they arrest teenage perpetrators.

Shifting Norms and a Need to Define the Lines:
The data in Chapter 2 confirms a general lack of attention to normative differences in the conceptual frameworks of DE Kids as compared to decision makers and politicians in positions of power who may not be as technologically

savvy, which can leave, and has left, gaps in the complex puzzle of evolving online social interactions (boyd & Jenkins, 2006; Gee, 2009, 2010; Tapscott, 2009). It also confirms that the DE Kids who participated are relatively confused about notions of fun versus harm; acceptable boundaries of communication; legal liability for online expressions; intentional and unintentional harm; and ownership of shared content (Shariff, 2014). Their responses illustrate why it is no surprise that we continue to grapple with navigating a balance between free speech, privacy, protection, supervision, and regulation. As I noted in the conclusion of *Confronting Cyberbullying*, when we fail to understand cyberbullying as fundamentally rooted in endemic social attitudes and hegemonies (Gramsci, 1994, 1971; Giroux, 2004; Freire, 2000; Foucault, 2012), we tend to respond in reactive ways to control and manage it through stricter rules and laws, harsher punishment, and threats to withdraw online privileges. And yet, if we stopped to think about the potential impact of such responses, we might find that not only do censorship and autocratic responses result in increased bureaucracy, they often cast too wide a discretionary net that could mistakenly implicate innocent online users.

The youth perspectives in the DTL Research clearly illustrate the need for increased attention to helping them think through the impacts of their online postings. It demonstrates struggles with peer pressure via their motivations to participate, to gain status, and to entertain others for "fun." I interpret this as the need to speak louder through increasingly unconventional means to be heard over the competitive din of the Internet. This research highlights two specific areas where the perspectives of two groups of DE Kids raised implications for the development of legislation and public policy:

- *Jokes or serious harm:* DE Kids have difficulty distinguishing the difference between intentional online threats and threatening words that have no intent to harm. Given that under criminal law in Canada and the United States, *mens rea* (intent to harm) and the act connected to the threat (*actus reus*) are essential to establishing guilt and actual or tangible harm to the victim, the online environment becomes a difficult space in which to establish clear legal boundaries, especially where children and youth are concerned.

- *Blurred lines: Public or private?* Young people's comments disclose they have difficulty recognizing the difference between public and private online spaces because they have grown up immersed in online environments where these lines are blurred.

These findings suggest that rather than blaming kids for their online behaviors, we should be working very hard to give them stability and clear boundaries that can guide their moral and social compasses. We can work with them to use digital and social media in ways that promote accepting, inclusive, and respectful forms of communication. Working with DE Kids would likely promote leadership and community instead of divisive and demeaning communication for entertainment purposes. We might also consider a boredom factor that accounts for offensive online behaviors (Ashford, 1996; Giroux, 2003; Kincheloe, 2005). Schools have not kept up with technologies and DE Kids often find curriculum and modes of learning irrelevant in a digitized world where information and knowledge are at their fingertips. At the crux of research examining youth engagement in schools is the relationship between setting and identity; in that, research on these issues should take on an analytical lens, which includes the behavioral, cognitive, and affective components of engaging youth (Yonezawa, Jones & Joselowsky, 2009). This multi-prong approach mirrors students' lives and the different way they have invested in their everyday realities both on- and offline. However, simply integrating technology into the classroom is not the solution. A recent American report on technology's role in the twenty-first century classroom underscores the fact that classroom technology has yet to shift from teacher-centered instruction, leaving students little choice in how and what they learn (Kolderie & McDonald, 2009).

The context provided in Chapter 2 helps with the analysis of the DTL data. For example, some of the confused responses may stem from the fact that girls in contemporary society are subjected to conflicting messages about their sexuality and identities. They are expected to be successful in their lives. Young women now aspire to and have careers that were previously only held by men. There is agreement in the literature that men and boys often feel threatened by feminist power and respond through sexist actions and sexual harassment (Cleveland & Kerst, 1993; O'Connell & Korabik, 2000; Jones, 2006). More than ever before, young women have celebrity role models like Miley Cyrus, Lady Gaga, and Madonna who reinforce the message that sexual freedom will help them gain success and popularity. However, too much self-promotion can result in teen girls standing out too far from their peers – crossing that invisible line that is required to belong to their peer groups. Unfortunately, the confused messages that these girls receive result in highly public "slut-shaming" when their trust is breached in online forums. The humiliation and teasing they are subjected to thereafter can be devastating. It can affect their health, grades, careers, and in some cases, it can result in suicide. It is important to also point out that it is not only girls who are singled out for online abuse. Homophobic abuse is prevalent as adolescent males attempt to establish their "maleness" in peer groups. This line of discussion is also continued in Chapter 4, where I discuss a California case that illustrates this very clearly.

Scholarship on Moral Development, Empathy, and Moral Disengagement of Youth

Finally, in Chapter 2, I analyze the DTL findings within the context of current scholarship in psychology as it relates to the moral development, empathy, and moral disengagement of DE Kids. This literature, when considered in light of the discussion on rape culture, popular culture, and the DTL Research, fleshes out our understanding of DE Kids, placing the data within an informed framework for analysis of the issues to be considered. To that end, Chapter 2 provides a comprehensive platform from which to move onto discussions of the role of law and how it applies.

Chapter 3: The Irony of Charging Children with Distribution of Child Pornography

In Chapter 3, I discuss the irony of charging children with laws that were developed to protect them. I evaluate the futility of applying criminal law and child pornography sanctions to address the non-consensual distribution of intimate images by digital generations as young as eleven to thirteen years old. I look at what case law, especially in the United States, indicates about the utility of applying child pornography laws to the distribution of images by children to other children or teens. Is the "flirty fun" that kids engage in really child pornography? What is the difference between adult child pornographers who sexually exploit children for pleasure and kids who are pushing the boundaries because they have access to the tools to distribute such images? Can the law contain, manage, or control the motivations that cause DE Kids to distribute such images?

Applying Child Pornography Laws. "A Square Peg in a Round Hole"

Importantly, I discuss the misapplication of child pornography laws to children whom the law is meant to protect. The paradoxical nature of applying these laws in these instances is even more troubling when one recognizes the impulsivity with which DE Kids and even DE Young Adults share comments and media online. For example, in 2009, when Florida teen Philip Alpert just turned eighteen, he mass distributed a naked photo of his sixteen-year-old girlfriend after having an argument. Police in Orlando, Florida arrested and charged Alpert for distributing child pornography. He was eventually convicted and sentenced to five years' probation and was required by Florida law to register as a sex offender. While in this case Alpert was perhaps of appropriate age to be charged with this type of offense, the question really revolves around the intent of the teenager – can we really equate Alpert's actions with that of a pedophile to the point where both should be convicted of the same crime? In 2012, a Pennsylvania Court of Common Pleas judge threw out child pornography charges against teen C.S. who had posted a video on her Facebook of two other teens participating in a consensual sexual act. The judge argued that applying child pornography laws to this type of distribution is like "trying to fit a square peg in a round hole" (RE: C.S., 2012). The judge concluded that teenagers who engage in sexting "should not face the same legal and moral conundrum [as child pornographers]" (RE: C.S., 2012). Still, these cases are becoming more commonplace. In Canada, for example, the conviction of a British Columbia female student for distributing nude photographs of a boyfriend's ex-girlfriend is currently under appeal.

I further discuss instances of law enforcement insensitivity when engaging with youths. This includes the manner in which ten Laval students were reportedly handled during their arrests (CBC News, November 14, 2013; Huffington Post via CBC, November 14, 2013; Kotenko, 2013). The Laval boys (aged 13–15) convinced female classmates to send them intimate images via Snapchat, then took screenshots of the images, and distributed them.

The misapplication of child pornography laws and the insensitivity sometimes displayed by law enforcement when working with DE Kids necessitates the recommendations I make in Chapter 5, which include digital and legal literacy as well as training regarding child and adolescent moral development and social norms.

Big-Stick Sanctions Don't Work

Chapter 3 evaluates these big-stick sanctions (Kift, Campbell & Butler, 2010) in emerging legislation, such as Bill C-13, the *Protecting Canadians from Online Crime Act*, which aims to criminalize the non-consensual distribution of intimate images (including those distributed by children and teens). In particular, I discuss Section 162.1(1), which pertains to the non-consensual distribution of intimate images that comes with a five-year prison sentence, and the broader discretion this law would give to law enforcement personnel.

Highly publicized teen suicides have increased the pressure on governments to clamp down on children's online behavior with harsher laws and penalties. Strong lobbying from parents and teachers, and an increasing number of lawsuits, has resulted in governments and corporate intermediaries investing time and funds in evidence-based research from multidisciplinary perspectives.[10] Academics are often called upon to provide expert testimony at congressional and parliamentary hearings as to whether proposed legislation will have an impact on reducing cyberbullying. However, the issue has become one that is ironically known as a "sexy" or "hot" topic for public policy – one that will get governments more votes if they can demonstrate they are taking a hard-line on crime through harsher laws and longer sentences. The highly controversial Bill C-13 has become known as the "cyberbullying law." It was developed by the federal government as a result of pressure from the parents of Amanda Todd and a teen known as "Jane Doe", both of whom committed suicide.[11] The law seeks to update the Canadian *Criminal Code* to address the realities of digital and social media; however, it also grants large discretionary powers to police to search and seize computers and digital equipment. Critics of the bill argue that the government has snuck in

---

[10] Bill C-13 has been recently proposed by the Canadian government to update the *Criminal Code of Canada* and address cyberbullying. Similarly, over the years, provisions aimed at sexting have been included in different states' penal codes. For example, in 2011, Texas added § 43.261 to the state's penal code to specifically address sexting. Importantly, this section of Texas' penal code provides for increasingly harsh penalties depending on whether the defendant is a first-time offender whereas Bill C-13 does not distinguish between number of prior offenses.

[11] See note 7.

surveillance powers under the guise of a cyberbullying law.[12] Opponents of the bill also argue that before we begin to put teenagers in jail and load them up with criminal records, we need to ensure that they are the only culprits (Seidman, 2013; Seidman, 2014; Geist, 2014). While Bill C-13 has not yet passed the House of Commons, the Conservative government has already overridden numerous opposition amendments to the bill – some of which call for the removal of increased law enforcement and judicial discretionary powers. The Canadian government also implemented legislation that has moved the legislative agenda towards harsher and longer penalties for youth, such as the *Safe Streets and Communities Act*.

U.S. laws have also tended toward criminalization in the wake of increased sexting between minors. For example, Florida passed HB 75 in June 2011, which specifically delineates the offense of sexting and provides for both criminal and noncriminal charges. Also in 2011, Texas added §43.261 to their penal code to specifically address sexting. Interestingly, this section of Texas' penal code provides for increasingly harsh penalties depending on whether the defendant is a first-time offender.

Victims as Perpetrators

In Chapter 3, I also draw attention to empirical research that confirms perpetrators of various forms of cyberbullying are often victims of previous bullying or harassment. Although they fight back, this does not reduce the fact that they, too, experience harm and should therefore be protected as well. In *A.B. (Litigation Guardian of) v. Bragg Communications, Inc.* (2012), the SCC did not discuss whether the same privacy protection afforded to victims, such as A.B., ought to be afforded to victim-perpetrators who might find themselves as defendants in these types of cases. The harm for victim-perpetrators can be deemed discernible as well, as they might be expelled from schools or social groups, or have difficulty securing jobs if they are publicly known defendants in defamation suits. Furthermore, with new legislation like Bill C-13 being considered, should cyberbullying become "criminalized," there is the risk that victims will be charged as perpetrators when they might be retaliating to provocation. The term "victim-perpetrator" is not truly oxymoronic in cases of cyberbullying.

Perspectives of Legal Academics

I round off Chapter 3 with a discussion of the perspectives of legal academics, who present refreshing and positive ways in which the law can enhance, protect, and support DE Kids instead of punish them. These legal theories show us that the answers we seek do reside in established legal frameworks – we just haven't looked in the right places:

---

[12] Geist, Michael. (November 21, 2013). The Cyberbullying Bill Is A Virtual Big Brother in Disguise. *Huffington Post*. Retrieved from www.huffingtonpost.ca/michael-geist/harper-cyberbullying-bill_b_4317791.html.

a) *Need to Address Outdated Laws:* In a policy brief and report to a U.S. Congressional Committee, Palfrey (2009) outlined a range of aspects in which legal responses to cyberbullying and related digital concerns have not kept up. Calo's (2011) notion of "privacy harm" provides a more relevant and less outdated theoretical framework to consider *subjective* privacy harm (e.g., the subjective experiences of victims of sexting) and *objective* impact of privacy breaches (e.g., the sense of being watched on social networking service). Moreover, traditional forms of punishment do not always have the intended deterrent results on perpetrators (Shariff, 2005; DiGuilio, 2001). This is especially true when we consider that perpetrators of actions described as bullying and cyberbullying have often also been victims of similar abuse (Farmer *et al.,* 2012; Mason, 2008; Carlyle & Steinman, 2007; Black, Weinles & Washington, 2010; Mishna, Khoury-Kassabri, Gadalla & Daciuk, 2012).

b) *Legal Assumptions/Child complexity Theory (LACT):* This perspective argues that legal assumptions add complexity and inconsistencies in the way laws are developed; legal doctrines and rules applied; and precedents established. Legal professionals, policy makers, and judges, whose decisions impact young people's lives and futures, should be aware of their own assumptions and those that underlie legal responses. Contradictions in private law respect adolescents' worthiness as decision makers under some rules; and override their dignity, agency, and autonomy through articulation of other rules or doctrines. There is a need for consistency in accounting for social, personal, and familial contexts that recognize the turmoil of adolescence, as well as the influence of peer and parental relations. While the law tries to address the paradox of children's vulnerability and increasing independence, it sometimes fails to forgive mistakes. Scholars worry that in the digital age, unfettered usage and access to digital information will have untold effects on the core values of judicial independence and impartiality (Van Praagh, 2005, 2007; Eltis, 2011; Altobelli, 2010; Danay, 2010).

c) *Apply LACT Theory to DTL Research:* Provisions under current legislation and sanctions are juxtaposed against survey and focus group responses gathered anonymously from the DTL Research participants based on age, gender, legal literacy, empathy, notions of intent (joking versus harm), and notions of public versus private sharing of online postings. This framework will contribute to conclusions and implications in Chapter 3 with regard to the potential value of criminal sanctions in reducing or addressing cyberbullying. It will also identify the complexities, nuances, and the need to address context when applying criminal law to assess the culpability of DE Kids.

Hence, Chapter 3 highlights the range of concerns and legal theories that call for informed consideration by legislators before child pornography and criminal laws are applied or amended to address online activities among DE

Kids. It also sets the stage for discussion of a range of legal frameworks that also apply to the nuanced complexities of this phenomenon.

Chapter 4: Keeping Kids Out of Court: Jokes, Defamation, and Duty to Protect

In *Confronting Cyberbullying* (2009), I discussed each applicable legal framework in a separate chapter. In this book, despite the fact that I have dedicated Chapter 3 to discussions about criminal law and related child pornography laws, I address the remaining applicable legal frameworks (constitutional issues, tort/civil law issues, and human rights considerations), in Chapter 4. This is so that I can illustrate how similar forms of offensive online postings can be addressed through more than one legal framework depending on the circumstances; and also to explain how more than one framework can apply in certain cases.

For example, in the past, the courts dealt largely with cases that took place in the physical world – either through speaking or writing. In the online world, it is easier to remain anonymous for longer periods of time and the number of abusers can grow rapidly and exponentially. A lot of online activities take place on personal and private computers, off-campus, and after school hours. The cases are no longer cut and dry. It is increasingly difficult to assess whether existing laws and doctrines that have served the judiciary well, such as legal tests to establish negligence, a duty of care, foreseeable harm, reasonable person, and intent or perceived intent are relevant or suitable when it comes to online crime.

Similarly, it is less clear when an online form of expression might breach privacy, for example, because notions of "privacy" have evolved in the online context. The lines between public and private spaces merge and blend to such an extent that getting DE Kids and DE Young Adults to think about the separations may seem futile. I present examples of this in Chapter 3 in order to emphasize why it is so important to find ways to protect the privacy and vulnerability of DE Kids instead of always blaming and punishing them. As Van Praagh (2005, 2007) observes, children are at the same time vulnerable and responsible as they grow up to become more independent and exercise their powers of agency. As they grow and develop moral frameworks, they are better able to make informed and thoughtful decisions. The law is intended to protect children from the ills of society. However, when children imitate and engage in crimes that are regulated under adult legal frameworks, it creates a dilemma for the judiciary and policy makers. Nowhere is the situation more complex than when the law attempts to address online crime and offenses among youth. This might be the reason that although we as a society have known about cyberbullying over the last decade, it is only in the last three to four years that legislators have begun attempts to regulate it.

Thus, having discussed intentional harm and culpability under the criminal law in Chapter 3, I focus Chapter 4 on civil law considerations of children's liability under tort law as different from assessment of children's culpability under criminal law. Chapter 4 also continues the analysis of scholarly legal literature that was introduced in Chapter 3.

Civil Lawsuits

Cyberbullying as it is understood today includes the use of smart phones, texting, videos, apps, and social media, among other things, to spread rumors, gossip, threaten, harass, and tease peers and authority figures. In 2008, smart phones with the texting, communication, photographic, and online capabilities they have now, and mobile apps like Snapchat, Ask.fm, and YikYak, did not exist. Civil lawsuits are on the rise as victims stand up to perpetrators to seek damages for maligned reputations. One deterrent for defamation suits has been that young people do not like to be identified for fear of further bullying. The doctrine of the open court system and right to free press in both Canada and the United States requires that plaintiffs in defamation lawsuits disclose their identities. A recent SCC landmark case, *A.B. (Litigation Guardian of) v. Bragg Communications, Inc.* (2012), has begun the shift, at least in Canada, toward greater protection of victims of cyberbullying if they are minors while allowing the free press to report on details of the case without citing the plaintiff's name. I discuss the case in Chapter 4; however, whether a similar decision could be made in the United States remains to be seen as freedom of the press and free speech retain their priority as the most revered freedoms under the U.S. Constitution.

I begin with a discussion of the California case of *D.C. v. R.R.* (2010) that involved homophobic harassment and defamation. D.C., a budding musician had to give up his career and move to another school. His reputation was destroyed and his physical and emotional well-being was depleted. The details of the case as presented in Chapter 4 explain the motivations of DE Kids to participate in competitions about who can post the most outrageous comments online. This case showed the court's balancing process between free speech and expression that is offensive without substance. This leads to analysis of another American case, where lewd and abusive speech by a teenager against her principal was allowed because she was stating an opinion and protesting her schools ear piercing policy (*A.B. v. State of Indiana*, 2007).

I also discuss the media's right to freedom of the press and young victims' rights to protection of privacy in civil litigation where the plaintiff wants to remain anonymous. In *A.B. (Litigation Guardian of) v. Bragg Communications, Inc.* (2012), the plaintiff had to pursue a constitutional claim prior to commencing her defamation suit. More specifically, because of the plaintiff's desire to remain anonymous throughout her defamation suit proceedings, she first had to argue against freedom of the press. Interestingly, as we will see, while the applicability of various legal frameworks can lead to a wide array of legal avenues for victims to pursue, there can also be conflicts between legal frameworks in ways that the courts have never dealt with before.

Protection of Victim Privacy: In *A.B. (Litigation Guardian of) v. Bragg Communications, Inc.* (2012), the SCC issued an important decision relating to the privacy protection of young victims of cyberbullying and freedom of the press. A.B. wanted to sue her perpetrator for defamation and remain anonymous; however, the lower courts insisted she had to disclose her identity. The SCC described cyberbullying as a "toxic phenomenon" and described the harm experienced by cyberbullied victims as "discernible harm." The high court recognized that this harm is discernible because young victims might experience ruined reputations and psychological harm. There is also discussion of Calo's (2011) notions of privacy harm, as opposed to privacy breach under tort law and these notions are also interesting when discussed in the framework of the potential to sue for defamation and privacy harm. I include their views on defining the lines between public and private and their understanding of privacy harm (Calo, 2011).

Application of Human/Civil Rights Law to Cyberbullying: In 2012, a Standing Senate Committee on Human Rights in Canada conducted inquiries into whether Canada is meeting its obligations under Article 19 of the *International Convention of the Rights of the Child* (CRC) to protect victims of cyberbullying. The Canadian Senate Committee interviewed numerous experts and young people, resulting in a comprehensive report that is analyzed in Chapter 4 (Jaffer & Brazeau, 2012). The chapter also includes an analysis of reports by congressional committees in the United States that have also heard evidence on the law's role on reducing cyberbullying (see Palfrey, 2009; Willard, 2010). This chapter will also review legal-academic rights-based literature relating to the role of human (civil) rights in the United States. Moreover, international literature on this issue is relevant and will be brought in primarily to highlight the relevance of human rights law to protect victims and perpetrators (from over-regulation) in Canada and the United States. Articles 3 and 12 *inter alia* of the CRC will also be discussed. The children's perspectives from the DTL Research, as well as the responses of the legal community also inform this discussion.

Finally, I highlight provincial and state legislation that requires schools to provide safe learning environments. This includes Quebec's Bill 56, which requires schools and school boards to report to the provincial government on the number and kinds of cyberbullying incidents that occur in their schools, and a number of American laws and acts, including *Seth's Law* in California, the *Anti-Bullying Bill of Rights Act* in New Jersey, and the *Dignity for All Students Act* in New York.

Chapter 5: From *Lord of the Flies* to *Harry Potter*: Freedom, Choices, and Guilt
I conclude the book with the implications of overly harsh legislation and recommendations for innovative, creative, engaging, and non-arbitrary responses to the issues discussed. Chapter 5 presents recommendations for enhancing legal literacy, sensitization of the legal community and news media, improved public education, and informed policy development. I call for increased funding to support these

essential initiatives. The following summary of Chapter 5 does not reflect the exact headings in that chapter, but it gives a general overview of the kinds of implications and recommendations the concluding chapter contains. It brings together the key conclusions of preceding chapters to clarify the blurred boundaries.

I begin by highlighting the importance of children's literature to inform legal analysis and also to inform and enhance the legal literacy of children. I cannot stress enough that while it is not necessary for everyone to have legal expertise, the need for improved public legal education and awareness is long overdue. In 1973, Chief Justice Bora Laskin of the Supreme Court of Canada noted that without public legal education, it is difficult to sustain and live by constitutional and human rights principles. This in turn can impact democratic values and civil society.

Therefore, my last chapter emphasizes the importance of providing legal literacy to all adults and children and sensitizing legal, educational, and law enforcement communities to the lived realities and perspectives of DE Kids. This is the only way we will truly "empower" DE Kids instead of "disempowering" them through harsh laws and punishment. And, given that harsher laws are on their way, it is all the more important to inform DE Kids about what to expect if they break the law.

My analysis in this book, and the concept map in Chapter 5, provides policy makers with a frame of reference as they contemplate and develop legislative, policy, or judicial decisions. A non-arbitrary, informed approach is so crucial when political decisions to calm the electorate result in convictions and jail sentences for youth. There is no question that legal boundaries need to be firmer given the cases of suicide related to online abuse. Nonetheless, the review of relevant case law, as well as emergent and applicable legal frameworks in the context of responses obtained under the DTL Research, discloses enormous gaps in public legal literacy. The DTL Research and case law presented in this book also shine a light on the general lack of sensitivity within the legal community to the shifting norms of young people's social communication. I have also developed a workshop for postsecondary students, which engages them in thinking about rape culture and the role of law in addressing it. The workshop provides them with hypothetical scenarios that encourage them to think about when the line is crossed from jokes and hyperbole to criminal harassment, criminal threat, distribution of child pornography, or rumors and gossip that could result in liability for defamation, slander, or libel. The workshop is included as Appendix C.

We need to show DE Kids how quickly "flirty fun" (Seidman, 2013; Poltash, 2013) on digital apps like Snapchat can land them a criminal conviction for production, possession, and distribution of child pornography.[13] They need to understand that gossiping about someone online, spreading malicious

---

[13] In November 2012, ten teenage boys between the ages of thirteen and fifteen from Laval, Quebec, were arrested on a series of child pornography-related charges. More specifically, they used persuasion or intimidation to get girls to send nude photos of themselves. Some of the girls

information, or making "unfair comments" about others can result in lawsuits for defamation. I outline some examples and explain the use of video-vignettes to help children and youth think through their online postings. I also highlight some very interesting articles on the use of children's literature to help children learn complex legal concepts and how books, like those in the *Harry Potter* series, can help adults work out legal notions of accountability, culpability, moral development, and responsibility as children grow up.

It is important to be clear at the outset that I fully respect the free press and have never, in any of my more than fifty news media interviews, ever requested any member of the media to censor a news story, save for one exception that I explain in note 13.[14] As I wrote in my earlier books (Shariff, 2008 2009), while some journalists are careful to provide informed and well-researched reports, some editors might frame news stories in misleading ways. Although the news media have helped significantly in raising awareness of the devastating impact of cyberbullying, they too need to be sensitized to the harmful impact of over-sensationalizing news reports. They can provide a platform for perpetrators of social media sites to reach a wider audience and unwittingly re-victimize individuals who have suffered through online abuses. They can also present headlines on research in this "hot topic" area that might misrepresent what researchers say.

Similarly, teachers and school administrators are under increasing pressure, under state and provincial legislation, to provide safe school environments.

---

were tricked into believing that their pictures would be deleted immediately because they sent their photos via Snapchat. On a similar note, when Florida teen, Phillip Alpert just turned eighteen, he mass distributed a naked photo of his sixteen-year-old girlfriend after having an argument. Orlando, Florida police arrested and charged Alpert for distributing child pornography. He was eventually convicted and sentenced to five years' probation and required by Florida law to register as a sex offender. Importantly, there are those who argue, including me, that child pornography laws were never meant to be applied to sexting but rather to those who exhibit true pedophilic behavior.

[14] This happened to me when I had to request that a media article be pulled the day it was posted. It was on the day that Facebook wanted to engage in a publicity campaign regarding the Digital Citizenship Award they gave me, as one of four researchers globally, to engage in a portion of the DTL Research. The DTL Research presented in this book, as I have noted in the Acknowledgements, was partly funded by Facebook. I had been interviewed by a reporter with whom I spent an hour explaining the paradoxes of applying child pornography laws to convict children who engage in sexting or non-consensual distribution of intimate images. I emphasized that children need guidance to learn where to draw the line and that given the rise in arrests using child pornography laws to deter young people from engaging in sexting, it was important for young people to be aware of the potential risks. Namely, they could be charged with production, possession, and distribution of child pornography if they did not think through what they post online. The headlines on the day of the publicity launch across Canada read "Professor says Kids Need Child Porn"! Needless to say, I called the publicity director and had the article removed immediately. It could have been a typographical error; nonetheless, on a matter that is already so sensitive, it is imperative that such headlines are thoughtful and vetted for accuracy. Accordingly, I believe the need for media sensitivity is essential and it is one of the recommendations that are included in Chapter 5.

University teacher education programs need to include courses on digital and legal literacy, discrimination, and cyberbullying. In Chapter 5, I propose that additional funding needs to be made available to teacher pre-service programs, professional development, and legal literacy so that educators are better equipped to guide DE Kids. Moreover, educators also need to better understand children's moral development and the tendency of DE Kids to experience moral disengagement when pressured by peers. The scholarship of psychologists as it relates to moral development, moral disengagement, and cyberbullying should be included within curriculum modules to better prepare educators. I consider legal literacy to be so important for educators and policy makers that I include a course outline for a course I have developed at McGill University, in *Public Policy, Law and Digital Media*, as Appendix D. This course also pays attention to the need for critical media literacy by educators, parents, and policy makers. Related to this is the need to sensitize the news media itself.

My research (Shariff, 2012–14) discloses that particular attention needs to be paid to those in the legal community who are beginning to enforce the harsher laws and public policies to address cyberbullying. Understanding judicial assumptions, discretion, and the perspectives that inform law enforcement officers as they carry out the arrests, penalties, and jail sentences of a generation they do not quite understand is imperative. I draw the readers' attention to some important changes since I last wrote about these phenomena.

I also highlight the need for improved sensitization of the legal community to the realities of today's DE Kids. It is important that they are better equipped to address nuanced cyberbullying cases in the future. My analysis draws on a body of scholarly literature about how law makers, enforcers, and judges use their discretion in applying the law (Hawkins, 1992, 1997). Given that the legal community is now dealing with unprecedented situations where illusive legal boundaries shift with each digital innovation, it stands to reason that discretion in applying the law will play a stronger role.

Ultimately, I argue that *informed discretion*, awareness, and improved and sustained educational approaches show greater promise than harsher legal sanctions. Although I agree that boundaries are necessary to address extreme and harmful social behavior, such laws will need to be implemented by a better educated legal community. Moreover, it is not unreasonable to assume that the more literate children and teens are about their own legal obligations and legal risks, the more careful they are likely to be before engaging freely in offensive and demeaning online behaviors. To that end, laws against cyberbullying might serve a deterrent purpose in some cases; however, they are unlikely to make a large dent in its prevention. Moreover, it is the circumstances and manner in which such laws are implemented that will make the difference in reducing cyberbullying, as well as preventative and informed educational initiatives and policies that involve input from youth. It is imperative that law enforcement officers, prosecutors, defenders, and the judiciary who will apply and interpret these new laws are also sensitized to the shifting norms of online communication among youth, as well as the adult population.

In order to do this, we must understand the assumptions and discretion they bring to their daily professional practices in arresting, prosecuting, judging and sentencing young people, and applying new laws on cyberbullying as there is no turning back from such legislation. The next few years of my DTL Research will be focused on reviewing judicial decisions, cases, and scholarly articles that indicate the assumptions and biases regarding DE Kids that the legal community brings to its application of the law. Depending on what I find, I will develop sensitivity workshops and resources to address the gaps through empirically based research and legal analysis. Accordingly, this is another recommendation I have included in Chapter 5.

I am confident that readers will find my focused discussions of the role of law to support, protect, and empower DE Kids (as opposed to criminalize and punish them) useful and practical. It is meant to contribute to the current public policy debate. I expect it will be a valuable educational resource. In particular, it could be used as valuable text for use in pre-service, graduate education, and professional development. I will be further developing webinars and workshops along the lines of those appended to this book that bring out its key messages.

The book will inform government and educational policy makers as they engage in the background research to inform amendments to legislation or propose new legislation. In that regard, it could be used in "judge schools" (continuing legal education courses for judges to keep them apprised of social developments); continuing legal education courses; law schools; police academies and professional development for public and private school education, as well as university education programs; a policy brief summarizing the key elements of the book will be included with a link to the Define the Line (DTL) website at www.definetheline.ca.

In addition, the final chapter provides a concept map that I have used in hundreds of keynote presentations and workshops and in previous books. The general concept has always worked to support my key recommendations toward preventative versus reactive measures. The objective is to provide a framework that will facilitate policy development and sustained implementation. The concept map was drawn from graduate courses that I developed at McGill University on education, law, policy, and technology. It has been popular with law students, school administrators, parents, and teachers. Finally, Appendix A provides a chart that summarizes established and emerging laws and policies relating to online abuse. This appendix will be easy to update, as will the content of the course outlines and workshops in **Appendices C and D.**

Survival of the Fittest

At the end of Chapter 5, I return to William Golding's (1954) analogy of survival of the fittest and apply it to the online world. I conclude my book by highlighting the interesting tensions between fun and power. How we approach public policy and the practices related to reducing online abuse among DE Kids depends on how we work out these tensions, which include: the scholarly discourse on the relationships of power between genders (rape culture and the influence of popular culture), the friction between the desire of young women to employ their own agency to be professionally successful and sexually liberated (power and fun); the tension between "fun" as perceived and experienced by DE Kids and "fun" as conceptualized by older DE Young Adults. For both generations, fun can also stem from power relationships – teasing and joking are examples. It is how far that teasing and joking goes in imposing a power imbalance on the recipient of the teasing or jokes that determines when it stops being fun and starts being harmful. It is at that point that the power of adults who seek to curtail the fun can "disempower" or take away the power created by the teasing and joking because of its inherent legal risks and potential for liability. Finally, I draw attention to the power of literacy. In Chapter 5, I highlight the fact that children's literature, critical legal and media literacy, and improved knowledge about the assumptions and biases that inform legal action will enhance our power to address these issues in thoughtful, supportive, and protective ways. Knowledge is power from the perspective of how well we understand DE Kids and DE Young Adults and how empowered we as a society can become if only we work with (and not against) DE Kids to support their digital empowerment toward socially responsible leadership and digital citizenship. I hope you will enjoy the book as you embark on the journey toward keeping kids out of court.

REFERENCES

10 Boys Arrested for Allegedly Using Snapchat to Make Child Porn. (2013, November 14). *Huffington Post*. Retrieved November 14, 2013, from www.huffingtonpost.com/2013/11/15/snapchat-porn-photos-quebec_n_4275696.html.

Altobelli, T. (2010). Cyber-Abuse–A New Worldwide Threat to Children's Rights. *Family Court Review*. 48(3), 459–481.

Ashford, M. W. (1996). Boredom as a neglected issue in violence prevention programs in schools. unpublished doctoral dissertation, Simon Fraser University, Burnaby, British Columbia, Canada.

Bailey, J. (2008). Towards an equality-enhancing conception of privacy. *Dalhousie Law Journal*, 31, 267–309.

Bailey, J. & Hanna, M. (2011). The Gendered Dimensions of Sexting: Assessing the Applicability of Canada's Child Pornography Provision. *Canadian Journal of Women and The Law*, 23(2), 405–441.

Bailey, J. & Steeves, V. (2013). "Will the Real Digital Girl Please Stand Up?" in Hille Koskela and Macgregor Wise (eds.), *New Visualities, New Technologies: The New Ecstasy of Communication* (pp. 41–66). London: Ashgate Publishing.

Bailey, J. & Telford, A. (2008). What's So "Cyber" about It?: Reflections on Cyberfeminism's Contribution to Legal Studies. *Canadian Journal of Women and the Law*, 19 (2), 243–271.

Bennett, S. & Maton, K. (2011). "Intellectual Field or Faith-based Religion: Moving on from the idea of 'Digital Natives'," in Thomas, M. (ed.), *Deconstructing Digital Natives: Young People, Technology, and the New Literacies* (pp. 169–185). New York: Routledge.

Black, S., Weinles, D. & Washingston, E. (2010). Victim Strategies to Stop Bullying. *Youth Violence and Juvenile Justice, 8* (2) 138–147.

Blanchard, T. (2014, April 9). Cyberbullying linked to suicidal thoughts in children. *The International.* Retrieved April 10, 2014, from www.theinternational.org/articles/529-cyberbullying-linked-to-suicidal-thoughts.

boyd, d. (2009, May 27). When teachers and students connect outside school [web log post]. Retrieved May 28, 2009, from www.zephoria.org/thoughts/archives/2009/05/27/when_teachers_a.html.

boyd, d. (2014). *It's Complicated: The social lives of networked teens.* Connecticut: Yale University Press.

boyd, d. & Jenkins, H. (2006). "MySpace and Deleting Online Predators Act (DOPA)." *MIT Tech Talk.* Retrieved May 30, 2006, from www.danah.org/papers/MySpaceDOPA.html.

Buckingham, D. (2011). Foreword. In Thomas, M. (Ed.), *Deconstructing Digital Natives: Young people, technology, and the new literacies* (pp. ix–xi). New York: Routledge.

Calo, R. M. (2011). The Boundaries of Privacy Harm. *Indiana Law Journal, 86* (3), 1131–1162.

Carlyle, K.E. & Steinman, K. J. (2007). Demographic differences in the prevalence, co-occurence, and correlates of adolescent bullying at school. *Journal of School Health,* 77(9), 623–629.

Cassidy, W., Faucher, C. & Jackson, M. (2013). Cyberbullying among youth: A comprehensive review of current international research and its implications and application to policy and practice. *School Psychology International,* 34 (6), 575–612.

Child porn charges laid against 10 Laval teens. (2013, November 14). *CBC News.* Retrieved November 14, 2013, from www.cbc.ca/news/canada/montreal/child-porn-charges-laid-against-10-laval-teens-1.2426599.

Cleveland, J.N. & Kerst, M. E. (1993). Sexual Harassment and Perceptions of Power: An Under-Articulated Relationship. *Journal of Vocational Behavior,* 42(1), 49–67.

Danay, R. (2010). The Medium is Not the Message: Reconciling Reputation and Free Expression in Cases of Internet Defamation. *McGill Law Journal,* 56 (1), 1–37.

DiGiulio, R. (2001). *Educate, mediate, or litigate? What teachers, parents and administrators must do about student behavior.* California: Corwin.

Edwards, L.Y. (2005). Victims, Villains and Vixens. In S.R. Mazzarella (Ed.), *Girl Wide Web* (pp. 13–30). New York: Peter Lang.

Eltis, K. (2011). The Judicial System in the Digital Age: Revisiting the Relationship between Privacy and Accessibility in the Cyber Context. *McGill Law Journal,* 56 (2), 289–316.

Farmer, T. W., Petrin, R., Brooks, D. S., Hamm, J. V., Lambert, K. & Gravelle, M. (2010). Bullying Involvement and the School Adjustment of Rural Students With and Without Disabilities. *Journal of Emotional and Behavioral Disorders,* 20, 19–37.

Foucault, M. (1977). *Discipline and Punish: The Birth of the Prison.* New York: Pantheon Books.

Freire, P. (2000). *Pedagogy of the oppressed.* New York: Continuum.

Gee, J. P. (2004). *Situated Language and Learning: A Critique of Traditional Schooling.* London: Routledge.

Gee, J. P. (2009). Digital media and learning as an emerging field, part I: How we got here. *International Journal of Learning and Media,* 1(2), 13–23.

Gee, J. P. (2010). *New digital media and learning as an emerging area and" worked examples" as one way forward*. Cambridge: MIT Press.

Giroux, H. A. (2003). *The abandoned generation: Democracy beyond the culture of fear*. New York: Palgrave Macmillan.

Giroux, H. A. (2004). Education after Abu Ghraib. *Cultural Studies, 18*(6), 779–815.

Golding, W. (1959). *Lord of the Flies*. London: Faber and Faber.

Gramsci, A., Hoare, Q. & Nowell-Smith, G. (1971). *Selections From the Prison Notebooks of Antonio Gramsci*. New York: International Publishers.

Gramsci, A. & Rosengarten, F. (1994). *Letters From Prison*. New York: Columbia University Press.

Grenoble, R. (2012, November 10). Amanda Todd: Bullied Canadian Teen Commits Suicide After Prolonged Battle Online and In School. *Huffington Post*. Retrieved November 10, 2012, from www.huffingtonpost.com/2012/10/11/amanda-todd-suicide-bullying_n_1959909.html

Hawkins, K. (1992). The use of legal discretion: Perspectives from law and social science. In K. Hawkins (Ed.), *The uses of discretion* (pp.11–46). Oxford: Clarendon Press.

Hawkins, K. (1997). Law and discretion: Exploring collective aspects of administrative decision-making. *Education and Law Journal, 8*(2), 139–181.

Hinduja, S. & Patchin, J. W. (2010). Bullying, cyberbullying, and suicide. *Archives of Suicide Research, 14*(3), 206–221.

Jaffer, M. (Senator) & Honourable Brazeau, P. (2012). Cyberbullying Hurts: Respect for Rights in the Digital Age Standing Senate Committee on Human Rights. Parliament of Canada. Retrieved from www.parl.gc.ca/Content/SEN/Committee/411/ridr/rep/rep09dec12-e.pdf.

Jones, C. (2006). Drawing boundaries: Exploring the relationship between sexual harassment, gender and bullying. *Women's Studies International Forum, 39*(2), 147–158.

Juvonen, J. & Gross, E.F. (2008). Extending the school grounds?–Bullying experiences in cyberspace. *Journal of School Health, 78*(9), 496–505.

Kift, S.M., Campbell, M.A. & Butler, D.A. (2010). Cyberbullying in social networking sites and blogs: legal issues for young people and schools. *Journal of Law, Information and Science, 20*(2), 60–97.

Kincheloe, J. L. (2005). *Classroom teaching: An introduction*. New York: Peter Lang.

Kolderie, T. & McDonald, T. (2009). How Information Technology Can Enable 21st Century Schools. *Information Technology and Innovation Foundation*. Retrieved from www.itif.org/files/Education_ITIF.pdf.

Kotenko, J. (2013, November 14). Snapchat tied to child pornography investigation. *Digital Trends*. Retrieved November 15, 2013, from www.digitaltrends.com/social-media/snapchat-child-porn-problem/#!FUoG7.

Lankshear, C. & Knobel, M. (2006). *New literacies: Everyday practices and classroom learning*. Maidenhead: Open University Press.

Laskin, B. (1973). The Function of the Law. *Atlanta Law Review, 11*, 118–122.

Li, Q. (2006). Cyberbullying in Schools. *School Psychology International, 27*(2),157–170.

Li, Q. (2007). Bullying in the new playground: Research into cyberbullying and cyber victimization. *Australasian Journal of Educational Technology, 23*(4), 435–454.

MacKay, A. W. (2013). *Promoting a Culture of Safety, Respect and Consent at Saint Mary's University and Beyond. Report from the President's Council*, Halifax: NS.

Mansbridge, P. (2014, April 16). Class of 2014: Generation Screwed? *CBC News*. Retrieved from www.cbc.ca/player/News/ID/2449809181/

Mason, K. L. (2008). Cyberbullying: A preliminary assessment for school personnel. *Psychology in the Schools, 45* (4), 323–348.

Mishna, F. (2004). A qualitative study of bullying from multiple perspectives. *Children and Schools, 26*(4), 234–247.

Mishna, F., Khoury-Kassabri, M., Gadalla, T. and Daciuk, J. (2012). Risk factors for involvement in cyberbullying: Victims, bullies and bully-victims. *Children and Youth Services Review, 34*(1), 63–70.

O'Connell C.E. & Korabik, K. (2000). Sexual Harassment: The Relationship of Personal Vulnerability, Work Context, Perpetrator Status, and Type of Harassment to Outcomes. *Journal of Vocational Behavior, 56*(3), 299–329.

Olweus, D. (2012). Cyberbullying: An overrated phenomenon? *European Journal of Developmental Psychology, 9*(5), 520–538.

Palfrey, J. (2009). Hearing on Cyberbullying and other Online Safety Issues for Children (United States House of Representatives, Committee on the Judiciary, Subcommittee on Crime, Terrorism and Homeland Security). Retrieved from http://judiciary.house.gov/_files/hearings/pdf/Palfrey090930.pdf.

Poltash, N. A. (2013). Snapchat and Sexting: A Snapshot of Baring Your Bare Essentials. *Richmond Journal of Law and Technology, 19*(4), 1–24.

Prensky, M. (2011). Digital Wisdom and Homo Sapiens Digital. In Thomas, M. (Ed.). *Deconstructing Digital Natives: Young people, technology, and the new literacies* (pp. 15–29). New York: Routledge.

[Jane Doe], Canadian Girl Dies After Suicide Attempt; Parents Allege She Was Raped By 4 Boys. (2013, April 9). *Huffington Post*. Retrieved April 12, 2013, from www.huffingtonpost.com/2013/04/09/rehtaeh-parsons-girl-dies-suicide-rape-canada_n_3045033.html

Retter, C. & Shariff, S. (2012). A Delicate Balance: Defining the Line Between Open Civil Proceedings and the Protection of Children in the Online Digital Era. *Canadian Journal of Law and Technology, 10*(2), 232–262.

Rigby, K. (2007). *Bullying in Schools and What to Do about It: Revised and Updated*. Australia: Acer Press.

SACOMSS Media Watch. (2013, March 18). This is what rape culture looks like: The Steubenville Rapists [web post comment]. Retrieved from http://sacomssmediawatch.org/.

Salmivalli, C. & Pöyhönen, V. (2012). Cyberbullying in Finland. In Q. Li, D. Cross, and P.K. Smith (Eds.), *Cyberbullying in the global playground: Research from International Perspectives* (pp. 57–72). West Sussex: Wiley-Blackwell.

Seidman, K. (2012, September 19). McGill law students in project that aims to curb cyberbullying. *The Gazette*. Retrieved September 19, 2012, from www.montrealgazette.com/.

Seidman, K. (2013, November 20). Tougher laws not the answer to cyberbullying, conference told. *The Gazette*. Retrieved November 20, 2013, from www.montrealgazette.com/.

Seidman, K. (2014, April 4). University officials unsure of what future holds. *The Gazette*. Retrieved April 4, 2014, from www.montrealgazette.com/news/University+officials+unsure+what+future+holds/9715870/story.html.

Shariff, S. (2005). Cyber-dilemmas in the new millennium: School obligations to provide student safety in a virtual school environment. *McGill Journal of Education, 40*(3), 457–477.

Shariff, S. (2008). *Cyberbullying: Issues and Solutions for the School, the Classroom, and the Home.* Ablington, Oxfordshire, UK: Routledge (Taylor & Frances Group).

Shariff, S. (2009). *Confronting Cyberbullying: What Schools Need to Know to Control Misconduct and Avoid Legal Consequences.* New York, NY: Cambridge University Press.

Shariff, S. & Churchill, A. (Eds.) (2010). *Truths and myths of cyber-bullying: International perspectives on stakeholder responsibility and children safety.* New York: Peter Lang.

Shariff, S., Wiseman, A. & Crestohl, L. (2012). Defining the Lines between Children's Vulnerability to Cyberbullying and the Open Court Principle: Implications of A.B. (Litigation Guardian of) v. Bragg Communications Inc. *Education and Law Journal,* 21(3), 231–262.

Slonje, R. & Smith, P. K. (2008). Cyberbullying: Another main type of bullying? *Scandinavian Journal of Psychology,* 49, 147–154. doi:10.1111/j.1467-9450. (2007).00611.x.

Sonawane, V. (2014, March 11). Cyber Bullying Increases Suicidal Thoughts and Attempts: Study. *HNGN.* Retrieved March 12, 2014, from www.hngn.com/articles/26245/20140311/cyber-bullying-increases-suicidal-thoughts-attempts-study.htm.

Sugarman, D. B. & Willoughby, T. (2013). Technology and violence: Conceptual issues raised by the rapidly changing social environment. *Psychology of Violence,* 3(1), 1–8.

Tapscott, D. (1998). *Growing Up Digital. The rise of the net generation.* New York: McGraw-Hill.

Tapscott, D. (2009). *Grown up digital: How the net generation is changing your world.* New York: McGraw-Hill.

Thom, K., Edwards, G., Nakarada-Kordic, I., McKenna, B., O'Brien, A. & Nairn, R. (2011). Suicide online: Portrayal of website-related suicide by the New Zealand media. *New Media and Society,* 13(8), 1355–1372.

Thomas, M. (2011). Technology, Education and the Discourse of the Digital Native: Between Evangelists and Dissenters. In Thomas, M. (Ed.). *Deconstructing Digital Natives: Young people, technology, and the new literacies* (pp. 1–14). New York: Routledge.

Van Praagh, S. (2005). Adolescence, Autonomy and Harry Potter: The Child as Decision Maker. *International Journal of Law in Context,* 1(4), 335–373.

Van Praagh, S. (2007). 'Sois Sage'- Responsibility for Childishness in the Law of Civil Wrongs. In Neyers, J.W., Chamberlain, E. and Pital, S.G.A. (Eds.), *Emerging Issues in Tort Law* (pp. 63–84). Oxford: Hart Publishing.

Varjas, K., Meyers, J., Kiperman, S. & Howard, A. (2013). Technology Hurts? Lesbian, Gay, and Bisexual Youth Perspectives of Technology and Cyberbullying. *Journal of School Violence,* 12(1), 27–44.

Wade, A. & Beran, T. (2011). Cyberbullying: The New Era of Bullying. *Canadian Journal of School Psychology,* 26(1), 44–61.

Werner, N. E. & Crick, N. R. (2004). Maladaptive peer relationships and the development of relational and physical aggression during middle childhood. *Social Development,* 13(4), 495–514.

Willard, N. (2010). Ensuring Student Cyber Safety. (Subcommittee on Healthy Families and Communities, Committee on Education and Labor). Retrieved from www.gpo.gov/fdsys/pkg/CHRG-111hhrg56926/pdf/CHRG-111hhrg56926.pdf.

Ybarra, M. L., Diener-West, M., Leaf, P. J., Markow, D., Hamburger, M. & Boxer, P. (2008). Linkages between internet and other media violence with seriously violent behavior by youth. *Pediatrics*, *122*(5), 929–937.
Ybarra, M. L., Mitchell, K. J., Wolak, J. & Finkelhor, D. (2006). Examining character- istics and associated distress related to Internet harassment: Findings from the Second Youth Internet Safety Survey. *Pediatrics*, *118*(4), 1169–1177.
Yonezawa, S., Jones, M. & Joselowsky, F. (2009). Youth engagement in high schools: Developing a multidimensional, critical approach to improving engagement for all students. *Journal of Educational Change*, *10*(2–3), 191–209.

LEGISLATION

Anti-Bullying Bill of Rights Act (2011) P.L. 2010, c. 122.
Chapter 2011-180 (*House Bill 75*).
Dignity for All Students Act (2010), c. 482.
Safe Streets and Communities Act, S.C. 2012, c.1.
Seth's Law, Assembly Bill 9, 2011.
Texas Penal Code, § 43.261 (Acts 2011, 82nd Leg., R.S., Ch. 1322 (*Senate Bill 407*)).

CASE LAW

A.B. (Litigation Guardian of) v. Bragg Communications Inc., 2012 SCC 46, [2012] 2 S.C.R. 567.
A.B. v. State of Indiana, No 67A01 0609-JV-372, 2007 Ind. App. LEXIS 694 (Ind. Ct. App. Apr. 9, 2007).
D.C. v. R.R., 2010 WL 892204 (Cal. App. Ct. March 15, 2010).
Re: C.S. 2012 CP-39-JV-447-2012. Retrieved from www.krautharris.com/ documents/In-re-CS.pdf.

CHAPTER TWO

Sexism Defines the Lines between *Fun* and Power

[I]f it's like a close friend and he says something offensive then you know he could be joking.

They didn't think it would be taken seriously!

There's a point where even if it is a joke, it's not okay to say some of those things. If it's hurtful, like if any of my friends said something hurtful like that to me, I probably wouldn't be okay with that.

(DTL Research respondents)

INTRODUCTION

In this chapter, I set the context for my discussion of legal responses that seem out of touch with the complexities and nuances of current popular culture and its enormous influence on young people. Although I have defined young people as Digitally Empowered Kids (DE Kids), the influences I discuss in this chapter can "disempower" them, with devastating results. In order to protect, rectify, prevent, and reduce the risks of engagement in online behaviors that can get young people into trouble with peers, school, and the law, it is important that we, as adults, attempt to understand what goes through their minds. Accordingly, this chapter considers a range of social contexts and influences, the DTL Research where we heard from 1,083 participants, and scholarly literature on moral development and moral disengagement. I discuss these considerations in light of well-publicized cases of cyberbullying and sexting, some of which have come to public attention because of the tragic suicides that followed the extreme humiliation and persistent online abuse.

I would like to acknowledge the contribution of doctoral student Ashley DeMartini who provided the scholarly materials on "rape culture" and sexism, and both Ashley and doctoral student Arzina Zaver for their support with editing and referencing. I also acknowledge the contribution of Dr. Nelofar Sheikh in the data coding and production of the graphs and tables presented under the DTL Research in this chapter and others throughout the book.

GOAL OF THIS CHAPTER

After reading this chapter, you will have a basic appreciation of why reactive laws have little effect without supportive educational policies and programs to help young people recognize and redefine appropriate boundaries for their own behavior. As I explain here, the boundaries may be blurred and confused in some cases, but where acceptable norms and behavior within the peer group are concerned there are very clear social lines in the minds of these generations that should not be crossed. These lines for young people emerge both in the DTL Research findings, which I present here, and also in some of the high-profile cases that I analyze. When these normative lines among DE Kids are crossed, particularly in cases involving an assertion of sexuality, it can draw significant wrath and vitriolic public humiliation from the very peer group to which "offenders" previously belonged. This peer social context is largely influenced, but also complicated, by influences from adult-created and adult-modeled popular culture. Young people attempt to imitate adult role models, but also to establish their own identities. These norms can also be explained in part by considering stages of moral development and young people's ability to empathize with others. Therefore, to the extent that the research in this area is helpful, I have included it in this chapter. My framework for discussion comprises three parts.

WELL-PUBLICIZED CASES, INFLUENCE OF NEWS MEDIA, POPULAR CULTURE, AND "RAPE CULTURE"

First, I draw on scholarly literature that concerns popular culture's influences on youth as well as feminist perspectives on why girls and women are publicly subjected to humiliation when they attempt to assert their sexuality. I highlight the existence of "rape culture" in universities; a concerning issue that has been addressed in the courts and was similarly analyzed in my last book.[1] Within this context, I discuss a number of highly public cases. Some of these cases ended in tragedy and suicide, and others brought criminal charges and lawsuits against perpetrators. I do not address the legal issues here because I treat them in Chapters 3 and 4. However, I do draw attention to those legal aspects of such cases, that are important to remember when I discuss the role of law in later chapters.

After providing some context, I discuss the study findings of research undertaken with a grant from the Social Sciences and Humanities Research Council of Canada (SSHRC) and Facebook. The implications of these findings are analyzed with reference to the broader context of rape and popular culture. This discussion also sets the stage for addressing the legal considerations in Chapters 3 and 4.

---

[1] Ellen Kraft wrote about the social and legal implications of "juicycampus.com," in my book *Truths and Myths of Cyber-bullying* (Shariff & Churchill, 2010).

Finally, I conclude this chapter with a brief summary around the relevant scholarship on moral development, moral disengagement, and empathy that I have reported elsewhere with my colleagues Victoria Talwar and Carlos Gomez (Talwar, Gomez & Shariff, 2014). This discussion builds on the broader social context and research presented in this chapter, establishing a comprehensive contextual platform to facilitate the legal analysis about the role of law and its implications in Chapters 3 and 4.

It is not within the scope of this chapter to discuss in great detail the known facts of cyberbullying and sexting cases reported in the news media. I only highlight details that are pertinent to the scholarly and legal discussion. My objective is to draw attention to key issues and considerations in five North American cases. Each case received an inordinate amount of media attention, which I argue, might have caused more harm than good. Although I commend the news media in raising significant public awareness about the issues relating to sexting, as Edwards (2005) and I observe (Shariff, 2008; 2009; Shariff & Churchill, 2010; Shariff, Wiseman & Crestohl, 2011; Retter & Shariff, 2011), reports about cyberbullying often sensationalize the victimization. Ironically and sadly, no issue has been more often described as a "sexy topic" than the tragic suicides related to sexting.

Amanda's Story
Consider first the tragic case of Amanda Todd, a fifteen-year-old Canadian teen from British Columbia, who committed suicide in 2012. Her case was complex because it involved a Dutch adult who lured her on the Internet when she was in Grade 8 and convinced her to pose semi-nude in front of a webcam; the adult then took a screenshot of the image. It took almost two years for police to track down the thirty-five-year-old man in the Netherlands and charge him with extortion, Internet luring, criminal harassment, and possession of child pornography in relation to Amanda's case, in addition to numerous other cases involving children (Hager, Shaw, Culbert & O'Connor, 2014). One of the particularly devastating aspects of this case was that the photograph circulated online to Amanda's relatives, friends, and schoolmates resulting in incessant cyberbullying by her peers, as well as anxiety and depression and the need for Amanda to move homes and switch schools. She felt isolated and decided to share her story on social media by videoing herself holding up index cards and telling her story one card at a time. She documented her experiences of being harassed on Facebook and ostracized from peer groups at school, resulting in her isolation and suicidal thoughts. She wrote about the photograph that had been circulated, saying: "I can never get that photo back" (Hager, Shaw, Culbert, & O'Connor, 2014, p. A10). Regretfully, after posting this video, Amanda was confronted by a group of teens outside her new school. She was beaten up and the attack was filmed. The news story does not confirm whether that video was uploaded, but it was after this attack that Amanda went home and drank bleach.

Consider the perspectives of teens of the same age, in the DTL Research, vis-à-vis this type of situation. Participants told us that when peers have had a bad day, or if they are feeling hurt and isolated, the worst thing they could do is post their feelings of isolation online. This is because once it is done the teenagers believed that the person who posted the comment should be ready for the onslaught of insults and comments that follow. I vividly recall comments made by a group of teenagers between the ages of thirteen and eighteen during a focus group session as part of the DTL Research. I asked them what might trigger the kind of harassment and vitriolic bullying a teen like Amanda Todd experienced on social media, and what motivates such extensive negative feelings. All focus group comments were recorded verbatim and have been similarly provided herein to retain authenticity with only slight modifications for clarity. Here are some of their answers:

People will comment with either things like get over it, or they'll tell you [that] you are an idiot or something because you are giving that attention that feeds off the rest of that network and you're having all the negative comments posted onto your wall.

You want it so that people can feel sorry for you and things like that, and it always turns into a negative thing no matter what.

But when you post things that to them don't matter, they think of themselves. And they think, "I don't think that matters, so I'm just going to post this comment because I can." And then it's like "there should be a hate button."

That's what people want. They want to see like, people who post those comments. They want to see people getting hyped up. Like "Oh yeah F! that person" They want argument. So it's not just like you post something and then people bring the argument upon you, you're creating it for yourself.

Because they want to look big, unstoppable, and to make the other people look small and stupid. Because they think they are cool and they think they can do anything so they do anything and they place embarrassing pictures of other people on Facebook, Tumblr, Twitter, chat room, and other chat places.

Another main motivation for bullying, according to the focus group, is jealousy of other peoples' popularity. The participants noted that it is a lot easier to express this jealousy on social media rather than in person:

Because they are jealous or they are trying to make friends because they do not have any or they are just being mean.

It is probably because they are jealous, or unhappy in their lives. Making fun of others might be a way for them to feel better about themselves.

Because when you don't see each other you don't know who it is so you can't tell anybody it was "him" or "her" unless you see them.

I return to more analysis regarding Amanda's case and the DTL Research later in this chapter, but first, I want to address the media's generally insensitive handling of the case. When Amanda committed suicide in 2012, there were weeks and weeks of media coverage regarding the case. Granted, Amanda's mother had initiated some of that because she supported her daughter's attempt to inform people about the isolation and horror of sexual harassment and online bullying. But what really bothered me was the repeated display of Amanda's video showing the index cards, and also in some reports, her Facebook page (or other social media pages) after her death, where "trolls" wrote offensive messages about her attempts to die and the fact that she drank bleach. These media reports were disturbing for three reasons.

First, every time a news station or Internet site aired Amanda's message, it represented her as a victim rather than as the person she had been for the better part of her life. Very little was aired about the successes and happiness she had experienced in her short life. There is a body of discourse emerging in the wake of these types of suicide cases that suggests that the media "glorifies" suicide (Gould, 2001; Pirkis, Blood, Beautrais, Burgess & Skehan, 2006; Lokeinsky, 2011). Other teens that may be contemplating suicide may see the amount of media attention Amanda's case received and they might seek to achieve the same by committing suicide.

Second, each time news media aired Amanda's social media page displaying comments placed there by "trolls" after her death, it provided them with a platform to reach a wide audience. This re-victimized Amanda even in death.

Third, the repeated airing of Amanda's story created an effect of "moral panic." It increased the pressure on politicians to come down hard on cyber-bullying no matter how young the perpetrators. Despite the fact that Amanda's main perpetrator was a thirty-five-year-old male pedophile, the primary dialogue around the case was about cyberbullying by her peers. Certainly, the peer bullying contributed to her isolation at school. But once the "capper" made her photographs available online, there should have been some support available to her before she posted her message of isolation, and even immediately after. My research (Shariff & Churchill, 2010) disclosed that teenagers, in particular, self-isolate. This is because they are too afraid to report cyberbullying for fear of further ramifications. As my study of 800 Grade 6 and 7 students from the Montreal region found (Shariff & Churchill, 2010), 50 percent of teenagers will not report cyberbullying for fear that: (a) perpetrators will accuse them of "ratting" and the bullying will increase; (b) adults (especially teachers) they report to will not do anything about the reported cyberbullying; and (c) parents will withdraw their online privileges to keep them safe, which will result in even further isolation.

We also observed that 70 percent of eleven- through fifteen-year-olds reported being bullied or cyberbullied often, or occasionally, and 43 percent confessed to "pretending to be someone else" online to engage in bullying. Seventy-two percent of females reported being cyberbullied compared to 28 percent of males, noting that they would only report cyberbullying if they could do it anonymously (see also similar statistics gathered by Hoff & Mitchell, in Shariff & Churchill, 2010).

Jane Doe's Story, the Maple Ridge Case, and Steubenville

Two other well-publicized Canadian cases and the American case of Steuben-ville (referenced in Chapter 3) involved teenage girls who were either drugged or incapacitated by alcohol and gang raped with their assailants posting and distributing the videos or photographs online for all to see. The legalities in the Steubenville case are addressed in Chapter 3. For the purposes of the current chapter, it is important to note the common elements of all three cases and to highlight some considerations.

Jane Doe committed suicide after humiliating photographs and videos of her rape were circulated online. Her suicide followed at least six other teen suicides in Nova Scotia in 2013. The accused, who was under 18 at the time of the offense, but is now 20 years old, plead guilty in youth court on September 22, 2014 to charges for making child pornography. The accused's name is protected under the Youth Criminal Justice Act. Jane Doe's parents and extended family have all become involved in advocating for policy development and stricter regulations on the distribution of non-consensual images online. The hard work of Jane Doe's family paid off with the development of Nova Scotia's new *Cyber-safety Act*, discussed in Chapter 4. This new legislation holds parents of perpetrators responsible and designates the distribution of intimate images as an actionable cause for damages under tort law. As I point out in Chapter 3, the wording of this act has legal scholars concerned about the potential for misapplication of this law. Jane Doe's parents, along with Amanda Todd's mother, were also instrumental in convincing the Canadian federal government to develop a law that specifically addresses cyberbullying and the non-consensual distribution of intimate images online. On November 20, 2013, Canadian Minister of Justice Peter MacKay announced Bill C-13, the *Protecting Canadians from Online Crime Act*. This controversial bill has yet to be brought before a House of Commons or Senate committee but has already been met with very strong oppositions from various political parties. In Chapter 3, I detail the relevant sections and implications of this bill and highlight public concerns about its potential impact on children and youth, as well as on the privacy of Canadian citizens.

Unlike the case of Jane Doe, the Maple Ridge case,[2] in which the victim, whose identity is protected, was drugged and gang raped in 2010 after a rave, did not result in new legislation. However, it does raise important questions and consider-ations. In this case, a sixteen-year-old male watched the rape. It is not clear whether he was a friend of the rapists or a bystander. The disturbing part is that he decided to videotape the incident and pass it to an older friend to post on Facebook. What one would have expected him to do was to pass it on to the police so that the rapists could be arrested and punished. Once posted, the video spread like a virus to such an extent that Maple Ridge police and the RCMP (Royal

---

[2] The publicly known facts of this case are discussed in this book pending receipt of permission from the British Columbia Youth Court to access the court documents. We have applied for access, but in the meantime I reference media reports. Thus, there may be some discrepancies in reported facts, which will be corrected when court records are obtained.

Canadian Mounted Police) made public announcements that anyone caught with the video would be arrested for possession and distribution of child pornography.

The boy was charged with possession and distribution of child pornography and given a one-year sentence to conduct community work. In addition, the judge, who noted that the teen had shown sufficient remorse for his actions, requested that he write an essay on the "evils of the Internet" (Weisgarber, 2012). It is likely the boy's actions were motivated by the influence of rape culture as highlighted in the scholarly literature; in particular, the tendency to dehumanize the victim and justify the harm by blaming her for being drunk, or as in this case, drugged. After the video went viral, there was significant discussion on social media as to whether the girl had "asked for it" and whether the images in the video made it look as though she "enjoyed" it. The impact of the video on the victim's life would clearly be significant. She most likely could not return to her school; she might have had to move to another town or area; and because of the global reach of the Internet, she might be recognized well into the future as "the girl in the rape video." Thus, on top of the physical violation and abuse she suffered, the emotional and psychological harm could affect her confidence, sexuality, relationships, and achievement for many years to come. In this case it appeared that the victim had a supportive family, but for those who cannot turn to their families for support this type of an attack would be devastating.

A very similar rape case took place in Steubenville, Ohio, three years after Maple Ridge, in 2013. In this case, two teenage boys were found guilty of the rape of a drunken sixteen-year-old girl at a party. The act itself was shocking enough as images of the rape in progress surfaced online (Welsh-Huggins, 2013; Murphy, 2013). Equally shocking, however, was the backlash online. On Twitter, people made comments such as, "Shouldn't they charge the lil' slut for underage drinking?" and "I honestly feel sorry for those boys in that Steubenville trial, the whore was asking for it" (Binder, 2013). The public response to both the Maple Ridge and Steubenville cases is highly disturbing because no blame was accorded to the rapists, as I discuss in Chapter 3, and the victims were seen as deserving or bringing the "punishment" on themselves.

What is more, in all three cases all three girls were re-victimized every time the videos of their physical and sexual abuse were distributed, viewed, saved, and reviewed on email, smartphones, and social media. It is equally disturbing to know that this type of rape culture is thriving in postsecondary contexts (see study by Cassidy & Jackson highlighted in CBC News, March 11, 2014).

Rape Culture in Postsecondary Institutions
The fact that rape culture is well established in university campuses was evident from the controversial American website, "juicycampus.com," which was shut down in 2009. The website allowed its visitors to vote, compare, and discuss the looks and sexual appeal of female students on campus. As a result of harassment and obscene comments, the owner of the site was sued. Ellen Kraft (2010) provides a good detailed analysis of the

juicycampus.com cases in my book *Truths and Myths of Cyber-bullying* (Shariff & Churchill, 2010), therefore, I do not detail it here. However, rape culture still thrives across university campuses.

Consider the following examples of this unsettling culture: Frosh[3] chants that endorse non-consensual sex with underage girls at both the University of British Columbia and St. Mary's University in Nova Scotia (CBC News, 2013a, b), online discussions of the desired rape of a student council female president by her male colleagues on social media at the University of Ottawa (Feibel, 2014), and the ritual of hazing on university and college sports teams. In 2005, senior members of McGill University's football team used a broomstick to sexually assault a freshman player (Kryk, 2013). More recently, three fraternities at Marquette University faced allegations of sexual assault and hazing during one of their parties (Crowther, 2014). An analysis of the St. Mary's incident is provided in an interesting report by Dalhousie Law Professor A. Wayne MacKay (MacKay, 2013) and discussed in light of the incident's legal implications. The report identified 6 Cs of desired culture change at universities: (1) commitment, (2) consent, (3) critical thinking, (4) communication, (5) collaboration, and (6) caring. In light of the aforementioned 6 Cs, I would like to highlight some of MacKay's recommendations. Specifically, MacKay suggests: (1) developing a university-wide code of conduct, (2) revising the university's sexual assault policy, (3) increasing the understanding of consent, and, finally, (4) encouraging and creating the infrastructure for teaching and research excellence in areas related to sexualized violence (MacKay, 2013). These recommendations not only emphasize the importance of well-established norms and law in affecting cultural change but they also reiterate the importance of true engagement with the law –through education. The law is not something that should be inflicted upon us; rather, it should be something that we interact with. Increasing legal literacy among university students and the public more generally is paramount to our efforts to curb cyberbullying and rape culture.

The University of Ottawa had recently suspended its men's hockey team when shortly after that, allegations of sexual assault emerged around the team's conduct while in Thunder Bay, Ontario (Bradshaw, 2014). More recently, shocking evidence of rape culture surfaced within the student leadership at the University of Ottawa in Canada's capital city and the hub of law and policy. Following is an excerpt from the online conversation that took place about the University of Ottawa's student council President. These quotes come from the blog, *The Belle Jar*:[4]

---

[3] Frosh week at universities is the undergraduate orientation week where bonding activities are organized and often result in a large amount of social drinking and partying among students.

[4] Rape Culture at the University of Ottawa. (February 28, 2014). Retrieved April 26, 2014, from http://bellejar.ca/2014/02/28/rape-culture-at-the-university-of-ottawa/.

*A **non-elected student**:* Let me tell you something right now: the "tri-fluvienne" [nick-name for someone from Trois-Rivières, Québec] president will suck me off in her office chair and after I will fuck her in the ass on Pat [Marquis]'s desk.

VP social for the Criminology Student Association: *Someone punish her with their shaft.*

Member of the board of directors of the Student Federation of the University of Ottawa: *Well Christ, if you fuck [her] I will definitely buy you a beer.*

These are but a few examples of rape culture in postsecondary settings. Specifically, the Ottawa University case confirms that even when women do not assert their sexuality publically, but hold leadership positions that come with some power, or express feminist views, they can become targets of extreme sexual harassment and online ridicule.

"Rape Culture" Resides in Popular Culture

Sexist and misogynist attitudes are unfortunately endemic and embedded in popular culture within greater society, which is then reflected in institutional and corporate settings. This is especially true when women in positions of power use their agency to express informed opinions, or when they assert feminist perspectives that can be a threat to insecure males. For instance, Amanda Hess, journalist and frequent tweeter, received death threats online for writing about issues around sex. She encountered a barrage of tweets, which ranged from attacks on her appearance, "I see you are physically not very attractive," to physical threats on her life, "happy to say we live in the same state. I'm looking you up, and when I find you, I'm going to rape you and remove your head" (Hess, 2014, para. 2). Hess admits there have been too many instances of this kind of online intimidation to count, pointing to how frequently women endure similar and disturbing forms of misogyny. Anita Sarkeesian, feminist pop culture critic, had her Wikipedia page hacked repeatedly with obscenities and pornography after the launch of her campaign that examines the sexist and misogynistic portrayals of women in video games. One man even went so far as to create a video game that allowed players to beat up and inflict black eyes and cuts on a virtual Sarkeesian (Moore, 2012). Blogger and programmer, Kathy Sierra, received death threats too, which caused her to cancel a public appearance and freeze her blog (BBC News, 2007). These forms of harassment can be devastating, and the humiliation can affect women's health, academics, and careers.

There are also serious concerns about rape culture intertwining with popular culture and its impact on the behavior of girls in posting or forwarding intimate and nude photographs online or to peers in trust (Bailey & Steeves, 2013; Bailey & Hanna, 2011; Ybarra, Mitchell, Wolak & Finkelhor, 2006). Young girls who have trusted male peers and sent risqué photographs online have sometimes paid the heavy price of public humiliation, ruined reputations, and blame for bringing it on themselves through "slut-shaming," once those images are distributed. As seen in the Steubenville case, the rape was shocking enough as images surfaced online (Welsh-Huggins, 2013; Murphy, 2013). More frightening and equally shocking was the backlash on social media (Binder, 2013).

Why Do Girls Post Nude "Selfies" or Engage in Sexting?

Another question that eludes older generations is why teenage girls might post nude or intimate images of themselves online, or why they send them to friends knowing that despite promises of confidentiality, others could get hold of the images and distribute them. It is quite easy to take someone's smartphone and view the saved content. Moreover, the false sense of security provided by apps such as Snapchat, which promises that risqué images will only remain on screen for a few seconds, is not reliable. These apps cannot prevent screenshots from being taken. This was the case in the arrest of ten boys between the ages of thirteen and fifteen in Laval, Quebec in November, 2013. The boys convinced female classmates to send them intimate photographs because they would only remain on their phones for a few seconds. Thinking this was "flirty fun," the girls sent the images only to discover that the boys took screenshots and distributed them online and through social media. The boys have been charged with distribution and possession of child pornography. Two of the boys face additional charges of production of child pornography. All await court hearings, which have continued to be deferred (CBC News, 2013c; Magder, 2014). So why did the girls agree to do it?

Girls Receive Contradictory Messages from Society

The discourse within feminist scholarship highlights the fact that girls and women in contemporary society receive conflicting messages. On the one hand, women and girls are encouraged to take on leadership roles and careers and positions of power traditionally held by men and boys. Popular culture also depicts as powerful, celebrities such as Lady Gaga, Rihanna, Madonna, Miley Cyrus, and Beyoncé. All these women are paid large amounts of money to assert their sexuality by pushing existing social boundaries. They all appear publicly and send strong messages of sexual independence. The marketization of the *modern woman* – strong and sexually assertive – has been dominating popular culture storylines across the music, film, and television industries (Chen, 2013). Since the 1990s, ideas of "Girl Power" have hijacked mass media outlets as images of overtly sexualized women emerge as proof of women's empowerment and agency.

Young girls impressed by celebrity role models might want to achieve the same notoriety as their idols, and this could be what drives teens' tendency to engage in sexting. What these young women do not recognize are the alternate forces of male hegemony, misogynist attitudes, sexual objectification of women, and a thriving male culture that attempts to regain power over women through sexual violence, embarrassment, and victim blaming known as "slut-shaming" (Ringrose & Renold, 2012; Hirschman, Impett & Schooler, 2006). Thus, the young women who were coerced into posing for nude or semi-nude photos and sending those photos to male classmates on Snapchat may have been driven by the boys' flattery and a need to assert their sexuality. They assumed Snapchat was safe, and even though much is reported about the tendency of such photographs to spread online, they decided to take the risks, without realizing that the real objective of the boys was to assert their sexuality and power over the girls by taking screenshots of the images and posting them online.

These trends in popular culture are more indicative of the pervasive reach of neoliberalism, its principles of consumer choice and market supremacy, than the actual liberation of women's bodies from traditional, passive, and subjugated positions (Chen, 2013; Gill & Arthurs, 2007). Neoliberal marketing spins the notions of agency and independence as a part of a sexually liberated woman's choice to voluntarily self-objectify (Chen, 2013). For instance, Rihanna's music video for the song "Pour It Up" portrays the pop star as a stripper-pimp. The character in the video has power and influence, using her sexualized body to make money and obtain status. Miley Cyrus' video for the song "Wrecking Ball" shows the young singer naked while provocatively straddling a swinging wrecking ball as she sings about a troubled relationship. These sexually explicit pop music videos significantly influence the socialization of adolescent girls (Zhang, Dixon & Conrad, 2010; Levande, 2008). They believe that they too can assert their sexuality through the sharing of nude or intimate photographs online.

What they do not realize is that celebrity role models are doing this as a business. They receive enormous amounts of money to expose their nude bodies publicly. Instead, the reality is that when teenage girls post such photographs online, they risk being ridiculed and slut-shamed even by their female classmates, who are afraid to support them for fear of being harassed themselves (Poole, 2013; Holman, 2013; Khazan, 2013).

This comes through clearly in the DTL Research findings outlined in the sections that follow. When presented with hypothetical scenarios in which a teenage girl sent nude pictures to a boyfriend in trust, which were later distributed online without consent, 46.47 percent of the students said the teenage girl deserved to be harassed and demeaned because she behaved like a slut. This echoes the public online reactions to the Steubenville and Maple Ridge rape cases. However, when presented with the scenario of a drunken female student whose photograph was taken and posted online by someone else, students of both genders agreed that the posting was unfair and that she was unnecessarily humiliated online. Unlike the case of Jane Doe and the Steubenville and Maple Ridge incidents, this hypothetical scenario involving a drunken student did not involve sex. This suggests an undeclared line in teen digital culture with respect to the amount of agency girls can use to express their sexuality. Too much, and they are perceived as "sluts." Too little, and they become isolated from the popular peer group. They must navigate just the right balance.

As long as girls express their sexuality within the accepted norms of their peers, without standing out too much, they are accepted. However, when they are seen as crossing the line to assert their sexuality in ways that may create jealousy and envy, and where they might stand out from the crowd like celebrities do, they are labeled "sluts" that deserve to be humiliated publicly and put back in their place. This reminds me of the Japanese saying I included in my book *Confronting Cyberbullying* (2009): "The nail that sticks out needs to be hammered down" (Shariff, 2009, p. 69).

On the other hand, it is an acceptable youth norm to make the most outrageous comments and insults, and pass on humiliating photographs of others, to make the peer group laugh. The unwritten rule is that postings should not draw attention to oneself, but to someone else who "deserves" to be scapegoated (DTL Research, 2013). More than a decade ago, I quoted Sibylle Artz (Artz, 1998) who observed that, especially among teenage girls, the victim is singled out for doing something that deserves blame. She is then dehumanized and in contemporary contexts labeled as a "slut." This dehumanization and labeling then justifies the vitriol that follows. As I explain later as part of the discussion of a California case, *D.C. v. R.R.* (2010), this type of teenage peer behavior code also applies in cases where males are perceived to be (or are) gay, or seen to have stereotypically feminine personality traits. These traits are sometimes sufficient to attract the homophobic wrath of teen males who are also attempting to establish their maleness and power.

When it comes to rape cases where teenage girls have been drugged, gang-raped, and images of the assaults are then posted online, I suggest there are several influences at work. They include the following:

- The influence of pedophiles and cappers who take advantage of the Internet and vulnerability of young women to extort nude and intimate photographs.
- Peer pressure among male youth to prove their male sexuality to meet heteronormative standards of belonging to their peer groups (Pascoe, 2007). They may engage in sexual harassment and assault of females and homophobic harassment of males to assert their heterosexuality (Frank, 1996; Bender, 2001; Stein, 1995).
- Burgeoning sexuality, especially at the post-puberty age where hormones are raging, resulting in young men establishing their social relationships and becoming more aware of their own sexuality and that of others.

The data discussed in the next section as part of our DTL Research with children and teens between the ages of eight and eighteen is illuminating and interesting.

THE DEFINE THE LINE RESEARCH (DTL RESEARCH)

Here are some pertinent details of our research, together with a summary and analysis of our findings:

Background and Project Objectives

In 2012, I received two research grants that would help me gain an improved understanding of how two sets of digital generations think about their online engagement. The objectives of our project were as follows:

- To determine whether and how children aged 8–12 (pre-Facebook age) and teens aged 13–18 (Facebook age) define the line between online jokes, teasing, and actual harm. This included assessing their awareness of the harmful consequences of posting and distributing non-consensual sexual or intimate content online; knowledge of their legal responsibilities; empathy with those victimized by various forms of online abuse known as cyberbullying; and comprehension of the impact of offensive online postings and communication on others.
- To assess whether the participants can easily define the lines between public and private spaces and online content, and in relation to those considerations, analyze their understanding of ownership of content and culpability when content is misused or abused online. Although our original intent was to ask only the older group (aged 13–18) about these concerns, we also obtained interesting responses on notions of public and private spaces and content from the younger group.
- To engage both age groups in interactive projects including the development of video vignettes that illustrate how they define the lines of joking, teasing, and digital citizenship.

I focus largely on the findings of our first two objectives. Later in the book, I also discuss the research where we engaged participants in developing their own video vignettes to illustrate how they define the lines. These results are included in my concluding paragraph, culminating in a discussion of the overall implications of our study and recommendations going forward. At this point, it is important to provide readers with a brief description of the methodologies adopted in the research.

Methodologies

The methodologies for this portion of our research were qualitative and quantitative, as well as interactive in Phase 3.

Phase 1: Online Survey

The online surveys for pre-Facebook age (8–12) and Facebook age (13–18) participants were designed to gather information about their experience(s) of cyberbullying, sexting, online discrimination, and their perspectives on digital citizenship, with a view to assess their understanding of harmless versus harmful joking. A set of written hypothetical scenarios pertaining to sexting and private versus public spaces were provided to participants.

Phase 2: Focus Groups

A set of semi-structured questions was developed to conduct focus group sessions with the pre-Facebook age participants (8–12) and Facebook age participants (13–18). Additional questions were asked to further probe the children's and adolescents' legal literacy and the legal risks associated with joking, teasing, and sharing information.

Phase 3: Interactive Projects

A full day event was organized on December 6, 2013, to engage school-aged children (8–18) in collaborative activities. Arrangements were made with the National Film Board of Canada on a pro bono basis to conduct a video-making workshop with twenty participants at McGill University. The workshops prepared participants to develop video vignettes that helped them explore and express how they define the line between socially responsible behavior and forms of online abuse that they might categorize or define as cyberbullying, and the line between public and private spaces. Prior to the workshop, the participants engaged in a range of activities and interactive games to learn how they think about the lines between insults, jokes, rumors, lies, criminal harassment, threats, and defamation through contemplating a range of scenarios.

Data collection

Phase 1: Online Survey

For recruitment purposes, we sent an ethics approval form and introductory letter explaining our research to a number of schools. Schools that agreed to participate were located in Montreal and Vancouver, Canada, and Seattle, Washington, and Palo Alto, California. Upon approval, the teachers of the participating grades were provided with consent forms for students' parents to sign. Once a number of students were selected, their teachers were contacted with a schedule for completing the questionnaires and provided with instructions for accessing the survey online. To maintain anonymity of the participants, a code was assigned to each classroom instead of each participant. Each class was provided with password-protected access to the questionnaire on Polldaddy.com. After the responses were captured, they were exported into NVivo 10 qualitative research software for analysis.

Phase 2: Focus Groups

Twenty focus group sessions were held in schools in Montreal, Quebec and Vancouver, British Columbia, as well as Seattle, Washington and Palo Alto, California. Focus group sessions involved fewer children from each school, face-to-face with either the principal investigator present or a senior member of her team and research assistants. The sessions were held with groups of four to eight children for forty to fifty minutes. A video vignette was shown to the participants, and then questions were asked. The discussion was audiotaped and later transcribed for data analysis.

Phase 3: Interactive Projects

A total of three schools in Montreal were recruited for this phase, with nineteen students ranging in age from eleven through sixteen. The participants were divided into three groups. A participatory action approach was used to design the interactive sessions. We had originally asked more schools to engage in the development of online interactive activities that could include video vignettes, prototypes for social media apps, smartphone apps, and so on, especially for the Facebook age group. Unfortunately, this turned out to be a logistical challenge given the short one-year timeframe and the apparent lack of motivation by schoolteachers to include this in a lesson plan. Despite reassurances from one school board in particular that they would encourage creativity in this endeavor, it seemed that getting teachers to bring out that creativity was another challenge. Hence, we took it upon ourselves to work directly with the children and organized a summit of interested schools to participate at McGill University. This summit was much more fruitful and provided us with some rich and interesting data, which is discussed in the analysis presented later on. The breakdown of the sessions conducted by DTL staff on December 6, 2013, is explained in Chapter 5, reporting Phase 3 of the project.

Data Analysis

We used NVivo software to analyze the data generated from the online questionnaires, focus groups, and interactive sessions. In NVivo, themes and sub-themes were created to capture the respondents' thoughts primarily on motivation behind the various behaviors the students described as cyberbullying, their awareness of the consequences of their online postings, the ways they engage in digital citizenship, and how they define the lines between private and public spaces, and between harmless and harmful joking. I present only a portion of the overall data obtained from this study as it relates to the concerns I seek to highlight in this book. We are currently analyzing scores of related data from the project, which will be reported in my next publication with the new studies being conducted at the postsecondary level.

Results and Discussion

For the online surveys, 1,088 children in total were recruited from sixteen schools in Canada (Montreal, Quebec and Vancouver, British Columbia) and two schools from the United States (Seattle, Washington, and Palo Alto, California). Five participants' responses were excluded due to a high percentage of missing data (e.g. unanswered questions). Our final sample therefore consisted of 1,083 participants. The profile of their age and gender is shown in Graphs 2.1 and 2.2.[5]

---

[5] Other demographic data and graphs can be found in Appendix B.

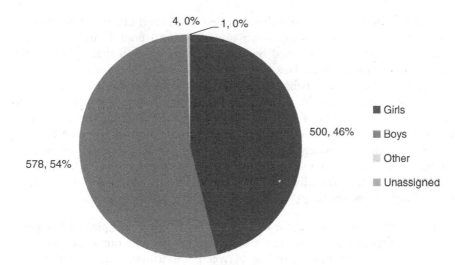

GRAPH 2.1: Gender profile of the participants for the online survey

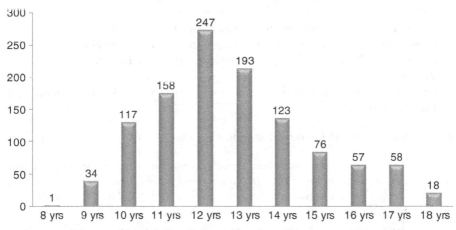

GRAPH 2.2: **Age profile of the participants for the online survey.** *Note:* Of the 1,083 participants, one participant did not disclose their age. Age distribute therefore represents only 1,082 participants. All other tables and graphs represent 1,083 responses.

Participants' Experiences and Thoughts on "Cyberbullying"

Although I have committed in this book to move away from using the words "cyberbullying" and "bullying," the accepted generic uses of both words required us to use them to communicate with the participants in our DTL Research. Thus, most of the analysis utilizes these words; however, in upcoming chapters, I have described the form of cyberbullying and the legal frameworks it might fall under, rather than generalize the behaviors under the heading of "cyberbullying."

First and foremost, the research confirmed that cyberbullying is an inevitable occurrence in society, serving as an impediment to digital citizenship. This sentiment is often accompanied by a sense of resignation that cyberbullying will probably never stop. This corroborates what I have noted earlier: that young people see hostile behavior modeled all around them, not only among children but also by adults and society in general. It was encouraging to see agreement among the pre-Facebook age children that offensive communication is not a positive way to interact and that it is worse than face-to-face bullying. What was more interesting was the theme that resonated throughout the data, namely, that social media sites could not protect them from being victimized.

The participants generally agreed on the following reasons for the difficulty in tracking and preventing cyberbullying:

- The challenge of verifying the motivation behind other people's online posts;
- Anonymity, or uncertainty that online threats will play out as actions;
- The difficulty of distinguishing between a harmless and harmful joke, especially on the Internet;
- The vast range of digital and social media that proliferate the online social sphere;
- Increased opportunities for participation by larger audiences;
- Observations that despite their interest in creating safe platforms, social media sites lack the ability to monitor offensive behavior and protect victims; and
- Concerns that "defriending" someone on Facebook may make the bullying worse.

Participant comments included the following observations:

It's on the Internet so if you would have seen the person and contacted them you would have seen them joking around and stuff, but it's through the Internet so you don't really know what they're thinking or if they're going to do anything...if they're actually going to do it.

The bully feels protected...by the screen...I think sometimes there's more cyberbullying because they don't have to confront the person.

With respect to the range of social media available and opportunities to join in or observe the offensive communication, participants noted that technology allows more people to join in the act of bullying. They also commented that it allows information to be shared very quickly on multiple websites; provides individuals with the ability to be anonymous; and facilitates the ability to hide behind screen names on some websites and applications. Participants acknowledged the problem does not reside in social media itself, but in *how* people use it and how perpetrators of bullying always find a tool to carry out their actions. Consider the following comment:

I think the problem is with cyberbullying, especially if it's on Facebook or Instagram or something, everybody sees. Let's say someone posts something bad about the other

*person but when other people see it they think that they could start doing something, like
start saying mean things to the person.*

There was a general sense that social media sites do not (or cannot) always help
much when it comes to reducing cyberbullying. Having worked with Facebook
and being aware of their concerted efforts to provide an improved safety
platform through their *Be Bold Stop Bullying* campaign, and their *Family
Safety* support pages, this data confirms that young people may not necessarily
be aware of such initiatives, and even if they are, many young people may not
turn to them because of their belief that it would not do any good. Moreover,
they may not be able to locate the information easily. Alternately, even if they
know of such initiatives, they still acknowledge the reality that it is difficult, if
not impossible, for social media sites to monitor for cyberbullying because of
the large number of accounts each of these sites has. Participants may not be
aware that legally in Canada and the United States social media intermediaries
are considered to be distributors rather than publishers and are not required to
monitor or take down content without a court order (*Zeran v. America Online,
Inc.*, 1997). Nonetheless, their observations on the challenges faced by social
media intermediaries in maintaining digital citizenship were also accurate.

...[A]nd there's always some kind of cyberbully situation or multiple [cyberbullying
situations], *so it's really hard to monitor every single account that people have.*

Moreover, participants explained that "defriending" someone on Facebook
can sometimes make things worse. The "defriending" procedure may be something Facebook can consider or revisit to make it safer for potential victims:
"If you defriend then they are going to find you and beat the heck out of you."

Motivation to Use Social Media

On questioning the *motivation* behind using social media, the majority of
participants in both the pre-Facebook and Facebook-age groups suggested that
social media is used to gain popularity, to be cool, or to feel good about oneself.
It is noteworthy that these comments were in response to a question that asked
nothing about cyberbullying or online abuse. Yet, they automatically connected
social media use with negative (rather than positive) postings. Consider the
following comments:

Because they want to look big [and] *unstoppable and to make the other people look
small and stupid.*

*Because they think they are cool and they think they can do anything so they do
anything and they place embarrassing pictures of other people on Facebook, Tumblr,
Twitter, chat rooms, and other chat places.*

I now move to look at some students' responses regarding the non-consensual
distribution of intimate images, which is largely the focus of this chapter.
The student responses are at the same time encouraging and alarming,

highlighting the dichotomy in their thinking about online postings and spaces. They illustrate why we need to pay much closer attention to how digital generations think about their postings and the norms that inform such postings before we proceed to implement strict policies and legislation.

Non-Consensual Distribution of Images (Intimate or Embarrassing)

The most common form of cyberbullying described by the respondents is someone posting an embarrassing picture of them that they had not previously approved. Respondents stated, for example: *"Someone posted an embarrassing photo of me on Facebook and I didn't like it."* Respondents described feeling angry or hurt by such actions. One respondent claimed: *"I've had a friend upload a picture of me on the Internet and I got really upset. Nothing bad happened but I felt humiliated."*

Many respondents simply claimed that these situations were quite common, saying, for example: *"This story* [referring to a hypothetical situation involving sexting] *sounds like something that actually happens all the time."* This comment came from the pre-Facebook age group, which is all the more alarming, especially hearing that it "happens all the time."

It was not clear whether some respondents simply distanced themselves from the situation or whether they really know that the actions described in our hypothetical scenarios were not so extraordinary. Personal experience with sexting was not discussed much in detail in the focus groups due to the sensitivity of the topic. However, some participants referred to incidents where they faced some level of harassment as a result of sexting. For example, one participant recalled an incident of being stalked by a friend on the Internet who sent threatening e-mails; however, the participant ultimately forgave the friend in the end because it happened only once. Meanwhile, another participant recalled an incident that took place on YouTube, which the participant decided to ignore based on a parent's advice. Another participant noted going to the police and reporting an incident of cyberbullying. This participant in particular identified and noted that cyberbullying involving sexting is a criminal offense to justify police involvement. These responses reflect the extent and level of seriousness of each participant's experiences with cyberbullying that inform their thinking about it as a matter that justifies legal intervention, or a matter that can be solved *ex-juris* (outside the legal justice system). It illustrates that there is a range of experiences and responses to the sexting of images and that responses should not be reactive, but thoughtful and informed.

Another personal experience with sexting was discussed in regard to how people use social media and how it can become unsafe when they add people to their social network that they do not know. In that incident, the participant noted that despite not accepting a friend request from a stranger, this unfamiliar person was able to view the participant's pictures and post inappropriate comments. This caused the teen to lose trust in the privacy settings of some social media sites. On the other hand, two participants noted that blocking a person or defriending them on social media sites is the best way to deal with these situations because they do not get bothered by others.

The fact that the non-consensual distribution of images was one of the key concerns about cyberbullying that surfaced in the data is important to the development of social media policies in this area. As noted in Chapter 1, governments are already putting in place legislation to address this issue in specific terms. Canada's proposed Bill C-13 reflects the Justice Department's attempt to update the Canadian *Criminal Code* and to avoid having to use child pornography sections when young people are caught sexting. Bill C-13 proposes amendments to the *Criminal Code* that include a new Section 162.1 (1) on the distribution of intimate images. In Chapter 4, I detail the wording of this and other sections of the proposed bill. I analyze them in the context of the sexist issues discussed here and in light of the findings of the DTL Research. When asked about their motivations to engage in forms of cyberbullying, and particularly distribution of intimate images, participants responded with the reasons described in the sections that follow.

"Harmless Fun": Jokes or Intentional Harm?

Both the surveys for pre-Facebook-age children and Facebook-age teens included questions aimed specifically at obtaining some perspective on the participants' understanding of motivations behind what they defined as "cyberbullying," which often involved the non-consensual distribution of intimate or demeaning and compromising images that might harm a person's reputation. We wanted to learn more about their understanding of defamatory postings and breach of privacy as well, which are discussed in greater detail in Chapter 4.

Participants were asked whether they or someone they know had ever spread rumors about someone else via text. While the data reveal that an equal amount of participants found themselves able to relate (38.4 percent) or not relate (36.52 percent) to the hypothetical story presented to them, what was of more interest was the follow-up question: "Why do you think this happened?" As expected, most students expressed that often these rumors are meant as a joke that is expected to die down eventually. Some of the most popular responses included comments that expressed this same sentiment: *"They didn't think it would be taken seriously!"* and *"It began as a silly joke!"*

Facebook-aged adolescents in particular appear to give their peers the benefit of the doubt in this regard, recognizing that comments and postings sometimes carry no initial ill-intent on the part of the individual who started the rumors. They often described "harmless fun" as the culprit rather than the other less discussed motivations such as jealousy, retaliation, othering or discrimination, venting and competition, and popularity. That said, it should be noted that some very interesting responses emerged from these subcategories as well, despite their lower representation within the sample. Several participants recognized the action of spreading rumors as a means to establish a power differential: *"Because they wanted to show they were more powerful than they were."* This corroborates the introductory discussion earlier in this chapter that power is a strong motivator for creating demeaning online posts.

Others expressed it as a normal way of getting back or getting even with their friends and/or enemies for a wrong they committed against them. This suggests that some perpetrators do have intent to harm others through social media and that their actions are intentional. What complicates this is, as the next comment highlights, is that perpetrators of cyberbullying often retaliate because they were victimized: *"[I]f someone was pissing me off very much, then since I'm so mad at them I'll just be like, yeah, well take this kind a thing and tell everyone."*

Despite the fact that these motivations were not as frequently brought up by our participants, their power to drive other children and adolescents to engage in cyberbullying behaviors should not be neglected. Again, this is especially pertinent in light of emerging legislation at global levels. Information on emerging legislation can be found on our website, www.definetheline.ca (and in Appendix A). Similar motivations behind cyberbullying were mentioned in the focus group sessions. For example, two participants noted:

It's more of like a weakness-intention thing. To make someone feel weak or some sort of insult like that involves making someone feel lesser than you.

Your best friend can turn on you because someone else is maybe more popular and stuff and they want to be on their side or something...so they just randomly make it, and they just follow other people, they don't stand up for themselves or stand up for their friends and say it isn't right.

Two hypothetical scenarios in the survey given to kids in the pre-Facebook-age group drew responses that warrant attention. Participants were provided with a fictitious story in which Diego, the new boy at school, e-mailed all of his classmates inviting them to be his friend. Brian, the most popular boy in school, used the e-mail to make fun of Diego's linguistic abilities. Unlike our older participants, when the pre-Facebook-age participants were asked about Brian's motives, a number of possibilities were represented and discussed.

The younger participants' responses (Graph 2.3) suggest that children between the ages of eight and twelve view motivations to engage in cyberbullying as the need to compete with each other (41 percent). As we had expected, there are concerns about the fact that quite often cyberbullying is viewed as being "fun" (26 percent). Discrimination and jealousy are considered to be the key motivations by 13 percent of the children. Only 5 percent of children considered improving one's status as a motivation for cyberbullying, perhaps because at the elementary school level status among peers is less important than it is in high school. In earlier questions, however, the younger group had responded that the motivations were not about gaining status. That response is at odds with the 41 percent who thought motivations were about competing for attention because attention usually provides status. Accordingly, these two sets of data need further follow up to clarify why status and competition mean different things to pre-Facebook-age children. This would have implications for ways in which they may use social media when they become old enough to join social networking sites.

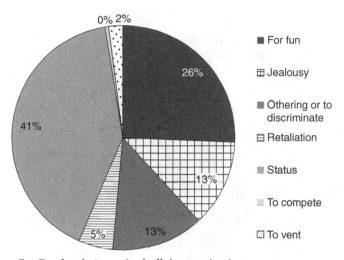

GRAPH 2.3: Pre-Facebook Age cyberbullying motivation

If we now look at Graph 2.4, which presents the data gleaned from the older children in the Facebook-age group, we see that 60 percent thought that the motivations behind cyberbullying are to have "fun." This is a significant finding, confirming our previous research that most teens between thirteen and eighteen years of age perceive sarcasm, jokes, threats, humiliation, and passing around non-consensual intimate or embarrassing images all part of the everyday norms of discourse. The threshold for normative online communications among this group has shifted because most of these young people are just beginning to establish their social relationships and sexuality. Indeed, the hormones are raging and belonging to a peer group and being perceived as cool and sexy are paramount.

If we compare this to the younger group for jealously (4 percent) and discrimination (7 percent) it becomes clear that most of these participants are not conscious that their expressions may be discriminatory (sexism, homophobia, racism, or other forms of "othering"), yet the distribution of intimate images for example is largely sexist or homophobic and definitely sexually charged. It causes concerns from the perspective that these kids do not appreciate the harmful effects of their online communication on others, or the fact that regardless of being unintentional, they can result in serious legal liability.

Moreover, 17 percent believe cyberbullying is often due to retaliation. This is also a concern because when victims do retaliate, they may now find themselves with a criminal record if charged and convicted for being perpetrators. In this regard, proposed legislation designed to protect victims inevitably falls through the cracks because it may in effect harm teens in this age group. This is a sign that significantly more attention and resources need

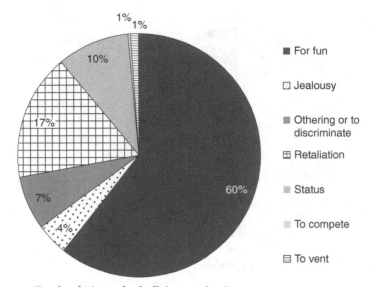

GRAPH 2.4: Facebook Age cyberbullying motivation

to be invested into raising awareness among this age group of the harm they can come to and cause, and to developing resources both on- and offline toward improved and sustained digital citizenship. It also suggests the need for longitudinal research to determine whether the pre-Facebook-age children shift their perspectives when they become teenagers and participate more frequently in social media sites.

Participants in the focus group sessions explained that motivation behind cyberbullying incidents and harmful versus harmless joking was dependent on the situation and the people involved:

The people who know the situation the best are the two people talking, and you like know what was called for and what was uncalled for.

[I]t's not like you can hear their voice like on the phone, you might understand their attitude and their intentions based on their tone and stuff.

[I]f someone says something online, you don't know how somebody is going to take it. If you say it to their face it's going to be way different…their reaction…cause they are not there on their computer.

Participants did not explicitly define the line between harmless and harmful joking but discussed how to tell when someone was joking or bullying through context, language and or symbolic cues used in messaging and the relationship between the person sending or making the joke and the person interpreting the joke. Further breakdowns by age and gender can be found in Appendix B.

Language and Symbolic Cues

Many participants pointed out how tone of voice and body language is lacking online: "*Online you can't hear tones of voices or things like that so you have to make sure that the person is really close to you and knows you are joking or just don't do it at all.*"

Some participants described how the use of popular Internet shorthand sayings or slang could be used to make up for the lack of physical communication. Participants described using emoticons to indicate whether or not it is a joke or the use of "lol" and "jk": "*People like to add like 'lol' OR 'jk'... like just kidding or whatever and to think that what their comment makes it seems like say sort of funny.*" Another respondent stated: "*Sometimes if it's a text or something they can add a smiley face and sometimes if it's a joke, they exaggerate a word by putting more letters in a word.*" However, it is significant that some participants pointed out that the use of "lol" and "jk" could also be a way of getting out of trouble, adding a *'just joking'* at the last minute: "*Sometimes they are really being serious they just say 'I'm joking' so they don't get in trouble or get caught.*"

This is an interesting observation, as it will inform legal definitions of "intent" to harm. Young people need to be alerted to the fact that even if you add "jk" or "lol" to your posting, case law confirms that judges will examine whether there was "perceived harm" by the victim; that is, if the victim truly believes they will be harmed when they receive an online threat, even if the letters "jk" are included the posting will still be considered as intentional. Hence, the opportunity to teach about digital citizenship would be to analyze these perceived loopholes in youth communication to help them understand the need to be sincere and honest; but also to explain, that with emerging legislation and case law, they will not get away with simply adding these abbreviations and/or smiley faces after hurtful comments and demeaning insults. I pick up on this observation again in Chapter 4 as I discuss emerging and impending criminal laws.

Jokes and Relationships

Whether participants considered a joke harmless or harmful might depend on the relationship between the sender and receiver of the joke. For example: "*[I]f it's like a close friend and he says something offensive then you know he could be joking.*" Others observed: "*Some might think it's a joke and some might not.*" One participant noted:

Usually people have a good core group of friends and let's say you would write on Facebook "oh you're such a bitch," you would usually know if they're joking or not but still people can take it differently.

The following quote indicates the participant is aware that the kind of relationship could soften the blow of the joke, but *could* still be taken the wrong way. Participants showed awareness that there is a line between harmful and harmless joking, even among friends:

There's a point where even if it is a joke, it's not okay to say some of those things. If it's hurtful, like if any of my friends said something hurtful like that to me, I probably wouldn't be okay with that.

This data illustrates why that line between jokes and harm is so tenuous and fragile. It also explains that even comments from friends can be perceived as harmful. It provides support for my sustained concerns over applying rigid laws to punish or control children or teens who engage in this type of communication. It also suggests that the participants themselves struggle to explicitly define the line between harmless and harmful joking. There was awareness in the focus group discussions that even a close friend could cross the line, and that the use of "jk" or "lol" was limited in softening the blow of a mean comment.

Posting of Non-Consensual Images and Contradictions in Empathy

Since most participation on Facebook involves posting of images, comments, and messages, it was important to present the participants with hypothetical case studies to analyze and gauge their responses to what took place. In the Facebook-age group survey, the participants were presented with the following two hypothetical situations to analyze:

1) The first involved the story of Dana and Louise. Dana passed out drunk at Louise's party, prompting Louise to take a picture of her and share it with others online.
2) The second considered the story of Brian and Angee. Angee sent Brian a sexually explicit photo, which he later sent to others.

The difference in responses between the two scenarios is very interesting. In the first case, participants were asked to check one of the following:

1) Dana had a right to object to Louise posting her photo online without her permission; or
2) Dana does not have the right to object because the photo was taken at Louise's party where others saw Dana.

Of the 530 teenagers who responded to the questions, 98.5 percent responded that Dana *did* have the right to object whereas only six responded that she did not have the right to object to her photo being posted online without her permission. The participants who responded in Dana's favor showed empathy for her situation. In the second scenario, participants were asked to check one of the following:

1) Angee has the right to object to her photo being shared online without her permission; or
2) Angee does not have the right to object to her photo being shared online because she sent it to Brian and now Brian can do whatever he wants with it.

In this particular case, only 53.53 percent of participants stated that Angee *did* have a right to object to her sexually explicit photo being shared. The disturbing aspect of our findings is that 46.47 percent (almost half) of the participants felt that Angee did not have a right to object because she sent the photograph to Brian. Clearly, in this situation, participants are not as convinced about Angee's consent (or lack thereof) and therefore, her vulnerability and culpability. This data explains so many of the highly publicized news media cases in which kids have forwarded non-consensual intimate images. This data certainly confirms that DE Kids between the ages of thirteen and eighteen actually believe it is acceptable to distribute non-consensual intimate images because the person who sent the photograph deserves the humiliation. Very little accountability or responsibility is given to the perpetrator of the humiliation, namely, the person who breaches trust.

These very different responses to the two scenarios create an interesting discrepancy. What makes participants sympathize with Dana as opposed to Angee? Are they not both victims? There appears to be some confusion in the participants' minds about consent and ownership of content, which explains the tendency of many teenage girls to send intimate images to trusted boyfriends or girlfriends. Sending a photograph or posting it on someone's Facebook page with privacy settings is perceived to be adequate consent. However, when that person passes it on, or it ends up on Facebook's timeline, it can have devastating effects.

The Justice Department's educational resources in support of the proposed Bill C-13 legislation at the national level may help youth navigate complex issues such as consent, privacy, and ownership of content. There is definitely the need for reflection, discussions, and increased dialogue about citizenship and digital citizenship in general, trusting relationships, and so on. However, many young people are gravitating to sites like Snapchat, which purport to only allow an image sent to someone's smartphone to remain on-screen for a few seconds. However, screenshots of those images can be taken and distributed very easily, as was the case of ten teenagers in Laval, Quebec who have been charged with non-consensual distribution of child pornography. The ten boys convinced female classmates to send them intimate images on Snapchat, took screenshots of the images, and then passed them on. Two of the boys are charged with production, possession, and distribution of child pornography and eight are charged with possession and distribution. Their cases are currently before the courts.

Consider the perceived differences between the two scenarios presented to the Facebook-age group. In the first fictitious story, Dana was under the influence of alcohol and therefore, perfectly vulnerable once she had passed out on the couch. When asked to comment on the first story, one student wrote: *"I don't think this is right or fair, because the person whose privacy is being violated had no choice."* Another student wrote: *"Shouldn't take advantage of people when they are drunk."*

In the second story, Angee appears to have put herself in that situation in an effort to impress Brian. In other words, Louise made Dana a victim whereas Angee has no one to blame but herself. To play devil's advocate, however, one might argue that Dana chose to drink alcohol thereby becoming inebriated and vulnerable to having her photo taken. It is important to recognize from this data discrepancy how children's assumptions about *agency and choice* might affect their willingness to empathize with the victim, especially from a feminist perspective. Somehow, the physical action of sending an image of oneself destroys one's right to privacy regardless of one's intention for the image or text to remain between the sender and recipient.

The foregoing responses are also an indication of a definite shift in adolescents' understanding of social norms. Social norms represent the types of behaviors that are perceived by DE Kids to be acceptable in a social media context and the types of behaviors that are not. The data suggest that for adolescent digital natives, getting drunk at a party may present itself as a more acceptable behavior than sexting. On the other hand, other data in this report indicate that sexting has become a very common "normative" aspect of online communication among both the pre-Facebook age and Facebook-age groups.

The responses to both stories confirm the kinds of assumptions that guide children's willingness to empathize with those who are victimized online. Tapping into these assumptions and attempting to debunk or humanize them is essential to enhancing and fostering socially responsible digital citizenship.

Sexting Perceived to be "Normal"

In the focus group sessions where participants viewed videos entitled "The Cell Phone" and "La Photo" on the Define the Line website (www.definetheline.ca), participants were asked to describe what was going on in the videos. In "The Cell Phone," a teenage girl is encouraged via text by a teenage boy to send him a photo of her breasts with the promise that the photo will remain private. The next day at school, the photo is circulated among students. Most recipients of the photo are shown having discussions with each other in which blame is solely placed on the girl who sent the photo in the first place. The French video "La Photo" is almost identical in content – the only difference is that in "La Photo," viewers are shown not only how the photo is discussed between students but also how the girl who sent the photo is directly taunted by her peers. Focus group participants described the depicted sexting incidents in the videos as standard scenarios:

It just seems like a standard scenario that's portrayed. Some guy or girl sends a photo of something and then it spreads all over the school.

Unfortunately it happens a lot. I think it's just something, a situation which we've seen over and over again, whether in real life or like on TV shows or videos like that.

Despite how sad it is and despite the awareness surrounding it, it still happens.

One result from the research that is especially important is the gender differences in perception of humor behind the postings of content of an intimate nature. Participants recognized the ingrained sexist responses between the genders. The female respondents empathized with the differing reactions of the male and female characters in the video. Participants viewed the girls as judgmental and sensitive to the picture being sent around: "*It was funnier for the guys, and like for the girls, it was a more serious thing.*"

A lack of empathy for the female victim in both videos can be found in some of the participants' reactions to the actors assigning more blame to the girl who sent the original photo, than the boy who passed it to his friends: "*I think it's 60 percent the girl's fault and then 40 percent the guy's fault because she starts the whole process of it being sent to everyone.*" Participants also seemed to empathize with the male perpetrator in the video who distributes the female's photo, stating: "*Sometimes it just spirals out of control.*"

These videos were used to jumpstart discussions of the key themes. There were limited codes assigned in the analysis specifically to video vignettes as much of the conversation was assigned to the other main themes. That being said, it is important to note that focus group participants' consistently recognized sexting incidents as normal. Focus group participants also commonly referred to such incidents as instances of cyberbullying.

Empathy was not directly discussed with participants in the focus group sessions. However, the discussions provided insight into what they felt about cyberbullying in general, or what they thought about the situation in the video vignette they watched. One of the younger participants (8–12) noted:

Bullies are a big part of society and it's really important to hit hard on it because I think it's really rude and disrespectful and it makes people feel really badly about themselves when most of the times they shouldn't be feeling that way, so I think it's really important and I feel we should do a project...ma [ke] a video or watch a movie because most of the time people don't understand the seriousness of [it].

So far I have presented a context where the influence of popular culture and rape culture, being endemic in adult society, greatly influence the social communications decisions of DE Kids, "disempowering" them socially. Moreover, peer pressure and the unwritten codes of peer expectations on conduct and agency related to sexuality and the development of social relations in adolescence, clearly have significant impact on how young people make their decisions to post content online. When young people make a decision to post content online, they have told us that sometimes, even though they know the consequences and impact will be negative, they do it anyway. What else informs that kind of thinking? Does it reside in the moral development or perhaps the moral disengagement of young people? Consider what the literature has to say in this regard.

MORAL DEVELOPMENT, EMPATHY, AND MORAL
DISENGAGEMENT OF YOUTH

As I was writing this chapter, I received an op-ed about an Iowa teenager who was beaten and whose perpetrators posted photos of the beating online (Augustine, 2014). What kinds of moral considerations, if any, take place when youth engage in this type of behavior? Certainly a conscious decision is made to post the images online. Just as the teen who decided to pass on the rape video for posting on Facebook in the Maple Ridge case, so do these teens make a decision to publicly share their victim's pain. Do they think about how they will be perceived as the aggressors carrying out the assault? Why does that not register as a consequence? I have undertaken a brief review of the scholarly literature on moral development, empathy, and moral disengagement or boredom of youth. Elsewhere, I have written with colleagues Victoria Talwar and Carlos Gomez (Talwar, Gomez & Shariff, 2014)[6] that there is a dearth of evidence examining moral aspects of cyberbullying events, or their ratings of such events as actual incidents of cyberbullying, especially among younger adolescents.

It has been argued that we should investigate individual differences in bullying behaviors and that young people's moral understanding is an important aspect to consider when explaining the occurrence of bullying behaviors (Arsenio & Lemerise, 2004; Hymel, Schonert-Reichl, Bonanno, Vaillancourt & Rocke Henderson, 2010). For instance, research on traditional bullying finds that children who engage in it are more likely to use mechanisms of "moral disengagement" when evaluating events of bullying than victims or non-aggressive children (Bacchini, Amodeo, Ciardi, Valerio & Vitelli, 1998; Gini, 2006; Hymel, Rocke-Henderson & Bonanno, 2005; Menesini et al., 2003; Perren, Gutzwiller-Helfenfinger, Malti & Hymel, 2012). This might explain some of the comments among DTL Research participants with respect to people who post their feelings online deserving abuse. It may also explain the experiences of Amanda Todd, who I discussed earlier in the chapter. Laible, Eye & Carlo (2008) identified the level of internalization of moral values as being negatively associated with bullying behavior. Furthermore, youth who frequently engage in aggressive behaviors or speech may not view their own behavior or similar behaviors by others as a moral transgression (Harvey, Fletcher & French, 2001; Tisak & Jankowski, 1998).

To date, only a few studies have explored moral aspects of cyberbullying and even fewer have looked specifically at sexting (Bauman, 2010; Menesini, Nocentini & Calussi, 2011; Perren & Gutzwiller-Helfenfinger, 2012; Pornari & Wood, 2010; Steffgen, König, Pfetsch & Melzer, 2011). Similar to traditional bullying, experts have discovered that those who engage in online forms

---

[6] I have received written permission from my co-authors Victoria Talwar and Carlos Gomez to use excerpts from the article with minor modifications to fit the context of this chapter.

of sexting or sexual harassment are more likely to use moral disengagement mechanisms when evaluating the online behaviors than those who may not engage (Perren & Gutzwiller-Helfenfinger, 2012). Not surprisingly, it has also been observed in the research in this field that adolescents who perpetrate online abuse display lower levels of empathy than those who refrain from offensive postings (Steffgen, König, Pfetsch & Melzer, 2011).

This suggests that both perpetrators of bullying and cyberbullying share some characteristics when evaluating their own or others' choices to distribute non-consensual images or online content that is potentially harmful. It may explain the spiteful responses to the sexting scenario in the DTL Research. Those who are most likely to support the distribution of non-consensual images to embarrass peers validate their actions through moral disengagement mechanisms and lower levels of empathy. But if this is the case, why is there empathy for Dana, the teen girl depicted in the drinking scenario? It might be that the majority of participants identified drinking as something they might be more prone to do and be punished for by parents; hence, a common sense of empathy may exist. Furthermore, the element of sexual assertion or identity is absent from the scenario. Had this element been present and combined with the drunkenness, we might expect to have found similar responses to the hypothetical situation that did involve sexting. In fact, it might have drawn out responses similar to those experienced in the Steubenville case, where people tweeted that the victim should have been punished for being drunk and that her behavior was asking for rape (Welsh-Huggins, 2013; Murphy, 2013; Binder, 2013).

Influence of Age on Moral Understanding
It is interesting to summarize what the scholarship on age and moral understanding suggests. In terms of the moral understanding of the elementary school children aged eight through twelve years old and high school children aged thirteen through eighteen years old, developmental trends indicate that with age children increasingly understand morally relevant situations like transgressions, teasing, and peer harassment as negative behaviors. They do judge them as wrong and are able to anticipate the emotions of people involved (Krettenauer, Malti & Sokol, 2008; Malti, Gasser & Gutzwiller-Helfenfinger, 2010). The bulk of research on moral development has found that such behaviors are judged as falling within the moral domain and are considered unfair and hurtful (Horn, 2005). More relevant to the context of our discussion however, moral judgments are also affected by the context of the peer relationship (Killen, Lee-Kim, McGlothlin & Stangor, 2002). This might explain why 50 percent of the DTL Research participants confirmed that they understood the consequences of negative or risqué online postings, but posted them anyway because of peer pressure, which could have affected their moral judgment.

Research on bullying also suggests that with age, youth become more tolerant of bullying and less empathetic towards the victim (Menesini *et al.*, 1997) – a finding that has been corroborated by the DTL Research. Children in the younger group showed more of an interest in reducing bullying and taking leadership to do so. Not only were the elementary school children more sympathetic, they also expressed the desire for a more friendly, supportive, and socially responsible online environment. Thus, examining moral evaluations of young people's attitudes to offensive online communication is important as acts of violence, aggression, and demeaning and defamatory postings are often viewed as moral transgressions. Such an examination will lead to an improved understanding of their online intentional victimization behavior (Arsenio & Lemerise, 2004). This is also a little disturbing because it implies that adults can be expected to be the least empathetic and the most likely to engage in demeaning and defamatory online behaviors. Indeed, such behaviors are often modeled both on and offline. We live in a violent world where in many countries political leaders kill their own people. Children witness wars, violence, rape, and murder committed by adults in movies and, unfortunately, in the real news that comes directly into their homes. It is not surprising they are confused by the mixed messages they receive about where to draw the lines.

Little is known about the role of developmental trends in the way young people evaluate different types of events as either being cyberbullying or harmless teasing or unintentional acts. For purposes of assessing the relevance of legislation, this knowledge is essential, but unfortunately not available. In our DTL Research, we expected that older participants would be more aware of the consequences of their online actions, reflecting perhaps increased moral development relative to their younger counterparts. However, clearly at least 42 percent of the Facebook-age participants, as shown in Graph 2.5, did not

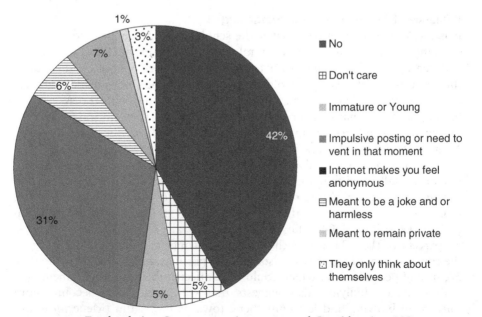

GRAPH 2.5: Facebook Age Consequence Awareness and Consideration- NO

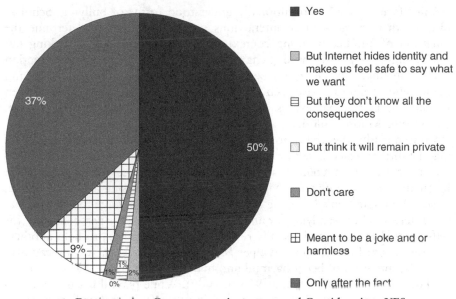

- Yes
- But Internet hides identity and makes us feel safe to say what we want
- But they don't know all the consequences
- But think it will remain private
- Don't care
- Meant to be a joke and or harmless
- Only after the fact

GRAPH 2.6: Facebook Age Consequence Awareness and Consideration- YES

think about the harmful consequences and significantly, even when 50 percent did consider the harmful consequences, most said they went ahead with or supported negative postings anyway (Graph 2.6). Further breakdowns by gender and age can be found in Appendix B.

Type of Offense Can Influence How Kids Define the Line

Several elements have been explored as most salient when it comes to evaluating the severity of traditional face-to-face bullying events. The research in this area finds that adolescents and adults judge physical events to be more negative than verbal or online forms of harassment, threats, and abuse (Bauman & Del Rio, 2006; Monks & Smith, 2006). Additionally, offending behaviors repeated over time were rated as more negative than those that happened once (Hazler, Miller, Carney & Green, 2001). In the case of cyberbullying, evidence suggests that adolescents consider as more severe those events involving graphic information (videos or pictures) displaying violent acts or private scenes (Menesini, Nocentini & Calussi, 2011). However, there is no consideration in the literature of what other characteristics of traditional bullying, apart from repetition over time, play in "cyberbullying." These can include power imbalance and intention (or lack of intention) to harm, which might have significant negative impact during online communications.

As the DTL Research disclosed, many youth fail to discriminate offensive online communications that have a negative psychological impact from acts that they consider to be harmless or fun (Shariff DTL Research, 2014). The DTL findings are especially important in considering that online abuses are not face-to-face like traditionally understood forms of bullying. Scholars observe that in face-to-face interactions one can sometimes determine the intention of another by using contextual behavioral cues (e.g., sticking out one's tongue, laughter, singsong chants, smirking) to infer teasing or deception (e.g., fidgeting, shifting eye gaze). Research suggests that children's and adolescents' abilities to use such behavioral cues, and inconsistencies between verbal and non-verbal expressive behavior, increases with age (Rotenberg, Simourd & Moore, 1989).

Consequently, the ability to judge the intentions and falsity of statements may be further exacerbated by the nature of online communications, which do not have the same contextual information face-to-face interactions have. It remains unclear how youth view such behaviors as teasing and lying online. Research on children's lie-telling shows that from an early age they appreciate the differences between lying for antisocial purposes (i.e., for personal gain, for self-oriented reasons) and socially responsible purposes (i.e., to help another) (Bussey, 1992; Bussey, 1999; Walper & Valtin, 1992). Their teasing can also carry the intention of being harmful and malicious or playful (Barnett, Burns, Sanborn, Bartel & Wilds, 2004; Warm, 1997). While playful teasing can help youth develop social skills and foster positive interpersonal encounters (Eisenberg, 1986), hostile, harmful teasing increases as children and adolescents become more aware of the social context and social norms. This can lead to a focus on norm violations within peer groups (Keltner, Capps, Kring, Young & Heerey, 2001). As we saw with the unwritten codes relating to sexual agency, it is possible that those who cross the invisible line to assert their sexual agency are punished most severely online, consistent with the nail and hammer Japanese proverb cited earlier. It is important to note that with age, children are increasingly able to judge the intentions of others when assessing the acceptability of their statements and actions (Heyman, Sweet & Lee, 2009).

SUMMARY AND CONCLUSION

The research findings presented in this chapter in the context of the discourse on rape culture, misogyny, and gender power relations illustrate how normative and rooted in the values of society DE Kids have become. The youth perspectives in the DTL Research clearly illustrate the need for increased attention to addressing sexist stereotypes; critical analysis of popular culture and negative roles models in society; and the need to guide younger digital generations to think through the potential impact of their online postings. It calls for increased critical media literacy.

There is also a clear need for improved legal literacy because these attitudes and subsequent actions are likely to result in litigation under civil lawsuits and criminal liability under child pornography. The DTL Research data and moral development scholarship are important because they illustrate the effect of peer norms, the role of moral disengagement, and the confusion that comes from mixed messages in popular and rape culture.

In Chapter 4, I highlight the DTL Research findings with respect to the participants' notions of the difference between public and private postings and ownership of online content. Their responses are analyzed in the context of Ryan Calo's work on helping us think through "privacy harm" and "privacy rights" as compared to "privacy breach" (Calo, 2011).

Finally, the data demonstrate the strong role of peer pressure and children's and adolescents' motivations to participate, to gain status, and to entertain others for "fun." In other words, children and adolescents engage in harmful online behaviors as they often feel the need to speak louder through increasingly unconventional means to be heard over the competitive din of the Internet. *D.C. v. R.R* (2010), a California case about homophobia detailed in Chapter 4, is a good example of how teens compete for the most outrageous postings without even thinking about the psychological impact on the person they are joking about, or the defamatory content in their comments that can result in civil law suits. Before I move on to that discussion, I address in Chapter 3 the implications of this research in relation to the proliferation of statutory responses that are aimed at criminalizing cyberbullying. In particular, I am concerned about the application of existing child pornography laws to criminalize children without a full understanding of the contextual and developmental influences highlighted here.

REFERENCES

Arsenio, W. F. & Lemerise, E. A. (2004). Aggression and moral development: Integrating social information processing and moral domain models. *Child Development, 75*, 987–1002.

Artz, S. (1998). Where have all the school girls gone? Violent girls in the school yard. *Child and Youth Care Forum, 27*(2), 77–109.

Augustine, I. (2014, April 22). Op-Ed: Teen beaten and brutalized online: Social Media to blame?. *Digital Journal Reports*. Retrieved April 22, 2014, from http://digitaljournal.com/news/crime/op-ed-teen-beaten-and-brutalized-online-social-media-to-blame/article/381806.

Bacchini, D., Amodeo, A. L., Ciardi, A., Valerio, P. & Vitelli, R. (1998). La relazione vittima-prepotente: Stabilita' del fenomeno e ricorso a meccanismi di disimpegno morale [Bully–victim relationship: Stability of the phenomenon and use of moral disengagement]. *Scienze dell'Interazione, 5*, 9–46.

Bailey, J. & Hanna, M. (2011). The Gendered Dimensions of Sexting: Assessing the Applicability of Canada's Child Pornography Provision. *Canadian Journal of Women and The Law, 23*(2), 405–441.

Bailey, J. & Steeves, V. (2013). Will the Real Digital Girl Please Stand Up? In Hille Koskela and Macgregor Wise (Eds.), *New Visualities, New Technologies: The New Ecstasy of Communication* (pp. 41–66). London: Ashgate Publishing.

Barnett, M. A., Burns, S. R., Sanborn, F. W., Bartel, J. S. & Wilds, S. J. (2004). Antisocial and prosocial teasing among children: Perceptions and individual differences. *Social Development, 13*, 292–310.

Bauman, S. (2010). Cyberbullying in a rural intermediate school: An exploratory study. *Journal of Early Adolescence, 30*, 803–833. doi: 10.1177/0272431609350927.

Bauman, S. & Del Rio, A. (2006). Preservice teachers' responses to bullying scenarios: Comparing physical, verbal, and relational bullying. *Journal of Educational Psychology, 98*, 219–231. doi:10.1037/0022-0663.98.1.219.

BBC News. (2007, March 27). Blog death threats spark debate. *BBC News Technology*. Retrieved from http://news.bbc.co.uk/2/hi/6499095.stm.

Bender, G. (2001). Resisting dominance? The study of a marginalized masculinity and its construction within high school walls. In J. Burstyn *et al.* (Eds.), Preventing violence in schools: A challenge to American democracy (pp.61–77). New Jersey: Lawrence Erlbaum.

Binder, M. (2013, March 19). If you thought these unbelievable reactions to Steubenville would just peter out, I guess you can say you were pretty, pretty wrong. [Web log comment]. Retrieved from http://publicshaming.tumblr.com/day/2013/03/19.

Bradshaw, J. (2014, March 4). University of Ottawa men's hockey team suspended over alleged sex assault. *The Globe and Mail*. Retrieved from www.theglobeandmail.com/news/national/university-of-ottawa-suspends-hockey-team-over-serious-misconduct/article17201525/.

Bussey, K. (1992). Lying and truthfulness: Children's definitions, standards, and evaluative reactions. *Child Development, 63*, 129–137. doi:10.1111/j.1467-8624.1992.tb03601.x. (1999). Children's categorization and evaluation of different types of lies and truths. *Child Development, 70*, 1338–1347. doi:10.1111/1467-8624.00098.

Calo, R. M. (2011). The Boundaries of Privacy Harm. *Indiana Law Journal, 86*(3), 1131–1162.

CBC News. (2013a, September 7). UBC investigates frosh students' pro-rape chant: Chant condoned non-consensual sex with underage girls. *CBC News British Columbia*. Retrieved September 7, 2013, from www.cbc.ca/news/canada/british-columbia/ubc-investigates-frosh-students-pro-rape-chant-1.1699589.

CBC News. (2013b, September 4). Saint Mary's University frosh chant cheers underage sex: Frosh week leaders, student union executive sent to sensitivity training. *CBC News Nova Scotia*. Retrieved September 4, 2013, from www.cbc.ca/news/canada/nova-scotia/saint-mary-s-university-frosh-chant-cheers-underage-sex-1.1399616.

CBC News. (2013c, November 14). Child porn charges laid against 10 Laval teens–Police allege boys traded screen grabs of girlfriends' explicit Snapchat photos. *CBC News Montreal*. Retrieved November 14, 2013, from www.cbc.ca/news/canada/montreal/child-porn-charges-laid-against-10-laval-teens-1.2426599.

CBC News. (2014, March 11). Cyberbullying in university on the rise, study says. *CBC News The National*. Retrieved March 12, 2014, from http://www.cbc.ca/m/touch/news/story/1.2568315.

Chen, E. (2013). Neoliberalism and popular women's culture: Rethinking choice, freedom and agency. *European Journal of Cultural Studies, 16*(4), 440–452.

Crowther, K. (2014, April 15). Marquette fraternities face sexual misconduct, hazing allegations. *TMJ4*. Retrieved from www.jrn.com/tmj4/news/Marquette-fraternities-face-sexual-misconduct-hazing-allegations-255429421.html.

Feibel, A. (2014, February 28). Sexually aggressive group between student officials posted online. *Fulcrum*. Retrieved from http://thefulcrum.ca/2014/02/sexually-violent-conversation-between-student-officials-leaked-online/.

Frank, B.W. (1996). Masculinities and schooling: The making of men. In J.R. Epp and A.M. Watkinson (Eds.), *Systemic violence: How schools hurt children* (pp. 113–130). London: Falmer Press.

Hager, M., Shaw, G., Culbert, L. & O'Connor, E. (2014, April 18). Charges in teen-bullying suicide case. *Edmonton Journal*, p. A10.

Harvey, R. J., Fletcher, J. & French, D. J. (2001). Social reasoning: A source of influence on aggression. *Clinical Psychology Review*, 21, 447–469. doi: 10.1016/S0272-7358(99)00068-9.

Gill, R. & Arthurs, J. (2006). Editor's Introduction: New Femininities? *Feminist Media Studies*, 6(4), 443–451.

Gini, G. (2006). Social cognition and moral cognition in bullying: What's wrong? *Aggressive Behavior*, 32, 528–539. doi: 10.1002/ab.20153.

Gould, M. S. (2001). Suicide and the media. *Annals of the New York Academy of Sciences*, 932(1), 200–224.

Hazler, R. J., Miller, D. L., Carney, J. V. & Green, S. (2001). Adult recognition of school bullying situations. *Educational Research*, 43, 133–146. doi: 10.1080/0013188011005137.

Hess, A. (2014, January 6). Why Women Aren't Welcome on the Internet. *Pacific Standard*. Retrieved January 6, 2014, from www.psmag.com/navigation/health-and-behavior/women-arent-welcome-internet-72170/.

Heyman, G. D., Sweet, M. A. & Lee, K. (2009). Children's Reasoning about Lie-telling and Truth-telling in Politeness Contexts. *Social Development*, 18(3), 728–746.

Hirschman, C., Impett, E. A. & Schooler, D. (2006). Dis/Embodied voices: What late-adolescent girls can teach us about objectification and sexuality. *Sexuality Research and Social Policy*, 3(4), 8–20. doi:10.1525/srsp.2006.3.4.8

Holman, R. (2013, November 15). She's A Homewrecker: the website where women expose 'infidelity'. The internet just ate itself. *The Telegraph*. Retrieved November 15, 2013, from www.telegraph.co.uk/women/womens-life/10452482/Shes-A-Homewrecker-the-website-where-women-slut-shame-each-others-infidelity.-The-internet-just-ate-itself.html.

Horn, S. S. (2005). Adolescents' peer interactions: Conflict and coordination among personal expression, social norms, and moral reasoning. In L. Nucci (Ed.), *Conflict, contradiction, and contrarian elements in moral development and education* (pp. 113–128). New Jersey: Erlbaum.

Hymel, S., Rocke-Henderson, N. & Bonanno, R. A. (2005). Moral disengagement: A framework for understanding bullying among adolescents. *Journal of Social Sciences*, 8(1), 1–11.

Hymel, S., Schonert-Reichl, K., Bonanno, R., Vaillancourt, T. & Rocke Henderson, N. (2010). Bullying and morality. In *Handbook of bullying in schools: An international perspective* (pp. 101–118).

Keltner, D., Capps, L., Kring, A. M., Young, R. C. & Heerey, E. A. (2001). Just teasing: a conceptual analysis and empirical review. *Psychological bulletin*, 127(2), 229–248.

Khazan, O. (2013, November 20). The Evolution of Bitchiness. *The Atlantic*. Retrieved from www.theatlantic.com/health/archive/2013/11/the-evolution-of-bitchiness/281657/.

Killen, M., Lee-Kim, J., McGlothlin, H. & Stangor, C. (2002). How children and adolescents evaluate gender and racial exclusion. *Monograph of the Society for Research in Child Development*, 67(4), vii.

Kraft, E.M. (2010). "Juicycampus.com: How was this business model culpable of encouraging harassment on college campuses? In Shariff, S., and Churchill, A. H. (Eds.), *Truths and myths of cyber-bullying: international perspectives on stakeholder responsibility and children's safety* (pp. 65–104). New York: Peter Lang Publishing.

Krettenauer, T., Malti, T. & Sokol, B. W. (2008). The development of moral emotion expectancies and the happy victimizer phenomenon: A critical review of theory and application. *European Journal of Developmental Science*, 2, 221–235. doi:10.3233/DEV-2008-2303.

Kryk, J. (2013, November 9). Target in 2005 McGill hazing horror speaks out. *The Toronto Sun*. Retrieved from www.torontosun.com/2013/11/09/target-in-2005-mcgill-hazing-horror-speaks-out

Laible, D., Eye, J. & Carlo, G. (2008). Dimensions of conscience in mid-adolescence: Links with social behavior, parenting, and temperament. *Journal of Youth and Adolescence*, 37, 875–887. doi:10.1007/s10964-008-9277-8.

Levande, M. (2008). Women, pop music, and pornography. *Meridians*, 8(1), 293–321. Retrieved from http://search.proquest.com/docview/196904770?accountid=12339.

Lokeinsky, K. (2011, January 6). Recent suicides casts light on bullying. *The Lariat*. Retrieved from http://thelariatonline.com.

MacKay, A. W. (2013). Promoting a Culture of Safety, Respect and Consent at Saint Mary's University and Beyond. Report from the President's Council, Halifax: NS.

Magder, J. (2014, January 20). Laval teens charged in 'sexting' case back in court. *The Gazette*. Retrieved January 20, 2014, from www.montrealgazette.com/news/Laval+teens+charged+sexting+case+back+court/9408215/story.html

Malti, T., Gasser, L. & Gutzwiller-Helfenfinger, E. (2010). Children's interpretive understanding, moral judgments, and emotion attributions: Relations to social behaviour. *British Journal of Developmental Psychology*, 28, 275–292. doi: 10.1348/026151009X403838.

Menesini, E., Eslea, M., Smith, P. K., Genta, M. L., Giannetti, E., Fonzi, A., *et al.* (1997). Cross-national comparison of children's attitudes towards bully/victim problems in school. *Aggressive Behaviour*, 23, 245–257. http://dx.doi.org/10.1002/(SICI)1098-2337(1997)23:4<245::AID-AB3>3.0.CO;2-J.

Menesini, E., Nocentini, A. & Calussi, P. (2011). The measurement of cyberbullying: Dimensional structure and relative item severity and discrimination. *Cyberpsychology, Behavior, and Social Networking*, 14, 267–274. doi:10.1089/cyber.2010.0002.

Menesini, E., Sanchez, V., Fonzi, A., Ortega, R., Costabile, A. & Lo Feudo, G. (2003). Moral emotions and bullying: A cross-national comparison of differences between bullies, victims and outsiders. *Aggressive Behavior*, 29, 515–530. doi:10.1002/ab.10060.

Monks, C. P. & Smith, P. K. (2006). Definitions of bullying: Age differences in understanding of the term, and the role of experience. *British Journal of Developmental Psychology*, 24, 801–821. doi:10.1348/026151005X82352.

Moore, O. (2012, July 11). Woman's call to end video game misogyny sparks vicious online attacks. *The Globe and Mail*. Retrieved from www.theglobeandmail.com/news/world/womans-call-to-end-video-game-misogyny-sparks-vicious-online-attacks/article4405585/.

Murphy, M. (2013, March 19). The Steubenville rape case: This is masculinity. [Web log comment]. Retrieved from http://feministcurrent.com/7339/the-steubenville-rape-case-this-is-masculinity/

Pascoe, C. J. (2007). *Dude, you're a fag: Masculinity and sexuality in high school*. Berkeley: University of California Press.

Perren, S. & Gutzwiller-Helfenfinger, E. (2012). Cyberbullying and traditional bullying in adolescence: Differential roles of moral disengagement, moral emotions, and moral values. *European Journal of Developmental Psychology, 9,* 195–209. doi:10.1080/17405629.2011.643168.

Pirkis, J., Blood, R. W., Beautrais, A., Burgess, P. & Skehan, J. (2006). Media guidelines on the reporting of suicide. *Crisis: The Journal of Crisis Intervention and Suicide Prevention, 27*(2), 82–87.

Poole, E. (2013). Hey Girls, Did You Know? Slut-Shaming on the Internet Needs to Stop. *USFL Review, 48,* 221–221.

Pornari, C. D. & Wood, J. (2010). Peer and cyber aggression in secondary school students: The role of moral disengagement, hostile attribution bias, and outcome expectancies. *Aggressive Behavior, 36,* 81–94. doi:10.1002/ab.20336.

Retter, C. & Shariff, S. (2012). A Delicate Balance: Defining the Line Between Open Civil Proceedings and the Protection of Children in the Online Digital Era. *Canadian Journal of Law and Technology, 10*(2), 232–262.

Ringrose, J. & Renold, E. (2012). Slut-shaming, girl power and 'sexualisation': Thinking through the politics of the international SlutWalks with teen girls. *Gender and Education, 24*(3), 333–343. Retrieved from http://search.proquest.com/docview/1013443636?accountid=12339

Rotenberg, K. J., Simourd, L. & Moore, D. (1989). Children's use of a verbal-nonverbal consistency principle to infer truth and lying. *Child Development, 60* (2), 309–322.

Shariff, S. (2008). *Cyberbullying: Issues and solutions for the school, the classroom, and the home.* Oxfordshire: Routledge (Taylor and Frances Group).

Shariff, S. (2009). *Confronting Cyberbullying: What schools need to know to control misconduct and avoid legal consequences.* New York: Cambridge University Press.

Shariff, S. & Churchill, A. H. (Eds.). (2010). *Truths and myths of cyber-bullying: international perspectives on stakeholder responsibility and children's safety.* New York: Peter Lang.

Shariff, S., Wiseman, A. & Crestohl, L. (2012). Defining the Lines between Children's Vulnerability to Cyberbullying and the Open Court Principle: Implications of *A.B. v. Bragg Communications, Inc. Education and Law Journal. 21*(3), 231–262.

Steffgen, G., König, A., Pfetsch, J. & Melzer, A. (2011). Are cyberbullies lessempathic? Adolescents' cyberbullying behavior and empathic responsiveness. *Cyberpsychology, Behavior, and Social Networking, 14,* 643–648. doi:10.1089/cyber.2010.0445.

Stein, N. (1995). Sexual harassment in school: The public performance of gendered violence. *Harvard Educational Review, 65,* 163–173.

Talwar, V., Gomez-Garibello, C. & Shariff, S. (2014). Adolescents' moral evaluations and ratings of cyberbullying: The effect of veracity and intentionality behind the event. *Computers in Human Behavior, 36,* 122–128.

Tisak, M. S. & Jankowski, A. M. (1998). Societal rule evaluations: Adolescent offenders' reasoning about moral conventional, and personal rules. *Aggressive Behaviors, 22,* 195–207. http://dx.doi.org/10.1002/(SICI)1098-2337(1996) 22:3<195::AID-AB4>3.0.CO;2-M.

Walper, S. & Valtin, R. (1992). Children's understanding of white lies. In W. Winter (Series Ed.), R. J. Watts, S. Ide, and K. Ehlich (Volume Eds.), *Politeness in language: Studies in history, theory and practice* (pp. 231–251). Trends in Linguistics: Studies and Monographs, 59. Berlin: Mouton de Gruyter.

Weisgarber, M. (2012, February 10). Probation in rave rape case called a 'slap on the wrist.' *CTV News.* Retrieved from http://bc.ctvnews.ca/probation-in-rave-rape-case-called-a-slap-on-the-wrist-1.766872

Welsh-Huggins, A. (2013, March 17). Ohio football players guilty in rape of 16-year-old girl, face year-plus in jail. *National Post*. Retrieved from http://news.nationalpost.com/2013/03/17/ohio-football-players-guilty-in-rape-of-16-year-old-girl-face-year-plus-in-jail/.

Ybarra, M. L., Mitchell, K. J., Wolak, J. & Finkelhor, D. (2006). Examining Characteristics and Associated Distress Related to Internet Harassment: Findings From the Second Youth Internet Safety Survey. *Pediatrics*, *118* (4), 1169–1177.

Zhang, Y., Dixon, T. L. & Conrad, K. (2010). Female body image as a function of themes in rap music videos: A content analysis. *Sex Roles*, *62*(11–12), 787–797. doi:10.1007/s11199-009-9656-y.

CASE LAW

D.C. v. R.R. 2010, WL 892204 (Cal. App. Ct. March 15, 2010).

Zeran v. America Online, Inc. 1997. 129 F.3d 327 (4th Cir. 1997).

CHAPTER THREE

The Irony of Charging Children with Distribution of Child Pornography

Those who are adjudicated or convicted of child pornography offenses are sexual offenders and often predators...Teenagers who engage in sexting should not face the same legal and moral conundrum.

(Judge Robert L. Steinberg at p.11 in *RE: C.S.*, 2012)

The statute at issue was designed to protect children, but in this case the court has allowed the state to use it against a child in a way that criminalizes conduct that is protected by constitutional right of privacy.

(Judge Padovano, dissenting at para 241 in *A.H. v. State of Florida*, 2007)

INTRODUCTION

The previous chapter addressed the difficult issues of sexism and misogyny as they are ingrained in contemporary society, or, as they have resurfaced with a vengeance through the uses of digital and social media, which enable (but do not cause) rapid proliferation and perceived anonymity. Chapter 2 also highlighted the perspectives of the participants in the DTL Research that reflected their confusion about the difference between expressions for "fun" and expressions that were intentionally harmful as they thought about how they define the lines between joking or teasing and criminal harassment, threats, and distribution of intimate images. I also presented research findings and theories on moral development, moral disengagement, and empathy that have been conducted in the field of scholarship on bullying. The DTL Research, as analyzed within those theories, confirms developmental differences among children as they grow up, which sometimes prevents them from making thoughtful ethical and empathetic decisions. As I explained in Chapter 2, Digitally Empowered Kids (DE Kids) are influenced by a context in which adult

I would like to acknowledge and thank the contributions of McGill University Law and MBA candidate, Alyssa Wiseman, who provided the legal research for the cases and statutes discussed in this chapter and participated in some of the legal analysis.

society sends very confusing messages about sex and sexuality, freedom of expression, and privacy through popular culture, news, and film media. Children and teens witness violent models of verbal and physical behavior and communication often perpetrated by adults. It is no wonder kids have difficulty defining the lines between jokes and potentially criminal offenses.

In this chapter, I review case law and emerging legislation that seeks to criminalize kids for their actions in reaction to public pressure and media focus on teen suicide. Admittedly, something needs to be done to prevent and reduce the sexualized behaviors discussed in Chapter 2. It is important to provide strong consequences and clear messages to children, especially in extreme cases that involve serious and persistent humiliation and related suicide. Nonetheless, it is also important to point out that we are headed down the wrong path if we charge kids with child pornography offenses. And it is *essential* to emphasize that children are not child pornographers! Amanda Todd's adult perpetrator was not "cyberbullying" as the Gazette (Sinoski, 2014) headlines suggest. He was a sexual predator.

This adult perpetrator, finally arrested in the Netherlands, was a habitual "capper" or online pedophile who preyed on children and teens like Amanda. It was his actions and extortion that eventually led to Amanda's semi-nude photographs being distributed online. Unfortunately for her, this also resulted in bullying from her peers. The fact that they bullied her does not mean that these teens were also sex offenders or child pornographers. As the DTL Research confirmed, many teenagers in the Facebook-age group (ages 13–18) are prone to post or forward offensive images online even when they realize the consequences because they perceive these acts to fall in line with the norms of their peer group's everyday discourse.

Despite the pressure on government and courts to take a hard-line on the non-consensual distribution of images online, American courts in general have at least thought about the maturity levels of the children, and in some cases, outright dismissed the charges of child pornography. However, there have recently been cases in both Canada and the United States where young people received criminal convictions. This trend appears to be on the rise. Criminal charges and the potential for an increased number of criminal convictions for youth can be expected should legislation such as Bill C-13, the *Protecting Canadians from Online Crime Act*, be passed into law. Before moving on to a discussion of relevant court cases, consider again some of the pertinent findings from the DTL Research that provide the context for my argument against the wisdom of charging kids with distribution of child pornography.

"JUST JOKING" SYNDROME

Quotes from participants in the DTL Research in Chapter 2 are encouraging and yet disturbing. The data confirm what I have always maintained – that many DE Kids are so focused on peer acceptance and entertaining friends online that they do not seriously think about the consequences of their actions on others, or intentionally seek to harm those victimized. Cases such as *D.C. v. R.R.* (2010), in which a male teen was harassed online with homophobic insults, clearly illustrate that the person targeted is often dehumanized and almost forgotten. The focus shifts away from the individual and moves to a competition of who can make others laugh loudest through the most vulgar comments and who can post the most outrageous photographs or insults. One of the reasons that apps like Ask.fm, Instagram, YikYak, Tumblr, Secret, and Snapchat thrive is because they indirectly encourage or enable people to take greater risks with their online postings. These apps and sites are attractive to a captive generation of youth who test social boundaries online as their hormones rage. This is no different from the 1950s when social relationships were developed in the back seat of a car at a drive-in. Sexual experimentation has moved online to cell phones and social media. In response, some social media sites have become more family oriented. For example, Facebook has created a family relations page and a *Be Bold Stop Bullying* page, which indicates the site's commitment to providing a safer social media platform.[1] As more adults use these "family-friendly" sites, teens migrate to other, newer sites and apps where they feel less restricted. Those who no longer find Facebook exciting migrate to sites on which offensive and insulting posts thrive. Teens do not want to be seen as social media friends with their parents (Martin, 2011).

With respect to non-consensual distribution of intimate images, I briefly take you back to the DTL Research, which disclosed worrisome statistics. Participating youth defined sexting as "normal" and up to 61 percent of the older group and 26 percent of the younger group engaged in offensive online postings for "fun" or "status." Graph 3.1 illustrates the responses of the older group when asked whether they thought about the consequences of their actions. While 50 percent said yes, another 37 percent said they thought about the consequences and impact after the fact, that is, after they posted or forwarded the offensive content.

Moreover, scenarios that we presented to the DTL Research participants indicate confusion about who is to blame when an intimate image is sent to a trusted peer in confidence, particularly when that image is posted and distributed online. Female participants indicated more serious concerns about non-consensual distribution of intimate images than male participants. Some female participants recognized a power component in the motivation of the boys to do this; nonetheless, female respondents were equally vicious when it came to "slut-shaming" other females who sent intimate images to boyfriends, even in trust, convinced that they deserved the punishment they received once the photographs were spread.

---

[1] Facebook's commitment to safer online spaces can be found at: www.facebook.com/beboldstop-bullying.ca

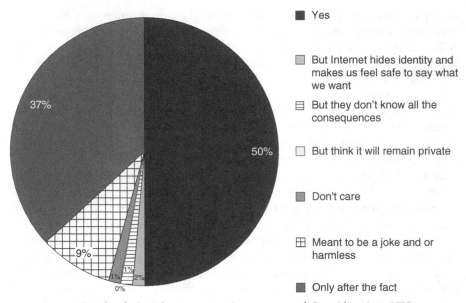

GRAPH 3.1: Facebook Age Consequence Awareness and Consideration- YES

Interestingly, distribution of photographs of a female peer who was drunk elicited more concern for the drunken victim because of worries that her parents would find out she had been drinking and that would result in her being punished. The fact that teens are less concerned about the psychological harm that comes from slut-shaming and more concerned about peers getting into trouble for drinking suggests a confused and selective hierarchy of priorities on their ethical or empathic frames of reference. Similar to traditional bullying, experts have discovered that those who engage in online forms of sexting or sexual harassment are more likely to use moral disengagement mechanisms when evaluating their online behaviors than those who may not engage (Perren & Gutzwiller-Helfenfinger, 2012). Not surprisingly, it has also been observed in the research in this field that adolescents who perpetrate online abuse display lower levels of empathy than those who refrain from offensive postings (Steffgen, König, Pfetsch & Melzer, 2011).

PRESSURE TO PUNISH

Policy makers have come under significant pressure to develop and implement stronger legislation and harsher punishment for young offenders who engage in sexting. Politicians and police have responded by applying child pornography laws to arrest and charge youth as young as eleven years of age (Kimber, 2014; Schwartz, 2013). Court judgments in this chapter confirm the opinions of many judges that applying these laws to children's behavior is like attempting to "fit a square peg in a round hole" (*RE: C.S.*, 2012). The data from the DTL Research is important because it will, or ought to, inform and be taken into consideration by policy makers, police, judges, and prosecutors as they consider legal sanctions and legal sentences. Members of the legal community are being provided with increased discretion to apply child pornography laws and harsher penalties against children to control what has been described by the Supreme Court of Canada as a "toxic phenomenon" (*A.B. [Litigation Guardian of] v. Bragg Communications Inc.*, 2012). The extent to which legislators and the judiciary will take into consideration the potential impact of criminal convictions on children and their families is yet to be seen. Some of these impacts would relate to their education and acceptance into college; reputation; difficulty finding jobs; economic burden to pay legal fees; disruption and embarrassment in the family, and so on.

It is also notable that in Canada very little discussion among politicians or the news media has revolved around the role of the *Youth Criminal Justice Act* (S.C. 2002, c.1) (*YCJA*), which was adopted to ensure young offenders are reintegrated into society as soon as possible with minimal impact on their future abilities to become contributing members of society. Moreover, the role of another piece of relatively recent legislation, the *Safe Streets and Communities Act* (S.C. 2012, c.1), has not been discussed. Nonetheless, in relation to any new cyberbullying legislation, its potential to impact youth lurks in the background. The legislation was introduced by the federal conservative government to meet election promises to take a hard-line on crime. It calls on judges to give young offenders longer and harsher sentences. In some cases, judges have protested and balked at meting out longer sentences for juvenile crimes that do not deserve harsh penalties.[2] In light of the foregoing, the cases I present in this chapter should be contemplated with the following considerations in mind:

• Given that the two age groups of DE Kids in the DTL Research consider offensive, demeaning, and sexualized postings largely "fun," and given that a significant number of them only think about the consequences after the fact, and even then post the offensive content anyway, it is important to examine whether "big-stick sanctions" like child pornography laws are appropriate or applicable.

• As we consider whether child pornography laws apply, it is essential to analyze the difference between the motivations and activities that engage adult pedophiles, cappers, and child pornographers and the activities of youth when they post, view, and distribute sexualized images online.

---

[2] Accused bully found not guilty in Ontario case. (March 5, 2012). Retrieved March 6, 2012, from www.cbc.ca/news/canada/toronto/accused-bully-found-not-guilty-in-ontario-case-1.1245484.

- It makes little sense for governments and policy makers to apply existing laws or create new laws to curb sexting and cyberbullying activities among youth without first making an effort to consider the potential impact on their lives and those of their families.

- It is essential to ensure that expanded discretionary powers of police to engage in increased surveillance and search and seizure do not compromise due process, especially where children are concerned. Police, who are the first responders to complaints by schools and parents, need to follow the rules of due process and respect constitutional and human rights. To that end, in the next chapter, I also address children's rights under the *International Convention of the Rights of the Child* (CRC), and Canadian and American obligations to protect children under those treaty provisions. While the United States has signed the CRC, it has yet to ratify it. Politically conservative groups have posed strong opposition to the treaty's ratification up to this point, which perhaps explains why the United States is among the last UN members to have not already ratified the CRC (Gunn, 2006).

IS "FLIRTY FUN" CHILD PORN?

To address the aforementioned concerns and clarify our thinking about them, I looked at North American scholarship and case law. Cases heard in the United States disclose judicial concerns about the utility of applying child pornography laws to the distribution of images by children to other children or teens. Is the "flirty fun" that kids are engaging in really "child pornography"? What is the difference between adult child pornographers who sexually exploit children for pleasure and kids who are pushing the boundaries because they have access to the tools to distribute such images? Can the law contain such distribution?

It is also important to examine emerging legislation, such as Bill C-13, the *Protecting Canadians from Online Crime Act*. In particular, I analyze Section 162.1(1), which relates to non-consensual distribution of intimate images. This infraction comes with a five-year prison sentence. With respect to ensuring due process, I also look at sections relating to broader discretionary powers this law would give law enforcement personnel. The Quebec news media reported that the ten male Laval students, who captured and distributed screenshots of intimate images sent to them by female classmates via Snapchat and were eventually charged with the production and distribution of child pornography, were handled insensitively during the arrests (Derfel, 2013). I relate what the media considered insensitive and expand on an analysis of American cases where judges have argued that applying child pornography laws to convict children is like "trying to fit a square peg in a round hole" (*RE: C.S.*, 2012). Finally, I conclude this chapter by reviewing the perspectives of legal academics and theorists on the role of law in addressing these issues.

AMERICAN CASE LAW AND SCHOLARLY DISCUSSIONS

There are a large number of American scholarly articles and a few cases on the inappropriateness of using child pornography laws to prosecute teens for sexting. The majority of the articles raise concerns, which I discuss in the sections that follow.

Lack of Intent to Engage in "Pornography"

There is significant concurrence in American scholarship that youth do not have the criminal intent necessary (because of their moral and cognitive development) to be charged with child pornography. Scholars concur that under both American and Canadian criminal law the prosecution has to establish two things:

1) *actus reus* (the act was committed); and
2) *mens rea* (criminal intent).

In cases involving youth and the non consensual distribution of sexualized photographs online, *mens rea* is difficult to prove. Our DTL Research corroborates this perspective. We now have evidence from children and teens between the ages of eight and eighteen that sexting has become a common way to embarrass peers and fit in with peer groups, and that pictures are often distributed as a game or joke between friends without a thought given to the harm it causes to those in the photograph. For adolescent boys, it is about their hormones raging and establishing their sexuality and social skills, and about power over the other gender (Sacco, Argudin, Maguire & Tallon, 2010; Levick & Moon, 2009). A disturbing finding was that even among the younger group of eight- to twelve-year-olds sexting is considered to be a "normal" part of growing up (Levick & Moon, 2009).

McLaughlin (2010) places teen sexting in perspective. She offers statistics on sexting, including disclosures that 39 percent of teens send or post sexually suggestive messages. She argues that prosecuting sexting as child pornography does not advance the legislative intent of the laws because there is no evidence of psychological trauma associated with some of the depictions or publications at issue. In cases where the photograph was self-taken or voluntary (known in popular culture as a "selfie"), there is no evidence that it is an intrinsic form of child abuse.

I am of two minds with respect to McLaughlin's opinion. On the one hand, I agree that with self-sent and consensual photographs, when this can be established, there appears to be no psychological harm. But when photographs are distributed online, even with consent, and they lead to serious cyberbullying or fall into the hands of pedophiles and cappers, as was the case of Amanda Todd (Morris, 2012), the courts would need to address the issue of psychological harm, intentional or otherwise. In my doctoral dissertation I argued that even though it is difficult to establish, the legal notion of "mental shock" or "mental anguish" has made its way into legal considerations under tort law (Linden & Klar, 1999). Under criminal law, the notion of "perceived harm" has been addressed (*R. v. D.W. and K.P.D.*, 2002). And under constitutional law, which is discussed in Chapter 4, but important to mention in connection with psychological harm, is the fact that the Supreme Court of Canada recently agreed that "cyberbullying" caused "discernible harm" in the case of fifteen-year-old A.B. (*A.B. [Litigation Guardian of] v. Bragg Communications Inc.*, 2012).

Impact and Need for "Zone of Teen Privacy"

Considering much of the literature on child pornography, McLaughlin (2010) advocates for a "zone of teen privacy" (p. 173). I agree with this suggestion. The need for a zone of teen privacy is clearly demonstrated in Weber and Mitchell's (2008) South African study. The teenage girls who participated in the study created what they called "public-private" diaries, which they posted online for their friends to see. They thought what they were posting was private within their zone of teen privacy – a zone in which only intended recipients and viewers are able to access the shared content. Unfortunately, the online space in which they posted did not afford them the privacy they expected. In Chapter 4, I address privacy considerations in greater detail, and address this notion of a zone of teen privacy as one that makes a lot of sense. The online world is a place where many teens feel sufficiently comfortable sharing information with friends, but not necessarily with adults. Therefore, a zone of teen privacy, contemplated and incorporated into legislative and government policy responses to sexting, might protect teenagers not only from actual pedophiles and sexual predators, but also from overzealous law enforcement. Charging teens with child pornography would not be appropriate if they were only engaging in "flirty fun" or sharing personal online diaries with friends within a protected zone.

For example, Richards and Calvert (2009) detail a sexting case from Florida where a young man, Phillip Alpert, was convicted of sending child pornography for distributing nude images of his ex-girlfriend who was sixteen years old. Alpert was eighteen at the time and is now a registered sex offender. He also cannot get a job because he has to disclose his felony conviction on employment applications. He had to move out of his father's house (since it was near a high school), was expelled from his college, and was harassed by his classmates. Alpert has given a number of in-depth media interviews discussing the harsh impact of these laws on his life and ability to succeed (Richards & Calvert, 2009; Mabrey & Perozzi, 2010; Orlando Sentinel, 2010).

Gifford (n/d) also outlines criticisms of using child pornography against youth who are sexting. She agrees with McLaughlin that charging teens with child pornography goes against the legislative intent, which is to "protect minors from sexual abuse committed by adults" (p. 2). Gifford observes that misapplied laws turn victims into perpetrators and points out the inconsistency in charges across the United States as far as who is charged, what charges are filed, and the types of sentences given. She briefly examines cases where teens were prosecuted for sending selfies or consensual photographs, as well as cases where teens were prosecuted for posting or forwarding images online without the subject's consent, and analyzes how states have reacted to the criticisms. Her analysis includes the state of Vermont, which introduced special legislation decriminalizing sexting between two people if they are between the ages of thirteen and eighteen so long as they are first-time offenders. Whether repeat offenders are tried under child pornography and exploitation laws is at the discretion of the prosecution (*An Act relating to expanding the sex offender registry*, 2009; Gifford, n/d, p. 5). Other states including Ohio (*Senate Bill 103*, 2009), Utah (*House Bill 14*, 2009), Illinois, (*House Bill 4583*, 2010) and Nebraska (*Legislative Bill 97*, 2009) have either passed or proposed bills rendering sexting a misdemeanor. New Jersey enacted a juvenile-diversion program for first-time offenders (*An Act concerning diversionary programs*, 2011). Consider the American case law in this regard:

American Case Law
Case 1: *RE: C.S.* (2012)
In this case, Pennsylvania Common Pleas Judge Robert L. Steinberg threw out the charges of sexual abuse of children filed against a teenager, identified by the initials C.S., who posted a video on her Facebook page of two other teens participating in a consensual sexual act. Judge Steinberg referred to the use of child pornography statutes in sexting cases as a "round hole/square peg approach." He noted that[3]:

Those who are adjudicated or convicted of child pornography offenses are sexual offenders and often predators...Teenagers who engage in sexting should not face the same legal and moral conundrum. (p. 11)

Judge Steinberg said sexting should be addressed by the legislature. He referenced bills that were pending in Pennsylvania to designate sexting and cyberbullying as misdemeanors and not the felonies with which the state was seeking to charge C.S.

Judge Steinberg deemed the charges against C.S. "void [by reason of] vagueness." He explained this as follows:

The juvenile, C.S., has been charged with crimes that could be interpreted as those committed by a deviant sexual offender. What heinous acts has she allegedly committed: the posting to her Facebook page of the consensual sexual acts of L.C. and M.T., who are ages 16 and 17."

---

[3] N.B. Full citation unavailable but case can be found online at www.krautharris.com/documents/In-re-CS.pdf.

Case 2: *Miller, et al v. Skumanick* (2009)

In *Miller, et al v. Skumanick* (2009), the American Civil Liberties Union (ACLU) of Pennsylvania filed a lawsuit in 2009 against a district attorney (DA) for threatening to charge three girls with producing child pornography for taking pictures of themselves nude or semi-nude. The DA asserted that the girls were complicit in producing child pornography since they allowed themselves to be photographed. One photograph was of two of the girls, wearing bras, at a sleepover. A judge granted the ACLU's motion for a temporary restraining order against the DA, while the Third Circuit Court of Appeals ruled that the prosecutor could not charge the girls simply based on the fact that they appeared in the photos.[4]

Miller, et al. v Skumanick evidences the fact that oftentimes children and adolescents do not recognize where their privacy begins and ends. A study by Weber and Mitchell further illustrates the blurred lines of the private-public divide. Weber and Mitchell (2008) asked adolescent girls in South Africa to create personal diaries. The girls created what they described as "public-private" diaries, in which they posted photographs of themselves in their bedrooms in short night-dresses and various states of undress like those of the girls in the *Miller* case. They had stuffed animals on their beds and pictures on the walls of semi-nude male or female celebrities that they idolized. Weber and Mitchell concluded that the adolescent girls were in a transition stage where they still held on to the stuffed and cuddly animals they loved as little children, but were also beginning to assert their sexuality, and the semi-nude photographs and baby-doll nightdresses suggested their experimentation with images, now known as "selfies." When asked why they used the oxymoron "public-private" diaries, these young women stated that their diaries were meant to be shared with friends. They did not realize that when posted on social media, even with privacy settings, the diaries might be accessed by predators and those who could misinterpret or use them as evidence of some form of child pornography.

Case 3: *State of New Jersey v. Dharun Ravi* (2012)

Tyler Clementi, eighteen, committed suicide after his roommate, Dharun Ravi, used his webcam to secretly film Clementi kissing another man. Ravi disclosed the content of the footage to his peers via Twitter. Ravi was later tried in a court of law and was charged on all criminal counts, including privacy invasion, tampering with evidence, and bias intimidation. The sentence was expected to be ten years in prison but he got one month in jail and a fine. The trial judge said that although he was "grossly insensitive," Ravi could not be held guilty for Clementi's suicide and should not pay for this with the rest of his life

---

[4] Miller, et al v. Skumanick (2009). Retrieved from www.aclupa.org/our-work/legal/legaldocket/milleretalvskumanick/.

or be deported from the United States; Ravi immigrated to the United States from India when he was six years old.[5]

Elsewhere (Retter & Shariff, 2012), I have explained that this case is particularly interesting because of the symbolism it held within the United States and around the world. Specifically, news headlines revered the judge and jury for the verdict – it was celebrated "as a symbol for an end to cyberbullying" (Retter & Shariff, 2012, p. 249). Despite its positive nature, this type of media exposure is troubling because it places so much importance on the outcome of the case so as to diminish the underlying problem altogether. In a reflection piece, danah boyd criticized society's praise for the outcome, noting that rather than "curing" cyberbullying, it only served to ruin a young adult's life:

This case is being hailed for its symbolism, but what is the message that it conveys? It says that a brown kid who never intended to hurt anyone because of their sexuality will do jail time, while politicians and pundits who espouse hatred on TV and radio and in stump speeches continue to be celebrated. [...] No teen that I know identifies their punking and pranking of their friends and classmates as bullying, let alone bias intimidation. Sending Ravi to jail will do nothing to end bullying. Yet, it lets people feel like it will and that makes me really sad. (boyd, 2012)

As my colleague and I explain, in our efforts to embrace technology, we have diminished any value we place on relationships, "thus eroding our sense of respect and responsibility towards others" (Retter & Shariff, 2012, 249). Our obsession with technology has prevented children from developing fundamental social skills, such as empathy, and the age gap between parents and DE Kids further prevents the facilitation of learning otherwise. The verdict in the case against Ravi did not solve cyberbullying – rather, it overshadowed an underlying societal issue in need of a systemic solution. To think otherwise is to be naïve. The first step to curbing the problem is to acknowledge it for what it is, which is much larger than any individual law or judicial decision.

Case 4: Steubenville High School Rape Case (2012)

In August 2012, a high school girl who had been drinking was publicly and repeatedly sexually assaulted by classmates, some of whom recorded the assaults and shared the recordings via social media. During the trial, the plaintiff testified that she had no recollection of the period during which the rapes occurred. The day after the assault, the plaintiff woke up naked next to two high school football players, Ma'lik Richmond and Trent Mays. Both boys were sixteen years old at the time of the crime and they were later convicted in juvenile court for the rape of a minor.

---

[5] Zetter, K. (2010, March 18). Court Slaps Prosecutor Who Threatened Child-Porn Charges Over 'Sexting'. Retrieved March 19, 2010, from www.wired.com/threatlevel/2010/03/sexting-lawsuit/.

During the case, six adults were indicted for offenses ranging from serving alcohol to a minor to tampering with evidence and obstruction of justice. Assistant football coach, Matt Belardine, is the only one of the six adults to be convicted up to this point. Belardine was sentenced to ten days in jail, forty hours of community service, and $1,000 in fines. William Rhinaman, the IT director for the Steubenville city schools, is still facing charges for tampering with evidence, obstruction of justice, obstructing official business, and perjury (Levitt, 2014).

Beyond the atrocities committed by the girl's assailants, what is more shocking is the general public's reaction to the case. Because images and videos of the assaults were posted online for all to see, some of the public took this as an opportunity to weigh in and pass judgment – in fact, some members of the local community even blamed the girl for being raped. Others suggested that the plaintiff was merely crying "rape" as an excuse for her late-night partying antics. Nick Hubbard, a volunteer coach for the Steubenville High School football team, said: "What else are you going to tell your parents when you come home drunk like that and after a night like that? She has to make up something. Now people are trying to blow up our football program because of it" (Macur & Schweber, 2012).

Perhaps more outrageous was the controversial manner in which the media covered the case – many reporters also seemed to be painting the perpetrators in an almost-angelic light. Upon breaking the news of the boys' rape convictions, CNN's Poppy Harlow discussed how it had been "incredibly difficult" to watch "as these two young men—who had such promising futures, star football players, very good students—literally watched as they believed their life fell apart" (Edwards, 2013). Harlow was one of many reporters that sympathized with the rapists rather than focusing their attentions and sympathies on the victim.

This case serves as a further reiteration of a persisting rape culture – issues of perpetuating misogyny and the objectification of women (Bailey & Steeves, 2013; SACOMSS Media Watch, 2013; Bailey & Hanna, 2011). Put in the context of the Steubenville rape, Bob Cook, a contributor to Forbes, writes:

[Importantly,] rape culture doesn't require a rape to happen. It merely is a culture ingrained into sports-playing youth that they get to do whatever they want, to whomever they want, with impunity. Rape culture is one gruesome step beyond jock culture. (Cook, 2013).

While the aforementioned quote may pose somewhat of a generalization to all sports leagues and athletes, its principal message rings true: Rape culture is a systemic failure; accountability does not lie solely with those who commit the wrongdoings but rather with all who stand idly by or perhaps even facilitate irresponsibility.

Case 5: *A.H. v. State of Florida* (2007)
The irony of charging children with child pornography was noted by a dissenting judge in the case of *A.H. v. State of Florida* (2007). This case is of critical importance to my argument against criminalizing children under child pornography legislation.

A.H. was sixteen when she and her seventeen-year-old boyfriend took digital pictures of themselves engaged in sex and emailed the pictures from A.H.'s house to her boyfriend's home computer. The couple never intentionally shared the pictures with a third party – how a third party eventually became aware of the pictures is not discussed within the court decision. Despite no intent to share the photos, both teenagers were charged as juveniles for "producing, directing or promoting a photograph or representation of sexual conduct of a child" (McLaughlin, 2010, p. 153). The trial court rejected A.H.'s challenge of the statute for violating her privacy rights and being too vague.

The Florida Court of Appeals rejected the appeal. However, in dissent, Justice Padovano objected to the majority's reliance on child pornography provisions to punish the minor defendant. He observed that the law had actually been designed to protect this defendant (McLaughlin, 2010). Justice Padovano wrote:

The statute at issue was designed to protect children, but in this case the court has allowed the state to use it against a child in a way that criminalizes conduct that is protected by constitutional right of privacy. (Judge Padovano, dissenting at para 241)

Turning now to the Canadian perspective we find many similarities to American case law, but there are certainly some emerging differences.

Canadian Case Law

The Canadian perspective is just as conflicted as the American one, with federal and provincial legislators intent on passing laws to punish or control kids and the judiciary somewhat reluctant to convict them. Nonetheless, recently several cases in Canada involving teenagers have led to criminal convictions. Some of those who were convicted are planning to appeal their convictions and one case in particular could make it all the way to the Supreme Court of Canada to establish a much needed precedent. Of course if Bill C-13, detailed later in this chapter, is eventually passed into law, the irony and dilemma of charging children with distribution of child pornography will be moot because the words "child pornography" have been cleverly removed from the section of the proposed law that addresses the "non-consensual distribution of intimate images." This section of Bill C-13 would still not let children or teens off the hook for engaging in sexting. It would however, avoid the court having to deal with the legal argument of whether or not children can be deemed child pornographers when sexting non-consensual intimate images.

For kids and teens who might share intimate images consensually, the Canadian approach to the harms of child pornography excludes the taking and sharing of sexual photos by minors over the age of consent. This means that as long as such photos are kept privately and for the mutual pleasure of the intimate partners involved in taking the photo (R. v. Sharpe, 2001), they cannot be charged with distribution of child pornography (Slane, 2009). The discourse in Canada also points to the irony of using child pornography laws against the very population the laws are supposed to protect.

Case 1: Maple Ridge, B.C., Case (2012)

In this case, a sixteen-year-old male filmed the assault of a teenage girl who was drugged and gang-raped at a rave. The teen then passed the video to a friend who posted it on Facebook. The video went viral and Royal Canadian Mounted Police (RCMP) charged the boy with production and distribution of child pornography. The boy pleaded guilty to the charges. The judge sentenced him to twelve months of probation and asked him to write an essay of at least 1,500 words on the "evils of the Internet" (Weisgarber, 2012). The judge noted that the boy had "matured significantly" while he awaited sentencing. The assignment of the essay suggests that the sentencing judge was quite out of touch. His ruling and the rulings of the Nova Scotia judges I discuss in Chapter 4, draw attention to the need to inform and sensitize judges about the lived realities of DE Kids. Far more useful to the boy would have been an essay that helped him think through the psychological impact his actions had on the female rape victim. If he could be made to appreciate that in addition to the physical sexual assault, the girl was "virtually raped" and re-victimized every time that video resurfaced, he might make better choices next time. He may have learned something from his conviction but not from his sentencing. It would have been valuable for him to be made aware of the significant cost to the victim and her family and the impact his impulsive decision to send the video had on the destruction of their lives. Two other boys were charged in the case; one with sexual assault, but the charges were stayed; and the other pleaded guilty to a lesser charge of distributing obscene material.[6]

Prior to analyzing the data from the DTL Research, I wondered why this teen would not have thought about passing the video to someone in authority so that they could bring the rapists to justice. It is not clear from the case whether he knew the rapists. If he did, he may have been afraid of retaliation. Nonetheless, passing on the video to a friend to put on Facebook indicated a conscious decision to further humiliate the victim and add to the physical abuse she had to endure, despite being drugged. Data from the DTL Research show that at least 45 percent of participants realize this kind of behavior is wrong. That is a high percentage. It suggests an urgent need to engage DE Kids in thinking through their decisions to post such content. In Chapter 5, I discuss skills we can provide and how we can engage youth in a number of processes that show great potential to help them define the lines between entertaining others for fun and committing a criminal offense, whether it falls into the category of child pornography or not.

[6] The full citation is presently unavailable but see http://definetheline.ca/dtl/sexting-or-child-pornography. Due to the age of the parties involved, the case is presently unavailable to the public. Therefore, in the meantime, I make use of media references for case facts. An application has been made to the court to access the court documents.

Case 2: Vancouver Island Sexting Discrimination Case

A sixteen-year-old in British Columbia was charged and convicted with possessing and distributing child pornography for allegedly sharing nude photos of her boyfriend's ex-girlfriend via text and Facebook posts. Youth court judge Sue Wishart noted in her judgment that the thousands of text messages the perpetrator sent were meant to intimidate the victim. She observed that the tenor of the messages was "mean, rude and antagonistic," concluding that "[t]he images in question come within the definition of child pornography" (as cited in Meissner, 2014). Through the news media, Crown prosecutor Chandra Fisher sent a message to teens after the hearing, saying:[7]

Always be careful of what you allow of pictures to be taken, what you send to whom. . . (Teens) need to be careful what they send, what they send to each other and where it might end up. (as cited in Meissner, 2014)

The prosecutor informed news media that the evidence included 36,000 texts, which forced the prosecutor to take a crash course in texting symbols and language used by many young Canadians (Meissner, 2014). The teen's lawyer, defense attorney Christopher Mackie, launched an appeal that challenged the constitutionality of the child pornography provisions under which his client was convicted. The legal basis of the challenge rests on the fact that such actions would not be illegal if the parties involved had been adults. Furthermore, defense argued: "The provisions were created to protect children. So is it now appropriate to use those provisions to prosecute children?" (Dickson, 2013). Mackie informed the court he would argue that it is unconstitutional to charge youths who engage in sexting with child pornography offenses because the process of sending erotic images by wireless devices is currently lawful for adults under *R. v. Sharpe* (2001). Outside court, Mackie informed reporters that his client and her family feel scapegoated by the law. He is quoted as saying:

We wanted to ideally avoid this kind of situation that we have now where my client has a conviction of child pornography . . . The concern being that if ultimately we succeed on the constitutional argument and it's found to be unconstitutional, then she's had to deal with the stigma of having been painted a child pornographer for the interim (as cited in Meissner, 2014).

Mackie said he is keenly aware that he will be making a constitutional argument to drop the convictions against his client while the federal government is moving to strengthen Canada's laws against cyberbullying. Referring to Bill

---

[7] Due to the age of the parties involved, court documents are presently unavailable. Please see Dickson, 2013 and Meissner, 2014 in the meantime. An application has been made to the court to access the court documents.

C-13, the defense lawyer noted that the proposed law will give police greater powers to investigate allegations of cyberbullying by giving courts (and thereby the police) the right to seize computers, phones, and other devices used in alleged offenses. In the interests of due process of youth, he noted that the constitutional argument is "a necessary step in the process of fighting this fight" (as cited in Meissner, 2014).

While I tend to agree that child pornography laws seem inappropriate when applied to children, I am skeptical of any real basis to the specific constitutional claim being presented, namely, the analogy being made to the sharing of intimate images. Although the original images where shared between the ex-girlfriend and her then boyfriend, the images that were texted by the defendant were not between two consenting teenagers. Rather, it was an act committed by one teenage girl without the permission of the other. In fact, Saanich Sergeant Steve Eassie claims that the charges against the teen were pursued in the first place because of this lack of consent. Eassie explained: "The accused began using the photos for the purpose of bullying. It's very unfortunate" (Dickson, 2013). To this extent, this case can be differentiated from the typical sexting situation between a boyfriend and girlfriend, both minors or otherwise. Notably, in handing down the judgment, Judge Wishart observed that this type of conviction was not the intent of child pornography laws and that hopefully cyberbullying laws that are more relevant to the offense will be passed, thereby avoiding the need to use child pornography laws.

In the meantime, child pornography charges have also been laid against the ten Laval teenage boys who captured and distributed screenshots of intimate images sent to them by female classmates. The boys' hearings have been postponed twice as of the writing of this book. The latest hearings have been deferred. I outline some pertinent details of this case in the section that follows.

Case 3: Laval Snapchat Case

In November 2013, ten teenage boys between the ages of thirteen and fifteen were arrested for possession and distribution of child pornography, having persuaded and intimidated their female peers to send nude photos of themselves via Snapchat. The investigation began in October when a teacher saw some of the boys in the hall looking at sexually explicit photos on one of the boy's phones.

Despite the police having warrants in hand, the details of the arrest are cause for concern. Police arrested the ten teens at 5:45 a.m. on November 14, 2013, waking the families up without warning. They seized laptops, cell phones, iPads, and tablets. The aunt of one of the teens described law enforcement's arrest methods as "humiliating and degrading" (Derfel, 2013). She even alluded to how the officers accompanied the boys to the bathroom as they got dressed that morning (Derfel, 2013). Importantly, while the actions of these boys are very serious, one should not forget that they are still children. The extent to which the court will address due process breaches during the arrests, and whether the boys' parents will argue this in court, is not known. It is important to point out however, that law enforcement officers who arrest teens for adult crimes should do so in a sensitive manner, bearing in mind that they are still children, and not adults. As I will soon argue, an effort should be made, perhaps in the form of workshops or training sessions, to educate both law enforcement and the judiciary further on how to engage with children and young adults, especially when they are faced with very serious charges.

The use of the Snapchat app to sext risqué photographs provided the girls with a false sense of security. They believed that the images would disappear seconds after being viewed by the recipients. That being said, the caveat to Snapchat has always been that the viewer is technically able to screenshot the image, at which point the sender will be notified that a screenshot has been taken. However, there are now similar applications, such as SnapHack, that allow recipients to capture screenshots of images without sending a notification to the sender.

Despite the incident occurring in November 2013, hearings have continued to be deferred. The case is taking quite a bit of time to be resolved, as police officers are still extracting information from the various devices confiscated from the teens. Interestingly, the case arose just days before the announcement of Bill C-13, the *Protecting Canadians from Online Crime Act*. While the bill covers a lot of ground, including stealing telecommunication services and computer data tampering, Canadian Justice Minister Peter MacKay insists the proposed law is intended to curb cyberbullying in an effort to prevent harm and further teen suicide. The bill plans to pass amendments to the *Criminal Code* to update its relevance to online crime. The proposed updates may even lead to less reliance on child pornography sections of the *Criminal Code*, particularly in light of a newly added section that focuses on non-consensual distribution of intimate images.

Under the act, the distribution of intimate images without the subject's consent or:

a) "being reckless as to whether or not the [subject] gave their consent" is deemed an indictable offense with a maximum of five years in prison [162.1(1)];
b) distributing false information with the "intent to injure or alarm a person," [372(1)] carries a maximum sentence of two years in prison; and
c) transmitting an "indecent communication" with the "intent to alarm or annoy a person" [372(2)], also risks a prison sentence of a maximum of two years.

Notably, the act has received much criticism up to this point, as many argue that the bill goes much further than addressing cyberbullying and updating the *Criminal Code*, as MacKay suggests (Rickwood, 2014; Southey, 2013; Mayer, 2013). Specifically, the general public is concerned about the additional discretionary powers it affords to judges and law enforcement, including new seizure and surveillance laws. For example, as per proposed Section 492.2(1):

A justice or judge who is satisfied by information on oath that there are reasonable grounds to suspect that an offense has been or will be committed against this or any other Act of Parliament and that transmission data will assist in the investigation of the offense, may issue a warrant authorizing a peace officer or a public officer to obtain the transmission data by means of a transmission data recorder.

Because of provisions like this, Bill C-13 has been deemed "omnibus" in nature by many critics and as an attempt to mask surveillance laws under the guise of an act aimed at cyberbullying. Cyberlaw expert, Michael Geist, argues that the bill provides law enforcement with access to metadata, which will allow them to survey each and every room in which digital media is used. Indeed, if this is the case it will result in serious infringement of the privacy and constitutional rights of Canadians. The discretionary aspect of the bill is more worrisome for many in this respect – and potentially unethical (Mayer, 2013). In any case, as with any piece of proposed legislation, the bill does have its strengths and weaknesses. Importantly, these will only be fully known once the bill passes, should it pass, and once its proposed amendments are applied in a court of law. Nevertheless, I would like to suggest some important considerations to bear in mind.

The DTL Research found that children and adolescents reported misdirected impulsivity and joking as a main motivation behind cyberbullying. The exceptional technological abilities that DE Kids are endowed with do not necessarily lead to exceptional moral reasoning. The instinctive or automatic neurological tendency to respond to e-mails or posts immediately creates a kind of "mind to keyboard" gap. I do not believe "big-stick sanctions" are the best method of filling the void. In the meantime, should further discretion be granted to the judiciary and law enforcement, an effort must be made to better understand social media and texting norms as adolescents engage in them. As the Honorable Andrew Becroft, Principal Judge of the New Zealand Youth Court, stated:

This is a qualitatively new challenge for my generation involved in youth justice. We must be trained to deal with the issues. We must do it, it is a non-negotiable part of our ongoing training. (National Centre Against Bullying, 2013)

On another note, as per the DTL Research, children and adolescents often displayed either having no awareness about the laws in place governing cyberbullying, or having some awareness, but little understanding of their implications. Awareness and understanding are two different things. So, I ask you: what good is a law for deterrence if no one knows about it or its effects? While wrongdoers will be punished for their actions, as we have seen in the cases described earlier, solutions that make a difference may come too late. It is essential to be ahead of the problem. Therefore, along with this proposed bill there should come an increased focus on legal literacy for all stakeholders including teachers and parents, but most importantly, for DE Kids. It is essential that children, adolescents and adults are aware of the various legal frameworks that govern their responsibilities and culpability, as well as those that can protect and guide them, through constitutional and human rights principles that contain lessons of inclusivity, acceptance, and shared respect for others in society. Providing young people with opportunities to engage with the law in meaningful ways will go significantly further than simply meting out criminal convictions and jail terms that contain no educational meaning at all for their actions both on and off-line. Indeed, enhancing legal literacy in schools will go much farther than the WITS program that the Canadian government has currently invested in to reduce cyberbullying. WITS stands for "Walk Away, Ignore, Talk it Out and Seek Help," none of which are helpful to victims of cyberbullying or sexting. What use would the WITS program be to a teenage girl whose rape is photographed and/or videoed and the compromising images distributed all over the Internet while her classmates ostracize, isolate, and ridicule her? Would it be possible for her to "walk away," "ignore," or "talk it out" with her peers or perpetrators? The only aspect of WITS that might be helpful would be the "seek help" option. Even that option is limited – because as I have demonstrated elsewhere in this book, young people do not readily report sexting or cyberbullying for fear of retaliation and further abuse or for fear of having their online privileges removed. Hence, it is frustrating to see that after so much comprehensive and informed research and empirical data that has been made available to the Canadian government, the Justice Department has decided to support a superficial program that ignores or overlooks the deep complexities of cyberbullying. It is no wonder then that proposed criminal sanctions remain unclear, despite several highly informed expert testimonies to the House of Commons Committee regarding the negative long- and short-term consequences of criminalizing young people.

Criminal Sanctions or Reintegrating Young Offenders into Society?

If the *Protecting Canadians from Online Crime Act* is passed, what needs to be made clear by the Justice Minister is the extent to which the *Youth Criminal Justice Act* (S.C. 2002, c.1) (YCJA) provisions will be amended or remain in place. If they are not amended, they will impact the sentencing of youth who are convicted under Section 162.1(1), and it will be important to monitor the length of any sentences they receive within the five years in jail rule.

In Canada, all sentencing procedures for adolescents are done through the YCJA. Section 38 of the YCJA states that the sentencing for an adolescent (aged 12–18 years old) must be lesser than that of an adult convicted for the same crime. Judges can base their sentencing decisions on other similar cases. They used to have a large amount of discretionary power for youth sentencing; however, two things have changed:

1. The introduction of the *Safe Streets and Communities Act*, which was brought in by the federal government to take a hard-line on crime including youth crime; and

2. The uncertainty of the extent to which the *YCJA* will be amended to meet the requirements of the *Protecting Canadians from Online Crime Act* if Bill C-13 passes into law. The main legal principle of sentencing for adolescents under the *YCJA* is to reintegrate them into society; whereas adult punishment is based on the gravity on the crime. The legal principles that judges use to determine sentences can vary, and as a result, there is no way of predicting what judges would decide for something like this.

It is interesting to note that sentencing guidelines for adults who are charged with possession, distribution, and production of child pornography necessarily requires a harsh penalty due to the nature of the crime. For a minor, section 38 of *YCJA*, and all of the case law we reviewed, emphasizes that the nature of the crime is not even included as a determining factor for sentencing when youth are charged with the same thing.

In brief, the punishment for the ten boys charged in Laval will most likely not be as severe as it would be for an adult. Without amendments, the principle of the sentence is to reintegrate them into society, whatever the punishment. Section 38 of the *YCJA* reminds judges to keep in mind the integration and rehabilitation of the young offender as the fundamental principle.[8] Even if judges must consider the proportionality of the crime with the sentencing, the fundamental principle of integration and rehabilitation of the young person should be considered.[9]

Legal Scholars on the Role of Law

It is important to briefly mention the perspectives of legal scholars who contemplate the role of law in addressing the complexities and nuances of online communication and the particularly difficult issues where online communications among youth are involved. As we have seen, this is even more difficult when vulnerable children and teens begin to engage in the public distribution of intimate images or "selfies", and even worse, when these are spread around as a joke or "flirty fun." The dilemmas and ironies of applying child pornography laws in their current form are enormous.

The following legal perspectives will inform the second stage of the DTL Research that I plan to complete in 2015, which is to better understand the role of law and its application through judicial and police discretion. As part of the upcoming research, I seek to understand law's potential to protect and empower young people toward socially responsible digital citizenship as opposed to exacerbating, without due attention, the confusion in their minds. I plan to contribute to public policy to help navigate a balance between free expression, privacy, protection, and regulation. Consider the following legal-academic perspectives.

---

[8] *R. v. Y.L.-S.G.*, REJB 2004-54838 (C.A.).
[9] *R. c. D.M.-L.*, [2003] J.Q. n°20498 (QL), J.E. 2004-540, REJB 2003-51984 (CQ).

Legal Assumptions/Child Complexity Theory (LACT)

This perspective argues that legal assumptions add complexity and inconsistencies in the way laws are developed, legal doctrines and rules applied, and precedents established. Law professionals, policy makers, and judges whose decisions impact young people's lives and futures should be aware of their own assumptions and those that underlie legal responses. In 2014, the DTL team is engaging in legal research to evaluate assumptions that underlie judicial decisions as they apply to DE Kids in the case of child pornography and cyberbullying criminal charges. We will also be surveying law students, police forces, and interviewing prosecutors, as well as analyzing relevant judicial decisions to gauge assumptions and level of knowledge and awareness the judiciary has with respect to today's youth. We propose to then juxtapose our results with the participant responses from the DTL Research, some of which is reported in this book, and develop educational resources and workshops to sensitize the legal community to the confusion in the minds of youth. This might lead to the development of more realistic and relevant judicial tests and doctrines in determining youth culpability going forward.

Legal scholars argue that contradictions in private law respect adolescents' worthiness as decision makers under some rules; and override their dignity, agency, and autonomy through articulation of other rules or doctrines (Van Praagh, 2005; 2007). There is a need for consistency in accounting for social, personal, and familial contexts that recognize the turmoil of adolescence and the influence of peer and parental relations. While the law tries to address the paradox of children's vulnerability and increasing independence, it sometimes fails to forgive mistakes. Scholars worry that in the digital age unfettered usage and access to digital information will have untold effects on core values of judicial independence and impartiality (Van Praagh, 2005; 2007; Eltis, 2011; Altobelli, 2010; Danay, 2010).

Need to Address Outdated Laws

Legal scholars, such as Palfrey (2009), have also argued that it is time to address the application of outdated laws and update them to be more relevant in a digital age. In a policy brief and report to a U.S. congressional committee that outlined a range of instances in which legal responses to cyberbullying and related digital concerns have not kept up, Palfrey argued the need for updated laws. He cautioned, however, that such updates need to be thoughtfully applied and cognizant of lived realities and unique perspectives of youth in a digital age – these words should be heeded by policy makers.

Although the Canadian government has taken the initiative to update the Canadian *Criminal Code* to be applicable to the Internet, digital, and social media, as I have noted, Bill C-13 has been criticized because the government is perceived to be sneaking in sections that provide it with increased powers of surveillance on unsuspecting citizens. Others have criticized the discretionary powers to search and seize digital equipment granted to police under the guise of clamping down on "cyberbullying" – this word is expressed repeatedly by the Justice Minister in the media (Rickwood, 2014; Southey, 2013; Mayer, 2013) but interestingly is not used as often in Bill C-13.

These additional discretionary police powers under Bill C-13 cause me concern as to the potential for abuses of due process when the police arrest and charge young people. The media reported several times (Banerjee, 2013; Seidman, 2013) on the fact that police who raided the homes of the Laval boys did so at 5:45 a.m. without warning. As explained in the case description, they arrived at the boys' homes very early in the morning, woke up their families, seized all their smartphones, iPads, computers and other technological equipment and insisted on remaining in the room while the kids got dressed (Derfel, 2013). The parents were overwhelmed and in shock with the sudden arrests.

Is the way this was done a breach of due process? It remains to be seen whether any of the parents will accuse the police of this or raise the issue. Nonetheless, it speaks to the need to develop a greater sensitivity among police to the rights and vulnerability of the children; to remind them they are arresting children and teens – not adults; and given the DTL Research, that most of the kids are confused and do not realize why they are being arrested or that they even did anything wrong. Not only that, due process is an obligation of the Canadian government under the *International Convention of the Rights of the Child* (CRC), which I discuss in Chapter 4.

Ironically, as I was putting the finishing touches on this chapter, I received another e-mail containing a news report that fits right into this conversation about teens, this time American, sexting nude photographs. I decided to reproduce the script to provide the essence of the report and illustrate the way in which police talk about teens who sext.

April 30, 2014 11:12 AM
  Regine Schlesinger[10]
  BATAVIA, Ill. (CBS) – Police and school officials in west suburban Batavia were investigating a sexting scandal at a local middle school. WBBM Newsradio's Regine Schlesinger reports investigators were looking into reports as many as two dozen or more Rotolo Middle School students, ages 11 to 14, took naked pictures of themselves.
  "Some inappropriate nude images were sent via social media," Batavia Police Det. Kevin Bretz said. "I think it's shocking. I think it's improper. However, with social media, the way cell phones are, the way technology has come about and improved and just jumped off in the last 10–12 years, a lot of these kids are very savvy with the electronic devices, and can figure things out."

[10] Schlesinger, R. (2014, April 30). Police Investigate Sexting Scandal At Batavia Middle School. CBS Chicago. Retrieved April 30, 2014, from http://chicago.cbslocal.com/2014/04/30/police-investigate-sexting-scandal-at-batavia-middle-school/.

It's unclear if anyone would face criminal charges, but Batavia Public School District 101 Supt. Lisa Hichens said students could face severe disciplinary action, but the district is waiting for the results of the police investigation before handing down any punishment.

Hichens said this kind of sexting scandal has become more common for schools with the continuing growth of social media.

"With students being so connected ... they're connected differently than we were in middle school, and it's so important that we partner with our parents," she said. "Hopefully parents are listening, and they take this as an opportunity to talk to their kids about Internet safety, and the permanence of things that they post on the Internet."

Bretz said parents need to be more aggressive about monitoring what their children do on sites like Facebook, Twitter, and Instagram.

"Find out what sites they might have, or what apps they might have on their iPhones or their Galaxies, or Facebook, or anything like that. Talk to your children. See what's going on there," he said. "You have every right to know what your young child is doing. You probably pay the bill for the phone and the computer."

This is at least the third time this month a suburban middle school has opened an investigation into sexting. Earlier this month, Barrington Middle School and Hadley Middle School in Homer Glen also investigated incidents of sexting among students.

The Batavia Police detective statements highlight exactly what I have written about in terms of the focus on the kids' behavior as though they were not living in a society without influences. The extent of the responsibility placed on parents is unrealistic. Kids can access the technologies anywhere and there are so many of them. As the research has shown in Chapter 2, DE Kids do not like to report these activities to adults – least of all parents. Moreover, the kids could face "severe disciplinary action," which suggests the possibility of criminal sanctions.

How Can the Law Help and Not Hinder?

The foregoing issues of surveillance, increased police power to search and seize digital technologies, and confusion in the minds of the DE Kids in the DTL Research all point to Calo's (2011) notion of "privacy harm." Calo provides a more relevant and less outdated theoretical framework to consider subjective privacy harm (e.g., the subjective experiences of victims of sexting) and objective impact of privacy breaches (e.g., the public's concern about being watched or under state surveillance). Objective privacy harm can also include stalking by pedophiles. Either way, privacy harm is inevitable if privacy protection and the privacy rights of vulnerable children and teens are breached. The irony is that adults, including law enforcement, promise children protection and yet could seriously harm them and impact their future if their privacy rights are not contemplated.

The forthcoming chapters address legal frameworks other than criminal law and consider the challenges and potential for the law in a supportive capacity. These include the rights of children and teens to protection of the state and the potential role of law in turning the tide toward defining reasonable boundaries that support constitutional and human rights principles. I also touch on private law as it relates to the potential for defamation and libel suits, the duty of care of educators, and emerging provincial and state legislation that places increased responsibility on parents.

Ultimately, I am building the case for adoption of a proactive and supportive stance that will, in effect, not only protect young people but enhance and facilitate their true potential as DE Kids. This, as I have repeated in many publications, will require thoughtful, non-arbitrary, informed, and proactive (as opposed to reactive) policy responses, education that sensitizes youth and the legal community, and active collaboration among all stakeholders.

REFERENCES

Altobelli, T. (2010). Cyber-Abuse—A New Worldwide Threat to Children's Rights. *Family Court Review*, 48(3), 459–481.

Bailey, J. & Hanna, M. (2011). The Gendered Dimensions of Sexting: Assessing the Applicability of Canada's Child Pornography Provision. *Canadian Journal of Women and The Law*, 23(2), 405–441.

Bailey, J. & Steeves, V. (2013). Will the Real Digital Girl Please Stand Up? In Hille Koskela and Macgregor Wise (Eds.), *New Visualities, New Technologies: The New Ecstasy of Communication* (pp. 41–66). London: Ashgate Publishing.

Banerjee, S. (2013, November 14). Child porn charges against teenage boys. *London Community News*. Retrieved November 14, 2013, from www.londoncommunitynews.com/news-story/4216791-child-porn-charges-against-teenage-boys/.

boyd, d. (2012, March 19). Reflecting on Dharun Ravi's Conviction. *Zephoria*. Retrieved from www.zephoria.org/thoughts/archives/2012/03/19/dharunraviguilty.html?utmsource=feedburnerandutm_medium=feedandutm_campaign=Feed%3A+zephoria%2Fthoughts+%28apophenia%29.

Calo, R. M. (2011). The Boundaries of Privacy Harm. *Indiana Law Journal*, 86 (3), 1131–1162.

CBC News. (2013, November 19). Laval teens' porn charges are 'extreme,' says parent committee chair. *CBC News*. Retrieved from www.cbc.ca/m/touch/canada/montreal/story/1.2431685.

Cook, B. (2013, March 17). Lesson From Steubenville Trial: How Jock Culture Morphs Into Rape Culture. *Forbes*. Retrieved March 17, 2013, from www.forbes.com/sites/bobcook/2013/03/17/lesson-from-steubenville-rape-trial-how-jock-culture-morphs-into-rape-culture/.

Danay, R. (2010). The Medium is Not the Message: Reconciling Reputation and Free Expression in Cases of Internet Defamation. *McGill Law Journal*, 56(1), 1–37.

Derfel, A. (2013, November 15). Laval Teens Face Porn Charges. *The Gazette*. Retrieved November 15, 2013, from www2.canada.com/montrealgazette/news/archives/story.html?id=9496f803-3579-44a3-ac43-c4f5562c481c.

Dickson, L. (2013, September 18). Vancouver Island 'sexting' case sparks challenge over charging youth with child pornography. *The Vancouver Sun*. Retrieved from www.vancouversun.com/news/Vancouver+Island+sexting+case+sparks+challenge+over+charging+youth+with+child+pornography/8928731/story.html.

Edwards, D. (2013, March 17). CNN grieves that guilty verdict ruined 'promising' lives of Steubenville rapists. *The Raw Story*. Retrieved March 18, 2013, from www.rawstory.com/rs/2013/03/17/cnn-grieves-that-guilty-verdict-ruined-promising-lives-of-steubenville-rapists/.

Eltis, K. (2011). The Judicial System in the Digital Age: Revisiting the Relationship between Privacy and Accessibility in the Cyber Context. *McGill Law Journal*, 56(2), 289–316.

Gifford, N. V. (n/d). Sexting in the U.S.A. *The FOSI Report*. Retrieved from www.wvisd.net/cms/lib/TX01001412/Centricity/Domain/12/sexting.pdf.

Gunn, J.T. (2006). The Religious Right and the Opposition to U.S. Ratification of the Convention on the Rights of the Child. *Emory International Law Review*, 111, 119–127.

Judges Need To Learn More About Cyberbullying. (2013, July 13). *National Centre Against Bullying*. Retrieved July 14, 2013, from www.amf.org.au/Assets/Files/MR_2013-13July(FF)-Media%20Release-Judge%20Becroft-Judges%20need%20to%20know%20more%20about%20cyberbullying(FF).pdf

Kimber, S. (2014, January 14). Why are we using child pornography laws to charge children? [Web post comment]. Retrieved from http://rabble.ca/blogs/bloggers/skimber/2014/01/why-are-we-using-child-pornography-laws-to-charge-children.

Levick, M., & Moon, K. (2009). Prosecuting sexting as child pornography: a critique. *Valparaiso University Law Review*, 44(4). 1035–1054.

Levitt, R. (2014, April 22). Volunteer coach gets 10 days in Steubenville rape case. *CNN*. Retrieved from http://edition.cnn.com/2014/04/22/justice/ohio-steubenville-rape-case/.

Linden, A.M. & Klar, L.N. (Eds.) (1999). *Canadian tort law: Cases, notes and materials* (11th). Vancouver: Buttersworth Canada Ltd.

Mabrey, V. & Perozzi, D. (2010, April 1). 'Sexting': Should Child Pornography Laws Apply? *ABC News*. Retrieved from http://abcnews.go.com/Nightline/phillip-alpert-sexting-teen-child-porn/story?id=10252790.

Macur, J. & Schweber, N. (2012, December 16). Rape Case Unfolds on Web and Splits City. *The New York Times* (The New York Times Company).

Martin, D. (2011, June 16). One Simple Rule: Why Teens Are Fleeing Facebook. *Forbes*. Retrieved from www.forbes.com/sites/davidmartin/2011/06/16/one-simple-rule-why-teens-are-fleeing-facebook/.

Mayer, A. (2013, November 21). New cyberbullying law has 'larger agenda,' expands police powers. *CBC News*. Retrieved November 22, 2013, from www.cbc.ca/news/canada/new-cyberbullying-law-has-larger-agenda-expands-police-powers-1.2434797.

McLaughlin, J. (2010). Crime and Punishment: Teen Sexting in Context. *Penn State Law Review*, 135–181.

Meissner, D. (2014, January 10). Sexting B.C. Teen Found Guilty of Child Pornography. *The Canadian Press and CBC, The National.* Retrieved from http://bc.ctvnews.ca/sexting-b-c-teen-found-guilty-of-child-pornography-1.1633678.

Morris, K. (2012, November 13). "The Daily Capper" exposes alleged culprit in Amanda Todd suicide. *The Daily Dot.* Retrieved from www.dailydot.com/news/daily-capper-amanda-todd-kody-viper/.

Orlando Sentinel. (2010, September 23). Sexting led to record as a sex offender. [Video log post]. *Orlando Sentinel.* Retrieved from www.youtube.com/watch?v=FssnkvIBdgg.

Palfrey, J. (2009). Hearing on Cyberbullying and other Online Safety Issues for Children (United States House of Representatives, Committee on the Judiciary, Subcomittee on Crime, Terrorism and Homeland Security). Retrieved from http://judiciary.house.gov/_files/hearings/pdf/Palfrey090930.pdf

Palfrey, J. & Gasser, U. (2008). *Born Digital: Understanding first generation of digital natives.* New York: Basic Books.

Perren, S. & Gutzwiller-Helfenfinger, E. (2012). Cyberbullying and traditional bullying in adolescence: Differential roles of moral disengagement, moral emotions, and moral values. *European Journal of Developmental Psychology, 9,* 195–209. doi:10.1080/17405629.2011.643168.

Retter, C. & Shariff, S. (2012). A Delicate Balance: Defining the Line Between Open Civil Proceedings and the Protection of Children in the Online Digital Era. *Canadian Journal of Law and Technology, 10*(2), 232–262.

Richards, R.D. & Calvert, C. (2009). When Sex and Cell Phones Collide: Inside the Prosecution of a Teen Sexting Case. *Hastings Communications and Entertainment Law Journal, 32*(1), 1–40.

Rickwood, L. (2014, January 14). Does Canada's Bill C-13 really tackle cyber-bullying? *Calgary Herald.* Retrieved from www.calgaryherald.com/news/Does+Canada+Bill+really+tackle+cyber+bullying/9386089/story.html.

Sacco, D. T., Argudin, R., Maguire, J. & Tallon, K. (2010) Sexting: Youth Practices and Legal Implications. Berkman Center Research Publication, No. 2010-8. Cambridge: Berkman Center for Internet and Society.

SACOMSS Media Watch. (2013, March 18). This is what rape culture looks like: The Steubenville Rapists [web post comment]. Retrieved from http://sacomssmediawatch.org/.

Schwartz, D. (2013, August 13). The fine line between 'sexting' and child pornography: Criminal Code may be too blunt an instrument to stop the practice of young people sharing sexually suggestive images. *CBC News.* Retrieved from www.cbc.ca/news/canada/the-fine-line-between-sexting-and-child-pornography-1.1367613.

Seidman, K. (2013, November 13). Child pornography laws 'too harsh' to deal with minors sexting photos without consent, experts say. *The National Post.* Retrieved from http://news.nationalpost.com/2013/11/16/child-pornography-laws-too-harsh-to-deal-with-minors-sexting-photos-without-consent-experts-say/.

Sinoski, K. (2014, April 14). Extraditing Dutch man for Amanda Todd case could take years expert. *The Gazette.* Retrieved from www.montrealgazette.com/technology/Extraditing+Dutch+Aydin+Coban+Amanda+Todd+case+could+take/9753678/story.html.

Slane, A. (2009, March 16). Sexting, Teens And A Proposed Offence Of Invasion Of Privacy. *IP Osgoode: Intellectual Property Law and Technology Program.* Retrieved

March 16, 2009, from www.iposgoode.ca/2009/03/sexting-teens-and-a-proposed-offense-of-invasion-of-privacy/.

Southey, T. (2013, December 6). Bill C-13 is about a lot more than cyberbullying. *The Globe and Mail.* Retrieved from www.theglobeandmail.com/globe-debate/columnists/maybe-one-day-revenge-porn-will-be-have-no-power/article15804000/.

Steffgen, G., König, A., Pfetsch, J. & Melzer, A. (2011). Are cyberbullies less empathic? Adolescents'cyberbullying behavior and empathic responsiveness. *Cyberpsychology, Behavior, and Social Networking, 14,* 643–648. doi:10.1089/cyber.2010.0445.

Van Praagh, S. (2005). Adolescence, Autonomy and Harry Potter: The Child as Decision Maker. *International Journal of Law in Context, 1*(4), 335–373.

Van Praagh, S. (2007). 'Sois Sage'- Responsibility for Childishness in the Law of Civil Wrongs. In Neyers, J.W., Chamberlain, E. and Pital, S.G.A. (Eds.), *Emerging Issues in Tort Law* (pp. 3–84). Oxford: Hart Publishing.

Weber, S. & Mitchell, C. (2008). Imaging, keyboarding, and posting identities: Young people and new media technologies. In Buckingham, D. (Ed.), *Youth, identity, and digital media* (pp. 25–47). Cambridge: MIT Press. doi: 10.1162/dmal.9780262524834.025.

Weisgarber, M. (2012, February 10). Probation in rave rape case called a 'slap on the wrist.' *CTV News.* Retrieved from http://bc.ctvnews.ca/probation-in-rave-rape-case-called-a-slap-on-the-wrist-1.766872.

LEGISLATION

An Act concerning diversionary programs for certain juveniles, amending P.L. 1982, c. 81, and supplementing Title 2A of the New Jersey Statutes (Assembly Bill 1561), 2011.

An Act relating to expanding the sex offender registry (Senate Bill 125), 2009, 13 V.S.A. § 2802b.

House Bill 14, 2009.

House Bill 4583, 2010.

Legislative Bill 97, 2009.

Protecting Canadians from Online Crime Act. R.S., c. C-46 [proposed bill].

Safe Streets and Communities Act, S.C. 2012, c.1

Senate Bill 103, 2009, s. 1 [proposed bill].

Vermont Statutes Annotated (Chapter 63: Obscenity), 13 V.S.A. § 2802b.

Youth Criminal Justice Act, S.C. 2002, c.1

CASE LAW

A.B. (Litigation Guardian of) v. Bragg Communications Inc., 2012 SCC 46, [2012] 2 S.C.R. 567.

A.H. v. State of Florida (2007), 949 So.2d 234 (Fl. Dist. Ct. App. 2007).

D.C. v. R.R., 2010 WL 892204 (Cal. App. Ct. March 15, 2010).

Miller, et al v. Skumanick (2009), 605 F.Supp.2d 634 (M.D. Pa, Mar. 30, 2009).

R. v. D.W. and K.P.D., 2002 BCPC 0096.

R. v. Sharpe, [2001] 1 S.C.R. 45, 2001 SCC 2.

Re: C.S., 2012 CP-39-JV-4470-2012. Retrieved from www.krautharris.com/documents/In-re-CS.pdf).

State of New Jersey v. Dharun Ravi (2012), N.J. Super. Unpub. LEXIS 1757.

CHAPTER FOUR

Keeping Kids Out of Court: Jokes, Defamation, and Duty to Protect

Contradictions in private law respect adolescents' worthiness as decision-makers under some rules; and override their dignity, agency and autonomy through articulation of other rules or doctrines.

(Van Praagh, 2005)

INTRODUCTION AND FRAMEWORK FOR DISCUSSION

In Chapter 3, I discussed how and why existing child pornography laws and emerging statutes that criminalize children and require harsher punishment are inappropriate for dealing with sexting and cyberbullying behaviors. My analysis was based on the data and scholarship presented in Chapter 2 to argue that criminal law is perhaps too rigid and reactive a response to apply to Digitally Empowered Kids (DE Kids). This is because, as the DTL Research data show, this generation of kids does not always have the required *mens rea* or criminal *intent* to harm others to the point of driving them to suicide.

I concluded Chapter 3 with reference to the perspectives of legal scholars on the role of law in addressing these issues. In particular, I mentioned the work of Van Praagh (2005) where she argues that contradictions in private law respect adolescents' worthiness as decision makers under some rules; and override their dignity, agency, and autonomy through articulation of other rules or doctrines (Van Praagh, 2005). This piqued my interest in knowing more about how the courts decide on children's culpability and accountability under tort law, human rights, and constitutional provisions designed to protect citizens and ensure due process. Basically, I wanted to learn the extent to which North American society is obligated to protect children from online forms of abuse. Numerous questions arose in my mind. These questions generally inform the discussion and analysis in this chapter, namely:

Once again, I acknowledge the legal research assistance and legal analysis contributed to this chapter by Alyssa Wiseman, McGill Law student and MBA candidate.

1. Which laws or legal frameworks protect children's vulnerability and which ones address their worthiness as decision makers?
2. In what ways might laws or their judicial application override children's dignity, agency, and autonomy?
3. What role does discretionary power play in the application of the law and on due process?
4. What are the roles and responsibilities of adults to oversee and regulate online communication among students, even when it occurs outside the physical school context, online and outside of school hours?
5. What types of laws have generally been implemented since I wrote *Confronting Cyberbullying* (Shariff, 2009) to address the responsibility of school and parents?
6. In what ways might current legal frameworks protect children's privacy and protect them from "privacy harm?" (Calo, 2011).
7. Finally, what are government obligations under international human rights treaties to protect children from abuse, and how do DE Kids fall through the cracks and commit suicide if such protections are in place?

In the discussion that follows, I use examples from Canadian and American legislative frameworks, legal doctrines, and case law. However, for the purpose of containing the discussion in this chapter, I focus more closely on Canadian constitutional and human rights obligations and Canadian provincial legislation to highlight some of the most critical legal, educational, and social considerations. The issues raised in the cases I present are also highly pertinent to the American context.

American state laws and judicial decisions in the areas of tort or private law, and civil and constitutional rights, are emerging at a rapid rate. The American legislation and case law disclosed in our review of the emerging legal landscape is included in Appendix A. It is not within the scope of this chapter to discuss all the statutes or judicial decisions; however, it will set the stage for a more comprehensive and in-depth discussion of state law and judicial decisions in the second edition of this book. In the second edition I will also expand on the analysis we are currently conducting as part of the DTL Research regarding assumptions and biases that might inform judicial decisions relating to the culpability and accountability of DE Kids.

It is also important to note that American and Canadian schools, the media, policy makers, judges, and legislators have approached cyberbullying issues using highly similar responses and approaches, as noted in my earlier books (Shariff, 2008–09). This is not surprising, as these responses are informed by common law practices and similar North American cultural norms. Despite nuanced cultural differences between the two countries, there are numerous parallels (see my earlier discussions in *Confronting Cyberbullying*, 2009). There might be a difference in the extra weight given to free expression and free press in the United States. One Canadian landmark decision in particular, (*A.B. [Litigation Guardian of] v. Bragg Communications, Inc.,* 2012) highlights some of these nuanced differences in the approach the Canadian Supreme Court took in applying the Canadian *Charter of Rights and Freedoms* (1982, c11) to free press and the rights of children to protection of privacy.

Also, my cursory review of American cases involving women's rights under *Title IX* for sexual harassment; school responsibilities, state laws, and constitutional rights; as well as emerging legislation to address Internet crime, confirm many similarities (Canadian laws such as *An Act to prevent and deal with bullying and violence in schools* (Bill 56) in Quebec; the *Accepting Schools Act* (Bill 13) in Ontario; the Nova Scotia *Cyber-safety Act;* and American state laws such as New Jersey's *Anti-Bullying Bill of Rights Act*, 2011; Minnesota's *Safe and Supportive Minnesota Schools Act,* 2014; and California's *Seth's Law,* 2011). American decisions such as those included in Chapter 3, by and large, inform Canadian judicial decisions, especially in emerging areas of law and technology where there are so few precedents.

Accordingly, the legislation and case law I present in this chapter sufficiently describe trends and trajectories in both countries. Moreover, with respect to relevant statutes (established, new, and emerging) in the United States, I have incorporated statutes from Hinduja and Patchin's (2014) U.S. legislation chart into Appendix A. In Chapter 2, I presented evidence from the DTL Research that corroborated my suspicions: DE Kids, regardless of their age range, engage in sexting and other forms of cyberbullying to fit into their peer groups. Not only do some children and teens perceive the purpose of these activities as "fun," they consciously attack those who air emotions of isolation, depression, or weakness on social media. Alternately, as some of the participant comments in Chapter 2 and my discussion of the *D.C. v. R.R.* California case in this chapter will show, DE Kids also single out for ridicule those who might assert their own sexuality or flaunt their appearance and talents too much on social media.

Although this generation of kids acknowledge what they are doing is wrong, they continue to do it to navigate the fine balance of fitting in with their peer group. As the early childhood psychology studies discussed in Chapter 2 confirm (CBC, July 4, 2013) children learn the difference between right and wrong, friendly and unfriendly, fair and unfair behavior, and lies and truth at very young ages ranging from between a few months' old and five or six years of age. However, research activities with very young children involving psychologists from Harvard University, Queen's University, and the University of British Columbia (Suzuki, 2012) show they will side with people they perceive to be more similar to them, even if the people have treated others unfairly. This might also explain children's fear of being ostracized and ridiculed if they stick out for any reason, especially during adolescence where social belonging and reputation are so critically important (Prout, 2005; Commachio, Golden & Weisz, 2008; Arsenio & Lemerise, 2004).

Sexual agency and sexual orientation appear to be the pivotal considerations that inform unwritten codes of conduct: individuals are included if they push the boundaries of ethical conduct online to entertain friends, but it means sacrificing former friends who might send them risqué content in the belief that they can be trusted. It is often those individuals who are scapegoated and viewed as overstepping the invisible line to stick out like a nail "that needs to be hammered down" (Shariff, 2009, p. 69; Senoo, 2007).

Nowhere was this more evident than in the libel case in California, *D.C. v. R.R.* (2010), which also addressed constitutional issues relating to free speech and the rare circumstances under which such speech can be limited.

JOKES AND HYPERBOLE CAN BE LIBELOUS: *D.C. v. R.R.* (2010)

D.C., fifteen, was an up-and-coming musician in California with Justin Bieber-like potential to succeed. His music was popular among pre-teenage girls and he had already secured a film contract and was working on a CD. He seemed to have everything going for him. He set up a guest book on his website, where he described himself as having "golden brown eyes," inviting people to comment. This is when his nightmare began. D.C.'s schoolmates began to post death threats and comments on his site.

A schoolmate who he had never met, R.R., posted the following threat: "I will personally unleash my man-seed in those golden brown eyes." (*D.C. v. R.R.*, 2010, p.5). This comment instigated a competition among D.C.'s peers as to who could post the most outrageous comments on D.C.'s guest page. A significant number of the comments implied that he was gay because of his description of himself as having "golden brown eyes."

As a result, D.C. suffered psychological harm and the threats became so vicious that the Los Angeles Police Department suggested he relocate to another school for safety. This relocation resulted in increased costs for his family because his parents had to drive further to work and drive longer to take him to school. His film contract was delayed and because of the types of comments on his website, people began to believe he was gay. D.C. ultimately underwent psychological treatment and his grades dropped, as did his confidence. Whether his music career ever recovered from this is not known; however, I do hope he regained sufficient confidence after the case to get a fresh start.

D.C.'s parents supported him in launching a civil action for defamation, with R.R. listed as one of the worst aggressors. In court, R.R defended his actions by testifying as follows:

- He maintained that he did not know D.C. or care if he was gay. A friend simply suggested he view the website.
- Irritated by D.C.'s arrogance and description of his "golden brown eyes," he began to post what he thought were "funny" comments.
- What followed was a competition to see who could post the most outrageous comments.

- R.R. described his own message as "[F]anciful, hyperbolic, jocular, and taunting." He explained that this was motivated by "[D.C.'s] pompous, self-aggrandizing, and narcissistic website – not his sexual orientation." *(D.C. v. R.R.,* 2010, p.10–11).
- R.R. described his other motive as "pathological" *(D.C. v. R.R.,* 2010, p.11). He wanted to win the one-upmanship contest that was tacitly taking place between the message posters, so he continued to post increasingly offensive (but what he described as "jocular") comments on the website.
- He argued that he assumed any rational person would understand his repulsion to D.C.'s self-promotional style. *(D.C. v. R.R.,* 2010, p. 10–11). This assumption evidences what I have explained as a shift in norms among DE Kids.
- R.R. and his parents filed affidavits saying R.R. is non-violent, a vegetarian, and a Buddhist.

R.R.'s behavior reflects the tendency toward mob mentality, exclusion, and dehumanizing and blaming the targeted individual to justify the harm (Kofoed & Sondergaard, 2009). The individuals who posted offensive comments on D.C.'s site did not care about or even consider the impact their posts would have on D.C. His description of himself as having "golden brown eyes" overstepped that hidden boundary of teen code of conduct that I discussed in the last chapter. He was calling attention to himself and his comment about his eyes went too far. Perhaps it was because he was seen to be competing for female attention. Whatever the case, as R.R. testified, that self description was seen as "arrogant" and deserving of ridicule. He had to be "hammered down" like the nail that sticks out too far in the Japanese proverb. He made his male peers feel less successful and insignificant and this could not be tolerated. The irony is that R.R. apparently lived by very non-violent and "Buddhist" standards. His parents testified in court that his comments were out of character. In a lower court ruling, the judge held for free expression and dismissed the claim of libel, suggesting that an online threat is not a "true threat" and that to allow the claim would be unconstitutional. However, the California Court of Appeal was not impressed with R.R.'s testimony or his offensive online comments.

The Court of Appeal ruled that there is a balance between free expression that is posted on a public website and the reputation of the victim. The court held that the content was indeed libelous and harmful to D.C.; it negatively impacted his reputation that he had worked hard to establish and curbed his blossoming career. The court held that though hyperbole and "mere jokes" (p.18) are protected by the First Amendment (to the U.S. Constitution), the banning of "true threats" is not unconstitutional. Moreover, the court explained that it is *not necessary for the speaker to intend the threat*. It is "perceived threat" or fear of the threat that disrupts lives *(D.C. v. R.R.,* 2010, p.17). The court held that limiting online threats protects against the "possibility that the threatened violence will occur" (p.17). In other words, we should not risk the possibility of such threats being physically carried out, and therefore it is important to address them, even if they are made in a virtual public space. Furthermore, the court noted:

[T]he further speech strays from the values of persuasion, dialogue and free exchange of ideas and moves towards threats the less it is protected." (D.C. v. R.R., 2010, p. 18)

This ruling is significant when it comes to offensive online communication among DE Kids and also among adults. Unlike the majority of American cases that tend to allow all forms of free speech because of First Amendment guarantees, the California Court of Appeal observed that in a democracy, free speech cannot be unfettered – there have to be limits. To that extent, the more threatening it is, and the more devoid of opinion, the less valuable it is as speech that deserves protection. In reaching its decision the court explained that impact on the victim, his family, and the perceived threat to safety must be considered. The court held that not only were these threats harmful, but the false information and untrue comments regarding D.C.'s sexual orientation (he insisted he is not gay) caused reasonable people to believe it as truth. Therefore, the expressions were held to be libelous.

In *Confronting Cyberbullying* (2009), I highlighted a 2007 case in Indiana in which the court also commented on the content of online expression and the limits that can be placed on free speech, especially when someone is stating an opinion or making a protest because then it has substance. In the case of *A.B. v. State of Indiana* (2007), teenager A.B. was upset about her school's policy on ear piercing. She posted the following message, aimed at her school principal, on her MySpace page, which was a popular social media site at the time:

Hey you piece of greencastle shit
What the fuck do you think of me [now] that you can[t] control me? Huh?
Ha ha ha guess what? I'll wear my fucking piercings all day long and to
School and you can['t] do shit about it! Ha ha fuckiing ha! Stupid Bastard!
(appellant's application, p. 69)

The next day, A.B. posted *"Die Gobert die!"* (appellant's application, p. 70)

Mr. Gobert, the principal, brought a charge of criminal harassment against A.B. and testified that he never received the postings directly but viewed them on MySpace and a website created by A.B.'s friend. The court responded this way (as referred to in the subsequent Court of Appeal reasons for judgment):

As the well-known U.S. Supreme Court decision "One knows Pornography when one see it," this court finds that such language is obscene in the context used by [A.B.]. [A.B.] was not exercising her constituted rights of free speech in such a tirade – but to use the most vulgar language she could. Moreover, she was not expressing her opinion in her writing."(A.B. v. State of Indiana, 2007, para. 1)

A.B. appealed the decision on the grounds that her free speech rights had been infringed. The Indiana Court of Appeal reviewed Article 1 of the Indiana Constitution and noted that for speech to be protected, the form of speech should constitute "the free interchange of thoughts and opinion." The appeal court found that A.B. was strongly protesting the school policy against ear piercing and that although she conveyed this message using foul language, she was still making a political statement. The second prong of the test was whether the principal, Mr. Gobert, had established that the harm he received was analogous to "tortuous injury." The court found that he had failed to do this and concluded that, indeed, A.B.'s right to free speech had been infringed. The court overturned the juvenile court probation for harassment, ruling as follows:

[W]e are mindful that political expression is not shielded from all criminal liability . . . As we stated before, "when the expression of one person cause[s] harm to another in a way consistent with common law tort, an abuse under Section 9 ha[s] occurred". . .Here the State failed to produce any evidence that A.B.'s expression inflicted particularized harm analogous to tortuous injury on readily identifiable private interests as required to rebut A.B.'s claim of political speech. Based on the evidence before us, we find that there is insufficient evidence to support that A.B.'s adjudication of harassment based on her posted message of February 15, 2006 is consistent with her right to free speech contained in Article 1, Section 9 of the Indiana Constitution. Therefore, we hold that A.B.'s conviction for harassment contravened her right to speak, as guaranteed by the Indiana Constitution. (*A.B. v. State of Indiana*, 2007, p. 9-10)

These two cases illustrate that on the one hand, offensive online speech that is engaged simply for the purpose of entertaining friends, without substantive opinion or political statement, is not considered to be a "free exchange of ideas." Lewd and obscene speech is only acceptable when it contains some kind of protest or states an opinion because then it can be considered a free exchange of ideas. Moreover, such speech should have a significant impact on the lives of those targeted. In D.C.'s case, the speech was indeed found to be libelous because it ruined his reputation and impacted his career, health, and education. In the case of A.B.'s school principal, he was found not to have been significantly affected in a "tortuous" manner to the extent that A.B.'s opinionated speech should be curtailed or that she should be punished for it.

There are interesting nuances in North American case law, many of which are surfacing as the floodgates to litigation are beginning to open regarding online speech. Consider also the challenge of balancing the "open court principle" or the right of the press to freely report civil actions to include the identities of plaintiffs whether they are adults or teens. The case I discuss next is particularly interesting because it involved the request by a teenage plaintiff for permission to bring a civil action against her perpetrator anonymously. This meant that an exception would need to be made to the "open court principle" in civil actions, which has been described as a "hallmark of a democratic society" (*Vancouver Sun (Re)*, [2004] at para. 23). The danger for the news media in this case was that if the court agreed to allow a media ban on reporting the plaintiff's name this would set a precedent, which would restrict a significant amount of their reporting and sensationalized approach to cyberbullying cases in Canada. Interestingly, this Canadian plaintiff was also known by the initials, A.B.

VICTIM PRIVACY AND THE "OPEN COURT PRINCIPLE": *A.B. (LITIGATION GUARDIAN OF) v. BRAGG COMMUNICATIONS INC.* (2012)

On Thursday September 27, 2012, the Supreme Court of Canada (SCC) solidified the rights of children victimized by cyberbullying in the landmark decision of *A.B. (Litigation Guardian of) v. Bragg Communications Inc.*, 2012. The decision, overturning the ruling of the Nova Scotia Court of Appeal, in part, centered on confidentiality order requests by A.B., a fifteen-year-old girl victimized by cyberbullying after a fake Facebook profile containing allegedly defamatory sexualized material was created in her name.

In its final ruling, the high court established an exception to the open court principle relating to free press coverage by partially supporting an appeal by the teenage plaintiff who was seeking to sue an online perpetrator anonymously for defamation. In recognizing the *objectively discernible harm* that children sustain from bullying or cyberbullying, the court balanced a child plaintiff's privacy rights in a cyberbullying case with the right of the news media to inform the public. The court acknowledged the potential for re-victimization when administration of justice fails to protect children's privacy but allowed all other aspects of the case to be reported by the media. In this regard, the case was also a victory for free press, limiting only their right to identify A.B. by name. I have written about this case with co-authors Alyssa Wiseman and Laura Crestohl in the *Education and Law Journal* (Shariff, Wiseman & Crestohl, 2012). My discussion of the case uses the following excerpt from that article, with permission from my co-authors:

In handing down its first decision on the publicly known issue of "cyberbullying," the SCC established an exception to the open court principle on free press coverage of litigation. The court partially supported an appeal by the teenage Plaintiff who seeks to sue her online perpetrator anonymously for defamation. The justices recognized the right of children to protect themselves from being bullied or cyberbullied, their vulnerability, and the objectively discernible harm they can sustain. The court acknowledged the potential for re-victimization if the administration of justice fails to protect their privacy. The ruling, however, did not compromise the open court principle, leaving intact freedom of the press to report all aspects of the case, including the contents of the false Facebook page created by the perpetrator (Shariff, Wiseman & Crestohl, 2012, p. 3).

Protection of Victim Privacy

The only caveat in the SCC decision was that nothing identifying A.B. could be published in the media. As noted, this is the first court ruling in Canada involving cyberbullying, which makes it significant, if only from that perspective. However, the issues of privacy, the particular vulnerability of children in online settings, and their right to protection (as weighed against open court principles and free press considerations) make this a landmark decision for many reasons. As Wiseman and Crestohl observe (Shariff, Wiseman & Crestohl, 2012), while the ruling clarifies some questions and begins to address the policy vacuum surrounding offensive online communications by DE Kids in Canada, it also opens the door to a range of additional questions and concerns that will likely remain unanswered until they are fully considered by future courts.

In this chapter, I want to highlight the implications of the A.B. ruling within the context of current research on cyberbullying presented in Chapter 2. Later on in the discussion, I also bring in some more data from the DTL Research whereby the DE Kids gave us their thoughts about privacy rights and their concerns about protection of privacy. I draw attention to complex considerations that the SCC was not required to address in the case, but that are essential to a policy debate about online communications and cyberbullying among DE Kids. My objective is to discuss the positive implications of the ruling as it stands and draw attention to questions and concerns that emerge from the ruling that remain unanswered. These questions are also at the core of the national debate that has raged in the media and Parliament since the suicide of British Columbia teenager, Amanda Todd, which, ironically, occurred only two weeks after the SCC decision. I have detailed Todd's circumstances in earlier chapters so I will not expand on it now. An important question that has not been widely debated in the media or in Parliament, but which I introduce for consideration in this article, relates to the protection of DE Kids whom I call "victim-perpetrators." These are children who experience the same anguish, and are as vulnerable to re-victimization or ruined reputations, as A.B. and Amanda Todd. Later, I also provide empirical evidence to highlight the fact that whether or not these child perpetrators become defendants in defamation lawsuits or if they end up being charged under the *Criminal Code*, the protection of their privacy and identities is equally important.

Fear of Being Identified and "Discernible Harm"

While tort law could feature strongly in cyberbullying cases, it had failed to do so in Canada until the SCC decision in A.B., a case originating in Nova Scotia. A.B.'s perpetrator constructed a Facebook page in a name similar to A.B.'s and posted lewd and sexual comments on it. The case generated significant interest from local and national news media, which challenged the publication ban on A.B.'s identity. A number of Canadian youth protection organizations, including Kids Help Phone and UNICEF Canada, intervened on A.B.'s behalf to argue for her privacy rights. As this case was the first of its kind on cyberbullying to be brought before any Canadian court, it is not surprising that the lower courts in Nova Scotia could not find the right balance between freedom of the press that supports the open court system and the harm that A.B. experienced.

As Wiseman and Crestohl note (Shariff, Wiseman & Crestohl, 2012), the Nova Scotia Court of Appeal ruling by Justice Saunders was particularly insensitive to A.B.'s fears, finding that her fear of "public embarrassment or a stated interest in privacy" was not sufficient for infringing on the open court principle and freedom of the press (*A.B. [Litigation Guardian of v. Bragg Communications, Inc.*, 2011, para. 73). Justice Saunders found that A.B.'s fears were not reason enough to grant her anonymity in the proceedings, holding that "subjective feelings of discomfort cannot be the test for anonymity" (*A.B. [Litigation Guardian of] v. Bragg Communications, Inc.*, 2011, para. 82).

The Court of Appeal further failed to recognize the special vulnerability that children face in the digital age. According to the court, "the mere fact of A.B.'s age did not establish any kind of special vulnerability such that the court ought to intervene and place her interests above the constitutional rights of others." (*A.B. [Litigation Guardian of] v. Bragg Communications, Inc.*, 2011 at para. 68). The court was charged with the task of balancing the privacy rights of Canadian citizens with freedom of the press, but failed to consider the special vulnerability of children, especially those who have fallen victim to hurtful cyberbullying. Regarding the open court principle, Justice Saunders had this to say:

In general terms, the open court principle implies that justice must be done in public. Accordingly, legal proceedings are generally open to the public. The hearing rooms where the parties present their arguments to the court must be open to the public, which must have access to pleadings, evidence and court decisions. Furthermore, as a rule, no one appears in court, whether as a party or as a witness, under a pseudonym." (*A.B. [Litigation Guardian of] v. Bragg Communications, Inc.*, 2011 at para. 75)[1]

The open court principle is inextricably tied to the rights guaranteed by s.2(b) of the Charter. Openness permits public access to information, which then fosters informed dialogue and criticism of court proceedings, practices and outcomes. Such values are seen as hallmarks of our democracy. Section 2(b) protects listeners as well as speakers to ensure that the right to information about the administration of justice in Canada is real and not illusory." (*A.B. [Litigation Guardian of] v. Bragg Communications, Inc.*, 2011 at para. 76)

He then tied freedom of the press into the value of the open court principle:

Freedom of the press is an essential cornerstone of a free and democratic society. Any measure which restricts the press in gathering information and disseminating it to the public, will, prima facie, be seen as an encroachment upon the freedom of the press."(*A.B. [Litigation Guardian of] v. Bragg Communications, Inc.*, 2011 at para. 77).

---

[1] Quoting Bastarache J. in *Application to proceed in camera, Re*, 2007 SCC 43, 2007 CarswellBC 2418, 2007 CarswellBC 2419 at para 81 (S.C.C.)

Regarding the harm A.B. suffered as a result of the victimization, and her reluctance to risk further harm if her identity were revealed, Justice Saunders first quoted the appellant's factum and then expressed disagreement with the submission therein:

Even if evidence of actual harm to a child is strictly required by the Dagenais test, the Appellant says that such evidence was before the Court. The defamatory statements themselves were sufficient evidence that the minor Appellant was at serious risk of harm. I am not persuaded by the appellant's submission. Respectfully, it confuses the steps required to satisfy the prerequisites for a publication ban under the Dagenais/Mentuck test with the stages of proof when trying a defamation action before a jury." (A.B. [Litigation Guardian of] v. Bragg Communications Inc., 2011, paras. 90–91)

Shariff, Wiseman and Crestohl (2012) noted that the SCC developed the Dagenais/Mentuck test specifically for the purpose of balancing public access to the courts with various other competing rights, including the parties' rights to privacy. In both *Dagenais v. Canadian Broadcasting Corp.* (1994) and *R. v. Mentuck* (2011) the court upheld the view that a publication ban should be ordered only if:

a) such an order is necessary in order to prevent a serious risk to the proper administration of justice because reasonably alternative measures will not prevent the risk; and
b) the salutary effects of the publication ban outweigh the deleterious effects on the rights and interests of the parties and the public, including the effects on the right to free expression, the right of the accused to a fair and public trial, and the efficacy of the administration of justice. (R. v. Mentuck, 2011, para. 32)

In *Canadian Newspapers Co. v. Canada (Attorney General)* (1988), preventing a newspaper from disclosing the identity of the parties was found to represent only a minimal harm to freedom of the press. Weighed against the harm that may ensue from A. B.'s inability to remain anonymous, an argument in favor of the overriding importance of freedom of the press cannot succeed. However, the Court of Appeal agreed with the way in which the Nova Scotia Supreme Court judge had determined the issue of demonstrable harm. Justice LeBlanc recognized the distinction in his decision. He said:

... I repeat that there is no evidence before the court of the harm that counsel for the applicant says will occur. While counsel suggests that no evidence of potential harm is necessary, I cannot agree. This conclusion does not depend entirely on the lack of evidence respecting future harm. The Facebook profile was published in March and this application was heard in late May, yet there was no evidence offered respecting any effects the publication had in the interim. I appreciate the contention by the applicant's counsel that if she were to proceed with a defamation suit and succeeded she would be entitled to a presumption of damages that would follow from the finding of defamation. However, it is my view that this is not sufficient to establish the harm, actual or potential, required to grant for this type of order. I therefore, deny the application for a publication ban and the use of pseudonyms.

It should have been a relatively easy thing for the appellant to produce evidence showing harm. A parent, a relative, a teacher, a nurse, or a doctor might easily have sworn an affidavit which would document the noticeable changes perceived in A.B. thereby offering evidence of past harm, which would then assist the court in predicting future harm or, at least, evaluating the risk of harm.

In my opinion, the appellant's failure to lead any evidence of harm or risk of harm to herself is fatal to both her request for a partial publication ban and that she be given permission to advance this litigation anonymously. (*A.B. [Litigation Guardian of] v. Bragg Communications Inc.*, 2011, para. 37)

The insensitivity shown by the Nova Scotia courts, and their failure to recognize the vulnerability of children, in effect impaired children's access to justice. They offered young victims the choice between subjecting themselves to further harm by revealing their identities to the court or not pursuing their perpetrators. Until the SCC decision, young plaintiffs were reluctant to sue perpetrators for compensation for unfair comments and ruined reputations (defamation and cyber-libel), breach of privacy, and identity theft of social networking profiles. Although Canadian courts have supported claims for cyber-libel involving defamation of adult reputations, very few cases of defamation involving children have reached the courts. Most have been settled out of court. It is important to explain briefly why plaintiffs might be afraid to sue their perpetrators. Plaintiff-victims are required to publicly disclose their identities in court documents. This can be problematic because they may not want to evoke additional hostility from their perpetrators.

Court backlogs can delay trials putting plaintiff-victims at risk for more abuse from angry defendants (Young, 2011; Lucock & Yeo, 2006; Danay, 2010). Consider the following factors that might add to this fear. First, a large number of people can view or engage in the cyberbullying. The difference between physical bullying and cyberbullying is that there can be an enormous number of cyber-voyeurs who watch the abuse or partake in it. Racist, sexist, or homophobic statements and compromising sexual photographs can be altered and sent to limitless audiences. Chu (2005) explains that incidents of online bullying are like cockroaches; for every incident that is reported, many others go unreported because they are difficult to track. What is most disturbing about this is that the person targeted is re-victimized every time someone new views the offensive postings. This form of harm has serious implications for focused research and attention needs to be paid to the variety of ways in which offensive and demeaning information is retrieved, viewed, used, saved, and distributed. Amanda Todd's case is a good example of this concern because, even after her death, the trolling has continued, and every time these abusive posts and videos are shown in the media Amanda continues to be re-victimized. Filters and bans are ineffective because the offensive information can be spread through so many online venues. In *A.B. (Litigation Guardian of) v. Bragg Communications, Inc.*, (2012), the SCC cites the Report of the Nova Scotia Task Force on Bullying and

Cyberbullying, chaired by Professor A. Wayne MacKay, the first provincial task force to focus on cyberbullying (MacKay, 2012), and describes cyberbullying as a phenomenon with "psychological toxicity." (*A.B. [Litigation Guardian of] v. Bragg Communications Inc.*, 2012, para. 20).

Quoting from the report, the SCC notes that cyberbullying's harmful consequences are "extensive," including loss of self esteem, anxiety, and school dropouts (*A.B. [Litigation Guardian of] v. Bragg Communications Inc.*, 2012 at para. 21). Researchers have found that teenagers in particular self-isolate because they are too afraid to report cyberbullying for fear of further ramifications. One of my Montreal studies (Shariff & Churchill, 2010) of 800 Grade 6 and 7 students found that 50 percent of teenagers do not report cyberbullying for fear that:

a) perpetrators will accuse them of "ratting" and the bullying will increase;
b) adults (especially teachers) they report to will not do anything about it; and
c) parents will withdraw their online privileges to keep them safe, resulting in even further isolation (Shariff & Churchill, 2010).

We found that 70 percent of eleven- to fifteen-year-olds reported being bullied or cyberbullied often or occasionally and 43 percent confessed to "pretending to be someone else" online to engage in bullying. Seventy-two percent of females reported being cyberbullied compared to 28 percent of males, noting that they would report cyberbullying only if they could do it anonymously. As the SCC noted, sexualized cyberbullying can add to the fear of being recognized and forcing children to disclose their identities could make them vulnerable to further abuse:

In the context of sexual assault, this Court has already recognized that protecting a victim's privacy encourages reporting: *Canadian Newspapers Co. v. Canada (Attorney General)*, *[1988]* 2 S.C.R. *122*. It does not take much of an analytical leap to conclude that the likelihood of a child protecting himself or herself from bullying will be greatly enhanced if the protection can be sought anonymously. As the Kids Help Phone factum constructively notes (at para. 16), protecting children's anonymity could help ensure that they will seek therapeutic assistance and other remedies, including legal remedies where appropriate. In particular, "[w]hile media publicity is likely to have a negative effect on all victims, there is evidence to be particularly concerned about child victims... Child victims need to be able to trust that their privacy will be protected as much as possible by those whom they have turned to for help. (Lisa M. Jones, David Finkelhor & Jessica Beckwith, "Protecting victims' identities in press coverage of child victimization" (2010), 11 Journalism 347, at pp. 349–50 in *A.B. [Litigation Guardian of] v. Bragg Communications Inc.*, 2012 at para. 25)

The court also referenced a UNICEF Innocenti Research Centre Report on Child Safety Online, which confirmed that allowing the names of child victims and other identifying information to appear in the media can exacerbate trauma, complicate recovery, discourage future disclosures, and inhibit cooperation with authorities (UNICEF Report, 2008) This report reflects exactly the sexualized harassment, extortion, and trauma that Amanda Todd experienced at the hands of her adult perpetrator, and then her peers. The court also cited *R. v. H. (D.)* (2002), a British Columbia case in which fourteen-year-old Dawn Marie Wesley committed suicide as a result of persistent bullying. She killed herself because of what the B.C. Provincial Court described as "perceived intent" to harm (Shariff & Churchill, 2010).

Increased Isolation and Emotional Distress

When victims of cyberbullying are afraid to come forward publicly, this increases their sense of isolation. Physical harm from bullying is tangible and easily identified as "real" violence. But threats and harassment in cyberspace, and their impact, are less tangible. This makes it more difficult to establish harm under tort law. There is no escape for victims who feel trapped knowing that an infinite audience can view their humiliation and identify them as the brunt of their jokes.

Libelous gossip and jokes about the incident would proliferate, making it very difficult for anyone to focus on learning. Relocating and changing schools make no difference because, wherever they go, there is the possibility that they will be identified as the victims whose pain was viewed so publicly (Danay, 2010). Abuse on the Internet creates emotional distress, psychosocial trauma, and serious mental health consequences for teenagers. Studies reported that 51 percent of students bullied at school are more likely to harass others in online environments, as are young people who experience high levels of depression or trauma in real life (Ybarra and Mitchell, 2004). Such young people also seek out close online relations to fill voids in their lives, further increasing their vulnerability to online exploitation. In 2010, a national study found that children who were cyberbullied were significantly more likely to experience risk behaviors, such as anger, physical injury, anxiety, eating problems, and drug use (Beran, Stanton, Hetherington, Mishna & Shariff, 2012).

Children may feel that their implicit sense of trust with an acquaintance has been violated just as they may feel that an explicit sense of trust with a friend has been broken. The study found that children who were cyber-victimized were more likely to bully others than children who were not. It is likely that becoming a target of cyberbullying creates an expectation among peers that harassment is normal, thus inviting reciprocating bullying behaviors in any form because "everyone does it." In the same report, a review of a range of research studies confirms that victims demonstrate a fear of leaving home; experience plunging grades; lose interest in school or drop out altogether; have disordered eating or sleeping habits; exhibit changes in dress and appearance; stop socializing with friends; and have suicidal thoughts. Hinduja and Patchin (2010) report that 20 percent of the respondents in their study reported seriously thinking about attempting suicide (19.7 percent of females and 20.9 percent of males), while 19 percent reported attempting suicide (17.9 percent of females and 20.2 percent of males). The authors coined the term "bullycide," which describes suicides by victims of bullying or cyberbullying. Cyberbullying itself may not always be the only cause of suicide, but where mental health issues exist, it could push victims over the edge (Hinduja & Patchin 2010).

Consider, for example, the case of *United States v. Lori Drew* (2009) wherein Drew and her daughter created a fake MySpace profile under the alias "Josh" and proceeded to befriend thirteen-year-old, Megan Meier (a classmate), via the social media site and send her hateful and threatening comments. The emotional distress caused by the comments later caused Meier to commit suicide.

While the Missouri district court was unable to hold Drew directly accountable for the harassment that led to Meier's suicide, for a number of different legal reasons, public outcry prompted federal prosecutors to apply the *Computer Fraud and Abuse Act* to the case, allowing the prosecution to apply the MySpace terms of service. Importantly, the terms of service necessitate "truthful and accurate registration, refraining from using information from MySpace to harass others [and] refraining from promoting false or misleading information" (*United States v. Lori Drew*, 2009). The jury therefore found Drew guilty of one felony count for conspiracy and three misdemeanors for unauthorized computer use.

The serious nature of the case prompted the state of Missouri to modify its harassment law to include cyberbullying. Importantly, the language of the law recognizes the emotional distress faced by victims of cyberbullying. More specifically, the law prohibits any electronic communications that "knowingly frighten, intimidate, or cause [victim] emotional distress" (Henderson, 2009).

An Expanded Meaning for "Objectively Discernible Harm"

The SCC has acknowledged that harm from cyberbullying can be objectively discernible. While considering the evaluation of harm in the case of A.B., Justice Abella, speaking for a unanimous court, noted, "absent scientific or empirical evidence of the necessity of restricting access, the court can find harm by applying reason and logic." *(A.B. [Litigation Guardian of v. Bragg Communications, Inc.,* 2012 at para. 16).

This welcome language provides a stark contrast to the lower courts' judgments, wherein A.B. was charged with the onus of proving that she had suffered tangible harm. Specifically, as I quoted earlier, Justice Saunders of the Nova Scotia Court of Appeal ruled that A.B.'s failure to provide evidence of risk or harm was "fatal" to her request for a publication ban (*A.B. [Litigation Guardian of] v. Bragg Communications, Inc.,* 2011 at para. 94). The SCC deemed the lower court rulings to be based on an error in law – a failure to recognize A.B.'s objectively discernable harm. The lower courts should have recognized that there could be a logical inference of harm under the circumstances of online offensive communication among DE Kids. Why is an analysis focused on court interpretations of "harm" so important?

In the case of such communication, it is essential that notions of harm are understood in the context of harm to both the victims and perpetrators of cyberbullying because often, as I have already mentioned, the latter are also victims of cyberbullying. This is all the more crucial, if, as my preliminary research found (Shariff, under review), DE Kids are unable to distinguish the point at which their normative lines of communication become so offensive that they risk liability.

As noted earlier, and as Wiseman and Crestohl remind us (Shariff, Wiseman & Crestohl, 2012), the Dagenais/Mentuck test established that a publication ban should be ordered only if it is necessary to prevent a serious risk to the proper administration of justice because other reasonable alternatives will not prevent it, and the salutary effects of the ban outweigh the deleterious effects on the rights and interests of the parties and the public (*A.B. [Litigation Guardian of] v. Bragg Communications, Inc.*, 2012 at para. 32). In other words, as the SCC put it, "the Dagenais/Mentuck test requires neither more nor less than the one from *R. v. Oakes*" (*A.B. [Litigation Guardian of] v. Bragg Communications, Inc.*, 2012 at para. 16). The court must simply apply logic to assess the relative harm associated with disclosing a child victim's identity as opposed to limiting the open court principle.

The constitutionality of A.B. proceeding anonymously is separate from the case of defamation that A.B. could later bring against the author of the fake Facebook profile. Because these are cases with different causes of action, the assessment of harm in each is perhaps typically counterintuitive and contradictory. As I noted earlier, the lower courts required *tangible* evidence of harm in order to consider granting A.B. the use of a pseudonym. In contrast, in defamation cases, harm is *presumed* and the onus shifts to defendants to substantiate defenses such as the truth of the statement.[2]

Generally, defamation suits are pursued publicly by nature of the claim being brought to the court as plaintiffs are seeking to clear their good names. Justice Saunders of the Nova Scotia Court of Appeal suggested that A.B. should not be fearful of pursuing her claim in an open court because if she succeeds she will

---

[2] Defamation: Where a person's reputation is put in a bad light because of false or twisted statements. By definition, defamation refers to a false statement that causes harm. For an action of defamation to succeed, the plaintiff must establish four things: a) That the statements were published in some form; b) That they were published by the defendant; c) That they refer to the plaintiff, and d) That the statements were defamatory, either in their normal sense or through innuendo. The test for this is whether the words lower the plaintiff in the estimation of right-thinking members of society or expose him or her to hatred, contempt, or ridicule: R.E. Brown, The Law of Defamation in Canada. 2nd ed. (Toronto: Carswell, 1994) at 15 noted: [A publication] may be defamatory in its plain and ordinary meaning or by virtue of extrinsic facts or circumstances, known to the listener or reader, which give it a defamatory meaning by way of innuendo different from that in which it ordinarily would be understood. In determining its meaning, the court may take into consideration all the circumstances of the case, including any reasonable implications the words may bear, the context in which the words are used, the audience to whom they were published and the manner in which they were presented (page 15).

be lauded for her courage in bringing her cyberbully to justice in the public eye (*A.B. [Litigation Guardian of] v. Bragg Communications Inc.*, 2011).

In the new media landscape, however, the public nature of digital communication and social media has transformed the face of defamation. The plaintiff is no longer an assertive adult or corporation, but instead a vulnerable child. This has created a situation in which, to proceed anonymously, the plaintiff would have had to provide tangible evidence of harm before continuing with a defamation case where harm would be presumed. The SCC rectified this by recognizing the vulnerability of children and the psychological consequence of cyberbullying through their interpretation of ostensible harm.

When one considers Calo's (2011) framework of privacy harm, the Dagenais/Mentuck test, as applied by the SCC, the court appears to strike the appropriate balance between A.B.'s privacy harm and the open court principle. The SCC's recognition of both objective and subjective privacy harm served to protect A.B.'s anonymity while simultaneously denying a complete publication ban. As such, the SCC's reason, coupled with social science evidence, brought A.B.'s potential and foreseeable harm to the forefront of the case, marking a monumental milestone for cases involving offensive online communication among DE Kids and, it is to be hoped, future policies in this regard.

Implications of the *A.B.* Ruling for Victim-Perpetrators

Perpetrators are often victims of cyberbullying. My primary concern regarding the A.B. decision relates to the fact that the court suggested privacy protection for victims of online harassment and cyberbullying. However, the research suggests that the lines between victims and perpetrators are not always so clear. Empirical studies discussed later confirm that perpetrators of cyberbullying are often victims of previous bullying or cyberbullying. Thus, there is the risk that victims of cyberbullying could be sued as perpetrators when they might, in fact, be retaliating to provocation. The term "victim-perpetrator" is not truly oxymoronic in cases of cyberbullying.

Consider the evidence: According to Farmer *et al.* (2010), 30 percent of children and youth across the United States report being involved in bullying in school either as a perpetrator or victim, or both. The term "bully-victim" refers to youth who both perpetuate bullying against peers and who are bullied by peers. Bully-victims tend to have the fewest positive interpersonal characteristics and are most likely to associate with unpopular peers. They also have the lowest rates of social acceptance and tend to be more emotive. Juvonen and Gross (2008) support these findings, noting that 28 percent of youth in their study of 1,454 teenagers between the ages of twelve and seventeen reported retaliating against bullying by engaging in bullying themselves, both in school and online. Their study found that of 48 percent of victims who reported retaliating against their presumed aggressors, 28 percent of school-based victims retaliated in school and online. They found that 90 percent would not tell an adult because they needed to learn to deal with it themselves.

The Impact of Media Reports on Child-Victims' Privacy

In earlier chapters I addressed my concerns regarding the impact of news media reports on the privacy of child-victims. I discussed this in the context of Amanda Todd's case and in the context of the moral panic over child suicides related to online communications among DE Kids. In this chapter I want to revisit that conversation in the context of A.B.'s plea to the SCC to protect her privacy.

The media spotlight on cyberbullying, sometimes through informed and sensitive reporting by news providers in Canada, has raised awareness of the related issues (Seidman, 2012; Lokeinsky, 2012). To that end, I support the SCC's decision to sustain the open court principle without compromising children's privacy rights. However, it is important to remain aware that the majority of media outlets continue to focus on the sensational aspects of extreme cyberbullying incidents, especially cases that involve suicide (Parker, 2012; Nies, Donaldson & Netter, 2010).

As I noted in earlier chapters, the publicity Amanda Todd's death received and continues to receive as her adult perpetrator from the Netherlands was arrested (Culbert & Hagger, 2014) is a case in point. Immediately after her death was reported (McGuire, 2012; Shaw, Sinoski & Quan, 2012; Reid, 2012) and the media became aware of her suicide note, Amanda's YouTube message was shown numerous times a day on most media outlets. The strong influence and role of the media in providing well-researched information to the public on the one hand, and indirectly fueling reactive public and police responses on the other, have been largely overlooked in the current debate and dialogue relating to offensive online communications among DE Kids. Consider the following concerns:

The Need for a Responsible Free Press

In the immediate wake of Amanda's story, eight female students were charged with criminal harassment for cyberbullying at a high school in London, Ontario, on October 19, 2012. Their names were obtained through an anonymous reporting option on the school's website. While this suggests a proactive initiative on the part of the school, it also raises concerns regarding the possibility that these young girls may be scapegoats in an angry, emotional, and reactive climate in Canada (CBC News, October 19, 2012).

Anonymous reporting in this reactive climate is also a concern because under the victim-perpetrator phenomenon discussed later in this chapter, there is always the possibility that perpetrators of cyberbullying could actually report victims as committing cyberbullying acts, placing their victims in a more precarious position vis-à-vis the law while the real culprits go undetected. Hence, I caution diligence and thoroughness in investigating anonymous reports that lead to the arrest of anyone, especially children.

Amanda's parents wanted her last words and the pain she suffered to be known in order to mobilize public and governmental responses to cyberbullying. While this was commendable on their part, as I have explained in earlier chapters, the effect may have been the indirect re-victimization of their daughter. The media and public attention focused on Amanda's YouTube suicide message, which indirectly resulted in providing a social media platform for the trolling that took place. Trolling perpetuated the cyberbullying against Amanda. For the trolls, this public media platform allowed access to a highly captive audience, re-victimizing Amanda even in death. In this regard, we have concerns that Amanda's privacy was breached in ways that might otherwise have been precluded.

While I endorse and respect freedom of the press, I maintain that the reporting could have been more thoughtful and sensitive in that once trolls were involved, the story could plausibly have been reported without giving them continued exposure. It could be argued that vigilantism from the reporting identified some of the trolls and one man lost his job as a result of proactive action. This situation of balancing free press with the need to protect Amanda's privacy after her death, is a difficult one, and needs to be debated to a much greater extent.

What Amanda's case contributes to my discussion of the A.B. case is that the SCC rightly acknowledged the discernible harm young people experience if their identities are disclosed in the free press. This harm is the same whether the victims are the plaintiffs in a court action or simply the victims of online sexual harassment who go public on social media to inform people about the isolation and devastating harm they have experienced.

The SCC's decision also points to the need for thoughtful media reporting that keeps the public informed. Clearly, the media coverage should not be at the expense of children's privacy rights or their safety. As I noted earlier, emerging scholarship suggests that the media glorifies teen suicides in ways that might encourage youth on the verge to commit suicide with the false impression that they, too, will receive a few days of celebrity and media attention. There needs to be significantly more research to understand the extent to which many young people, especially those in crisis, understand mortality (Gould, 2001).

Media Influence on Reactive Policy Responses

New media focus on extreme cases has resulted in the development of reactive policies and laws that specifically target cyberbullying in schools. While Canadian provincial laws such as *An Act to prevent and deal with bullying and violence in schools* (Bill 56) in Quebec; the *Accepting Schools Act* (Bill 13) in Ontario; the Nova Scotia *Cyber-safety Act;* and American state laws such as New Jersey's *Anti-Bullying Bill of Rights Act,* 2011; Minnesota's *Safe and Supportive Minnesota Schools Act,* 2014; and California's *Seth's Law,* 2011 are well intentioned, and direct schools to develop safe-schools plans, I have observed in the last ten years that without informed research, sufficient or sustainable resources to educate and prepare school officials and teachers for how to develop safe schools environments for DE Kids, these laws will make little difference in reducing cyberbullying. This is especially true when schools are provided with increased discretionary power to expel students who they suspect or "catch" perpetrating cyberbullying. Whether the arrest of the eight female students in London, Ontario, during the highest peak of media reporting of Amanda Todd's suicide, can be attributed in part to a reactionary response based on the public's emotional response to Amanda's case and the national debate taking place on the necessity for criminal consequences, remains to be seen (CBC News, October 19, 2012).

The A.B. case adds concretely to the debate about whether tort law is an appropriate vehicle for young victims of cyberbullying who are seeking a legal remedy. Legal scholars argue that current policies and legislation need to evolve to deal with the complexities of online communication among kids who are increasingly likely to be brought before the courts in a rapidly evolving digital society (Eltis, 2011; Arehart, 2007; Livingston & Brake, 2010; Altobelli, 2010), and that the legal community needs to be better sensitized to normative shifts in online communication among youth.[3] If the effect of the SCC decision is expected to open up the floodgates to litigation for defamation cases of cyberbullying, it is essential that the judiciary is better apprised of how DE Kids conceptualize their online forms of social communication. As part of the DTL Research, we asked participants how they define the lines of public and private online communication, privacy rights, breach, and harm. The results are presented in the sections that follow.

"Private" Venting in Public

DE Generations also often forget the "public" aspect of social media, such as that of Twitter. For example, in early 2010, a McGill University undergraduate student attended a political meeting on campus and became increasingly agitated. He "tweeted" about how he wished he had an M-16 gun to kill everyone. When confronted by the administration, he said he was simply venting his frustration – tweeting felt like he was confiding in someone; whereas, in actuality, the student was publicly threatening to kill his fellow students without realizing the potential impact of his words. Similarly, high school students have insulted and threatened their unpopular teachers on social media, making false sexual allegations. In 2012, an Olympic athlete was expelled from the London Olympics for tweeting racist comments about his opponents. This suggests that the athlete clearly did not appreciate the ramifications of tweeting these comments in a highly public forum. This example of an athlete thoughtlessly risking expulsion from the Olympics, after putting in an enormous effort and investment of time to get to the Games, makes it all the more important that youth are helped to restrain their impulsive comments in a highly public forum. In North America, a number of challenges have been brought against schools that suspended students for cyberbullying. The students claimed infringement of their rights to freedom of expression and

[3] Shariff, S. (Principal Investigator); Van Praagh, S., Beheshti, J., Talwar, V., Manley-Casimir, M., Beran, T., (Co-Investigators). Defining the Lines on Cyberbullying: Keeping Kids Out of Court by Comparing Legal Responses with Motivation, Moral Development and Legal Literacy of Digital Natives. Social Sciences and Humanities Research Council of Canada Insight Grant (Term of 5 years 2012–2017).

insisted that the schools breached their privacy. The privacy claim pertains to the students' belief that they were having private conversations with friends, but they had failed to realize that regardless of the putatively "private" settings on social media sites, the information shared online can be accessed quite easily. This again is an example of the patterns we see in the blurring of public and private spaces.

Girls and Personal Online Information

In Chapter 2, I discussed in detail concerns about why female DE Kids might post intimate content online without thinking about the public ramifications. Research by Weber and Mitchell (2008) confirms that social networking empowers teenagers, especially girls, to construct and produce strong and independent identities through online personal diaries that the girls describe as "public-private."

Although an oxymoron, this terminology reflects the way in which DE Kids think about themselves and view their world. I have already highlighted the insensitivity of the Nova Scotia judiciary in the A.B. case. To enable courts to make informed judicial decisions that take into account the realities youth face in the contemporary digital age, it is important that the judiciary become informed about how today's teenagers, especially girls, perceive, understand, and live in real and virtual time and space.

For DE Kids, there is no separation of the two lives. Their known online and offline identities and reputations are the most important aspects of their sense of confidence. In order to be heard over the din of a million online voices, youth need to construct strong digital identities that pass the judgment of their peers on social networking sites. When an individual is identified and singled out for ridicule, her entire world falls apart because she knows that every time she logs into her online world the embarrassment will persist. Weber and Mitchell (2008) explain that the trajectory from preadolescence to adulthood and social maturity is reflected in shared online conversations as preteens become sexually aware and intellectually mature and develop internal frameworks of moral and social responsibility.

Other scholars agree that while adults continue to view real and virtual spaces as separate, the digital identities of most young people are integral to and inseparable from their physical identities (Lankshear, Knobel & Peters, 2008). Weber and Mitchell (2008) observe that preteen girls can include cuddly animals and images associated with younger children but also take photographs or videos of themselves in sexy poses and combine them with images that more closely resemble children's cartoons. They point out that, to preteen girls, the word "sexy" can mean just "cute" in one posting and "sexy" in the most conventional adult sense, in another. They note that girls' "public-private" diaries can contain photographs, downloaded music, popular culture examples, and a range of other information about themselves and friends. All of these converge to create their identity and through their online postings, girls share ideas and gain a sense of belonging regardless of time and space. The communication is in a space they find safe. Therefore, when these online safe spaces are violated by cyberbullying, identity theft, or unwanted sexual comments, insults, or advances, they no longer feel safe anywhere – in their real or virtual world. Such violations result in what Calo (2011) refers to as "privacy harm."

When we consider the eight London, Ontario, female students who were arrested for cyberbullying in the wake of Amanda Todd's suicide, it is important to consider whether they were simply sharing information or actually engaging in cyberbullying (CBC News, October 19, 2012). In Chapter 3, I highlight *Miller, et al v. Skumanick* (2009) where three girls were charged with child pornography for posting photographs of themselves in bras and towels. As the court aptly ruled, this was definitely not a case of child pornography. Given this background research on how female teenagers communicate online and share their public and private information, any judges deciding criminal convictions, sentencing, and civil lawsuits need to take into account these complex and often conflicting tensions that teenage girls experience as they experiment with their sexuality and the tensions of growing up, sharing information, and communicating in highly public forums.

It is interesting that in sharp contrast to their admissions that they posted online for fun, and even realized the harmful consequences but posted anyway (see Chapter 2), the participants in our DTL Research appeared to be fairly clear about the lines between public and private postings, especially if they are intimate in nature.

DTL RESEARCH: LINES BETWEEN PUBLIC AND PRIVATE SPACES

Respondents to our DTL surveys seemed to grasp that things posted online were often not private in nature. They understood that information posted online could spread farther than was originally anticipated, as well as that information posted online could be: *"out there forever."*

Other than concerns regarding assumptions that young people make about photographs of friends participating in undesired activities, most participants acknowledged that certain content such as intimate images should not be posted publicly. As well, participants recommended that children and adolescents should keep their social network settings on "private" and not share any personal information online. Here is some advice that thirty-one of the respondents gave regarding privacy:

- Make sure you use privacy settings.
- Don't post anything *"you might regret later."*
- Don't post anything that you would not want anyone to see; fourteen participants in the study even mentioned specific people to think about, including grandparents, parents, teachers, and future employers.
- Use a nickname or pseudonym instead of a real name and never give out information such as your phone number or address.

In the focus groups sessions, participants discussed whether or not content remains private once it is posted online. There were consistent statements made by participants regarding the risk of posting something online, including comments such as the following:

It's public. Nothing is private on the Internet... There is nothing that is private on the Internet.

Anything you post on the Internet is accessible to almost anyone and you know that people will spread it no matter who owns it.

Specific to smart phone messaging, participants discussed how you can't revoke a sent message; therefore, you do not have control of the text:

But it's like not just the picture. Once you send anything, like a message, it's out there. You can't delete it unless you have the other person's phone.

Moreover, these participants voiced that they did not feel privacy settings were enough:

No matter how many privacy settings you put...you have all this technology...you're just going to be exposed.

Pre-Facebook Group More Thoughtful about Privacy
Interestingly, most of the explicit comments, which focused on social media during focus group sessions, came from the pre-Facebook group, or those who should not have accounts. Differences in opinion were apparent. For example, some participants felt that they had control over pictures of themselves that were posted by friends by whether or not they approved the tag:

I really like the idea of Facebook making you accept being tagged because like if you get tagged in a really embarrassing photo something you don't want other people seeing; you have the right to ask your friend to take it down.

Other participants felt that the very nature of Facebook or social media sites prevents privacy and enhances the chances of cyberbullying:

The problem is that when you post on Facebook...let's say that I am friends with somebody who is friends with somebody and my actual friend comments or likes [a photo], then their friends can see [it] and so then [people I am not friends with] can add on mean comments.

Participants felt that any message posted on a Facebook wall would be public because, for example:

Anyone can take it and put it on the Internet. Also, pictures they can get on Google. It can spread and anything can go online.

Still other participants believed that posting online could mean complete loss of control over the content:

I understand once you put something on Facebook it's out there. It's not even your property anymore. It's like Facebook's property.

The seeds of digital citizenship and an appreciation of the difference between public and private online spaces appeared to be more evident in the pre-Facebook age group, which is encouraging. This might be due to more awareness among parents of this younger age group and the general result of more focused educational awareness, especially with elementary school children. However, it would be important to engage in a follow-up longitudinal study that seeks their views on the same issues once they are the appropriate age to begin using social media (e.g., Facebook-age).

Aside from the difference in assessing blame for posting of intimate photographs online as discussed earlier, many Facebook-aged respondents characterized posting a picture of someone without first obtaining their permission as an invasion of their privacy. One respondent wrote:

It's not okay to be posting people's pictures online without their permission, because it infringes on their privacy.

Importantly, some respondents even acknowledged that simply taking a photograph of someone without their permission is an invasion of privacy, whether or not the photo is eventually shared. Sharing that photograph on a social network, then, was seen as a further invasion of the subject's privacy. One respondent wrote:

You should not take photos without the person's permission at all in the first place, let alone post them on Facebook.

Respondents recognized that invading someone's privacy in this way is not something a friend would do because it would be breaking the person's trust in their friend. Participants also concluded that the decision over whether information is public or private rests in the hands of the subject of that information, not the person sharing it. Respondents expressed a belief that the subject of the photo had either an ownership right of the photo, or a right to their image or reputation, and that these rights meant that it is ultimately up to that person whether to share the photo or not. This is true especially when the information being shared is a photograph. One respondent wrote:

The subject[s] of the picture should still have the final say over whether pictures are posted in a public place.

Accordingly, it is interesting to note in the research that DE Kids can, when encouraged to think about how they define the lines, think in terms of subjective and objective harm to their privacy. In this regard, Ryan Calo's (2011) legal framework through which we can think about online privacy as "harm" rather than "rights" or "breach of privacy" is relevant.

"Privacy Breach" or "Privacy Harm"?

Calo (2011) provides a framework that has enhanced our understanding of online information that causes privacy harm in the context of cyberbullying. Calo asserts that notions of online privacy can be better understood in terms of subjective and objective privacy harm. He argues that the law needs to evolve to recognize privacy *harm* as opposed to maintaining a continued focus on privacy *rights*. He describes the subjective category of privacy harm as the "unwanted perception of observation" (Calo, 2011) and objective privacy harm as the "unanticipated or coerced use of information concerning a person against that person" (Calo, 2011).

In the case of DE Kids' creation of false Facebook pages, sexting, and unwanted postings of photographs on social media Calo's framework is helpful in analyzing the impact of the emotional distress and fear that might occur when teenagers first have their information used against them, for example, through the creation of a false Facebook page, and even if the page is taken down, the subjective privacy harm that may come from their concern that they may be watched and harmed if people know their identity. This is especially pertinent to fear of a loss of privacy that could result in serious psychological harm. Having heard Calo's American perspective it is useful, in light of the A.B. case, to consider the Canadian debate on the protection of privacy and the open court system as it relates to DE Kids.

The Canadian Debate on the Protection of Privacy and the Open Court System

As I have already noted, the SCC's recognition of children's rights to privacy to protect further victimization is of significant importance. The open court principle was not substantively compromised, thereby addressing a debate that has come to the forefront as the courts attempt to grapple with evolving technologies. In the case of A.B., the court advanced this debate by articulating the following guidelines:

The open court principle mandates that court proceedings presumptively remain open and accessible to the media and the public. However, in the context of cyberbullying involving child-plaintiffs, there are sufficiently compelling interests, namely, the protection of children and privacy, that warrant restrictions on freedom of the press and openness. (Gould, 2001)

Courts do not require evidence of direct, harmful consequences to children in order to make a finding that they are *inherently vulnerable* and deserving of a heightened form of legal protection. Instead, children will be afforded such status based on their age alone and not because of characteristics attributable to their temperament (*A.B. [Litigation Guardian of] v. Bragg Communications, Inc.*, 2012 at para. 17).

The administration of justice requires that children be able to proceed anonymously in court against their cyber-perpetrators; otherwise, the Canadian judicial system will experience a chilling effect whereby children will refrain from coming forward in fear of experiencing further harm resulting from public disclosure (*A.B. [Litigation Guardian of] v. Bragg Communications, Inc.*, 2012 at para. 23). Even prior to the SCC decision, the plaintiffs' right to remain anonymous engaged significant debate in Canada. As early as 2003, Chief Justice Beverly McLachlin commenced the debate over the need to protect the privacy of plaintiffs while maintaining the open court system in the digital age:

In an age of mass media, electronic filing, and online access to court documents, it is becoming ever more difficult to reconcile concerns for the privacy, reputation and the well-being of individuals engaged in the justice system, with the principle of the open and public administration of justice. If we are serious about peoples' private lives, we must preserve a modicum of privacy. Equally, if we are serious about our justice system, we must have open courts. The question is how to reconcile these dual imperatives in a fair and principled way. (McLachlin, 2003, p. 4)

In a more recent speech, Privacy Commissioner Jennifer Stoddart commented on the same dilemma of protecting the privacy of victims in a digital age:

I am also concerned about the potential for a broader impact: Will the potential disclosure of their personal information cause people to be apprehensive about seeking recourse or justice because of the potential for humiliation and embarrassment, or even concerns for their safety? Certainly, parties and witnesses could face embarrassment or intimidation before the Internet came along... (Stoddart, 2012).

But, as Professor Karen Eltis warned in a recent McGill Law Journal article, these preexisting difficulties are "exponentially worsened" by the posting of court records online, word-for-word. Although the objective of online posting is to increase access to justice, it has the ironic consequence of deterring participation in the justice system, which actually frustrates the objective of access. According to Eltis, if we rethink privacy within the cyber context, it can be considered an ally of openness in the court system. If people are deterred from going to courts or tribunals to enforce their rights or seek justice, we, as a society, need to be extremely concerned about access to justice. Another important factor to consider before posting personal information online is its permanence. Once information is out there, it can be impossible to remove (Stoddart, 2011).

In light of this debate, it is important to move on to consideration of how the law should protect DE Kids when they are vulnerable to having their privacy infringed or when they are exposed to "privacy harm," in Calo's (2011) sense of the word. Recognition of the inherent vulnerability of children has consistent and deep roots in Canadian law. This results in protection for young people's privacy under the *Criminal Code*, which will be amended under Bill C-13 to incorporate digital crimes, the *Youth Criminal Justice Act*, and child welfare legislation, not to mention international protections such as the *International Convention of the Rights of the Child* (CRC), which are all based on age, not the sensitivity of the particular child. As a result, in an application involving sexualized cyberbullying there is no need for a particular child to demonstrate that she personally conforms to this legal paradigm. The law attributes the heightened vulnerability based on chronology, not temperament.[4]

ROLE OF INTERNATIONAL HUMAN RIGHTS LAW IN PROTECTING DE KIDS

It is worth addressing, briefly, the role of international human rights law in protecting DE Kids. The United Nations *International Convention of the Rights of the Child* (CRC) provides for treaty holders an obligation to ensure the protection, participation, and provision of children. Article 3 provides for the "best interests of the child," Article 12 places an obligation on member countries to ensure they enable participation of children in important areas of learning and decision making, and Article 19 provides that children will be protected from abuse and negligence. As a signatory to the treaty, Canada does a good job of protection and provision but not as good a job of encouraging participation in their learning or enabling youth to engage in the political process (Howe & Covell, 2001; 2007). Brian Howe notes:

[O]fficial commitment is not the same thing as actual commitment. Official commitment is when a government makes a pledge to pursue a particular course of action or policy. In ratifying the UN Convention, Canada's federal and provincial governments...were pledging to implement it. Actual commitment is when a government demonstrates its official commitment by taking concrete measures, be they in the form of laws, policies, or programs. It does so whatever obstacles and challenges stand in its way. (p. 1)

Howe and Covell believe Canada has fallen quite short of its commitment. The Committee on the Rights of the Child also found Canada's commitment to be lacking – more specifically, their 2012 report suggests that the government lacks comprehensive policies and strategies to cover the scope of the CRC that the government continues to fail to collect the appropriate data to inform these policies and monitor the country's progress regarding alignment with the CRC, and that the government has failed to properly disseminate and raise awareness about the CRC, especially given the government's extensive network of free

---

[4] see *R. v. D.R.*, [2008] 2 S.C.R. 3 at paras 41, 61 and 84–87; *R. v. Sharpe*, [2001] 1 S.C.R. 45, at paras 170–174.

web access providers (Committee on the Rights of the Child, 2012). In fact, in 2013, the Canadian Coalition for the Rights of Children (CCRC) made a call to action to the Canadian government to make a commitment to act on the 2012 recommendations of the Committee on the Rights of the Child by National Child Day, November 20, which represents the anniversary of the CRC (CCRC, 2013). Unfortunately, this was to no avail.

Meanwhile, the United States' commitment has not fared much better. While the United States has signed the CRC, it has yet to ratify it. The U.S. Constitution describes the ratification steps as follows: (1) the president begins by signing the treaty; (2) the treaty is submitted to the U.S. Senate for consent; and (3) the Senate votes. If a two-thirds majority approves the treaty, the president may then ratify it. Politically conservative groups have posed strong opposition to the treaty's ratification up to this point, which perhaps explains why the United States is among the last UN members to have not already ratified the CRC (Gunn, 2006).

APPLICATION OF HUMAN RIGHTS LAW TO CYBERBULLYING

Notably, although the A.B. case was brought under tort law, it is highly relevant to Article 19 of the CRC because it set the judicial standard in Canada for protecting young victims of cyberbullying who are afraid of being publicly identified. As the SCC observed, recognition of the inherent vulnerability of children has consistent and deep roots in Canadian law, but it is also present in international protections such as those within the CRC. It is important to summarize the CRC's protections for children as they pertain to this discussion because the Canadian Standing Senate Committee on Human Rights (Senate Committee) studied Canada's role under Article 19 of the CRC in protecting children from cyberbullying.[5]

In 2012, the Senate Committee conducted inquiries into whether Canada is adequately meeting its obligations under Article 19 of the CRC to protect victims of cyberbullying. The sections that follow discuss the relevant aspects of the CRC articles.

Article 2 of CRC: Non-Discrimination
Everyone should have the same right to grow up in a safe environment and to feel safe whether in school or at home (free from bullying based on gender, homosexuality, race, religion, appearance, or disability). Everyone has to work together to mobilize against bullying including parents, teachers, and other adults (e.g., in sports activities). Thus it is a collaborative effort by all stakeholders such as schools, parents, community organizations, parents,

---

[5] I have drawn upon an online article by the Swedish non-profit organization Friends, which highlights the relevance of Articles 2, 3, and 12 to bullying. See "Barns r̈attigheter, Centrala artiklar." www.friends.se/barns-rattigheter/centrala-artiklar.

corporations, and governments to ensure that children are learning and growing up in safe environments in school, at home, and in cyberspace through online social networking and digital media.

Article 3 of CRC: Best Interests of the Child

Bullying behaviorists often studied and responded to bullying and cyberbullying incidents through zero-tolerance approaches that do not take into consideration the best interests of perpetrators and victims (Shariff, 2012). The discussion in this book illustrates that the application of criminal sanctions to certain forms of cyberbullying and the introduction of harsher laws that take a hard-line on youth who engage in cyberbullying are incongruent with the best interests of the child. While it is in the best interests of society to deter youth from engaging in cyberbullying, a reactive and punitive approach to preventing cyberbullying may not always succeed as a deterrent and may, in fact, exacerbate the problem. The increased discretionary powers that will be given to police in Canada should Bill C-13 be passed into law could result in serious breaches of due process, which are not in their best interests, unless serious attention is paid to developing sensitivity programs for law enforcement officers, prosecutors, and even judges to sensitize them to the way in which DE Kids think about their world and online communications.

Article 12 of CRC: Right to be Heard

In addressing the best interests of the child under Article 3, it is also essential to consider the obligations under Article 12, which calls for giving children and youth participation rights and a voice that can help to shape the impact of adult decisions on their safety and wellbeing. It is important to talk to children and young people and to start a dialogue on how to resolve bullying situations. Children and youth have much to say about matters affecting their security. Article 12 emphasizes the importance of listening to children in order to ensure that their views are taken into account if and when specific laws and policies are developed and implemented to address cyberbullying.

Article 19 of CRC: Protection from Abuse, Violence, and Negligence

Under this article of the CRC it is important not only to consider whether countries are protecting children from peer-against-peer abuse and violence through cyberbullying, but also to ensure that this protection is afforded to all children who are growing up as digital natives and who may not fully appreciate the consequences of their actions. As I have emphasized, the SCC was silent on the protection rights of young victim-perpetrators because it was not required to consider that aspect of the problem, but the Court's decision certainly raises concerns about the need to ensure that perpetrators are protected as well. Whether it is in the application of tort law principles or criminal law, it is important to consider whether modified or new laws against cyberbullying that might call for harsher punishment and criminalization of bullying contravene CRC obligations to protect all, not just some, children and youth.

If young people do not realize that their actions are criminal, and if no effort is made to educate them about the legal ramifications of their actions, it is likely that some legal responses may be over-reactive and too harsh.

The Senate Committee interviewed numerous experts and young people, resulting in a comprehensive report to Parliament (Standing Senate Committee on Human Rights, 2012). The report's major conclusions suggested that Canadian children are not being adequately protected from online hate crimes, sexual abuse, harassment, and cyberbullying, and that even one suicide is too many. Its recommendations included the following:

- The need for appointment of a children's commissioner to monitor and ensure these protections.
- More emphasis on restorative justice and funding for increased research and educational initiatives rather than harsher laws and penalties.

The Canadian Parliament voted against the need for a children's commissioner and released Bill C-13, the *Protecting Canadians from Online Crime Act*, which is detailed in Chapter 3, proposing amendments to the *Criminal Code* to provide harsher penalties and increase police surveillance powers *inter alia*. The government did invest in a television public service ad directed at DE Kids that tells them to think before they post. The government has also invested significant funding in research projects that involve cyberbullying as a result. Congressional committees in the United States have also heard evidence on the law's role in reducing cyberbullying (see Palfrey, 2009; Willard, 2010)

More specifically, in 2009, John Palfrey suggested that the "most effective solution to cyberbullying is to combine a series of approaches to protect minors…education, intervention by social workers, technology, and law reform each have a role to play" (Palfrey, 2009, p. 3). Speaking to the prospect of new legislation, Palfrey asserted that it is only natural for various states to want to introduce new laws –government feels helpless and at the mercy of fast-moving technology. He suggested, however, that newly criminalizing various forms of online speech and actions is not necessarily the right approach and it is not the only type of consideration we must be making. Instead, he suggested we should also consider rethinking existing laws (Palfrey, 2009, p. 4). Namely, Palfrey called for a reconsideration of section 230 of the *Communications Decency Act* and the widespread immunity it affords Internet service providers (ISPs) – the idea being that if cyberbullying is a systemic problem, ISPs need to be a part of the solution. Extending liability to ISPs might "provide incentive for technology companies to do the right thing" (Palfrey, 2009, p. 5).

Before the Subcommittee on Healthy Families and Communities and the Committee on Education and Labor, Nancy Willard recommended that it be made clear via legislation that schools should address bullying activity that occurs both on and off campus – any activity that causes significant interference with a student's security and education rights must be dealt with by the institution in question (Willard, 2010, p. 68).

There is clearly an international obligation to protect DE Kids and an emerging duty to protect them at provincial and state levels as well.

ANTI-BULLYING LEGISLATION: CANADIAN PROVINCES

Canadian provinces have implemented laws that require schools to pay attention to bullying and cyberbullying that takes place in their learning environments. The province of Ontario took the lead with the *Accepting Schools Act* (2012). This required Ontario schools to report to the provincial government on the number of incidents in their schools and to create "gay-straight" alliance clubs to foster inclusion. Religious parents protested this aspect of the law to argue against the gay-straight alliance clubs.

In Quebec, Bill 56, *An act to prevent and stop bullying and violence in schools*, known as the anti-bullying law, created major panic in schools in 2012 when the provincial government required all schools to report on the incidents of bullying and cyberbullying at each school. Teachers are now required to complete reports that are then given to the school principal and then forwarded to school boards. The school boards then submit a final report to the ministry at the end of each year. With the new liberal government in Quebec, elected April 7, 2014, there is now a newly appointed "anti-bullying" minister.

The case of teen Jane Doe in Nova Scotia, and the efforts of her parents, had significant impact on that province's expedition of the Nova Scotia *Cyber-safety Act*. This legislation goes further than the other two in the following ways:

1. It provides for parents of perpetrators being held responsible if they know about their children's engagement in bullying and fail to stop it; and
2. It allows for civil actions being brought by victims to seek remedies, by declaring cyberbullying an actionable tort under Nova Scotia law.

Accordingly, even though the courts in both the United States and Canada have attempted to avoid the floodgates of litigation in this area, the potential for lawsuits under this type of provincial legislation is on the rise. Under Ontario and Quebec legislation, schools can be held liable for negligence if they fail to act effectively in responses to reports of traditional or cyber-bullying. Both pieces of legislation provide increased discretionary powers to school principals to expel students. This raises another area of concern for due process if kids are framed online and for the victim-perpetrator dilemma I mentioned earlier. New Brunswick, Manitoba, and the other provinces listed in Appendix A also have established and proposed anti-bullying legislation.

ANTI-BULLYING LEGISLATION: U.S. STATES

Similarly, there has been an effort on behalf of many U.S. states to impose requirements on schools to address cyberbullying. I highlight some of the more prominent laws that have been imposed; other state laws can be found in Appendix A, which includes Hinduja and Patchin's brief U.S. legislative overview (2014), as well as Canadian responses.

- New Jersey *Anti-Bullying Bill of Rights Act* (2010): The act describes bullying as a harmful act that impedes the child's security and education rights. Furthermore, it requires that every public school report cases of bullying to the state. Once made aware of the incident, families and the superintendent must be notified and a formal investigation must take place within ten days. The act also outlines how teachers and administrators are to recognize and respond to bullying. Importantly, the act also provides for preventive measures along with its more reactionary responses. Specifically, the act requires that every school have an anti-bullying specialist as well as a school safety team. It also stipulates that the first week of October will be deemed the "Week of Respect," during which schools will raise bullying awareness among the students and faculty.
- California's *Seth's Law* (2012): *Seth's Law* is named for a thirteen-year-old California student who committed suicide in 2010 after years of anti-gay bullying, which the school failed to deal with. As per the American Civil Liberties Union's (ACLU) fact sheet, the law requires school districts to do the following: (1) adopt a strong anti-bullying policy that concretely defines "bullying"; (2) adopt a specific process for receiving and investigating complaints and instances of bullying; (3) publicize the policy and complaint process; and (4) provide online resources to support bullying victims (ACLU, 2012).
- *Safe and Supportive Minnesota Schools Act* (2014): In 2012, Governor Mark Dayton established a Task Force on the Prevention of School Bullying for the purpose of issuing recommendations regarding anti-bullying policies and legislation. The act, which is an outcome of said task force, provides clear definitions of bullying, harassment and intimidation. Furthermore, it provides training and resources to students, staff, and school volunteers on prevention and intervention. Importantly, it also provides staff with a procedure to follow when recognizing and addressing bullying incidents.
- Connecticut's *Act Concerning the Strengthening of School Bullying Laws* (2011): The act concretely defines "cyberbullying." It further states that school policies "must include provisions addressing bullying outside of the school setting if such bullying (a) creates a hostile environment at school for the victim, (b) infringes on the rights of the victim at school, or (c) substantially disrupts the education process or the orderly operation of a school."

Elsewhere (Shariff, 2008–2009), I have detailed American court cases that established the legal obligations of schools to provide safe school environments, even if the cyberbullying and sexting incidents occur among students, teachers, and other school personnel outside of school hours, and on computers and smart phones. Therefore, I only provide a brief overview of that discussion here; the crux of said discussion is that there is increasing pressure on schools as new state and provincial legislation builds on already existing common law obligations. Schools may also be subject to negligence suits for failing to protect victims. It is not within the scope of this book to look into that aspect.

Importantly, school responsibility stemming from case law has centered on what has been deemed a "nexus" to the school environment and education. In other words, educational institutions' obligations arise when the actions and comments in question disrupt learning or otherwise oppose a safe school environment. A long line of case law have brought the courts to this under-standing, whereby the need to act and protect the student body is balanced with such constitutional rights as freedom of expression.

In *Tinker v. Des Moines Independent Community School District* (1969), three public school students were suspended from school for wearing black armbands to protest the war in Vietnam. The pupils sought out nominal damages and an injunction against the black armbands ban. The United States Supreme Court ultimately held in favor of the students, asserting that "[the school] did not demonstrate any facts which might reasonably have led school authorities to forecast substantial disruption of or material interfer-ence with school activities, and no disturbances or disorders on the school premises in fact occurred" (*Tinker v. Des Moines Independent Community School District*, 1969). In *Hazelwood School District v. Kuhlmeier* (1988), the United States Supreme Court found that the school was justified in its decision to withhold articles discussing divorce and pregnancy from publication. Specifically, the Court reiterated its stance on the standard for determining when a school may punish student expression that occurs on school premises:

Educators are entitled to exercise greater control over this second form of student expression to assure that participants learn whatever lessons the activity is designed to teach, that readers or listeners are not exposed to material that may be inappropriate for their level of maturity, and that the views of the individual speaker are not erroneously attributed to the school. (*Hazelwood School District v. Kuhlmeier*, 1988)

In *Hazelwood*, the majority of the Court recognized the school's right to act in order to curb foreseeable disruption and harm. Conversely, dissenting judges focused on the uncertain or unforeseeable nature of the future disruptions to school life.

Interestingly, these cases began as an exploration of whether schools can act only to transform into an exploration of when schools are obligated to act.

For example, in *J.S. v. Bethlehem Area School* (2000), the question arose as to whether a school could expel a student for creating a webpage that included defamatory and threatening statements about members of the school's administration. Importantly, the court ruled that the school's decision to expel the student was, in fact, justified as the public nature of the information posted, although posted outside of school, created an evident disruption of the school environment.

It is therefore evident that schools are empowered and at times obligated to act against the interests of some in order to protect the interests of many. Disruptions in the form of hurtful comments and actions have no place in educational institutions –the mission of many schools is the promotion of tolerance, kindness, and respect. As such, schools are now expected to "walk their talk" and engage in preventative as well as reactive responses to ensure a safe school environment.

The general discussion I have provided here now takes us to Chapter 5, which summarizes the main points I have tried to make throughout the book, discusses the implications of the legal, policy, and educational dilemmas raised, and makes recommendations on atypical and useful ways to address the dilemmas presented in these chapters. Ultimately, it is all about finding ways to navigate a balance between free expression, privacy, safety, supervision, and regulation, without reacting and over-regulating complex issues. It is important to ensure that all policies are developed and implemented with the constitutional and human rights considerations that are in place to protect children as they work through their vulnerability to gain strength and confidence as adults.

REFERENCES

ACLU. (2012). AB 9: Seth's Law—New Tools to Prevent Bullying in California Schools. Retrieved from www.aclunc.org/sites/default/files/asset_upload_file529_10688.pdf.

Altobelli, T. (2010). Cyber-Abuse–A New Worldwide Threat to Children's Rights. *Family Court Review*, 48(3), 459–481.

Areheart, B.A. (2007). Regulating Cyberbullies through Notice-Based Liability. *Yale Law Journal*, 117(41) 41–47.

Arsenio, W. F. & Lemerise, E. A. (2004). Aggression and moral development: Integrating social information processing and moral domain models. *Child development*, 75 (4), 987–1002.

Beran, T., Stanton, L., Hetherington, R., Mishna, F. & Shariff S. (2012). Development of the Bullying and Health Experiences Scale Interact. *Journal of Medical Internet Research*, 1(2), e13. doi: 10.2196/ijmr.1835.

Calo, M. (2011). The Boundaries of Privacy Harm. *Indiana Law Journal*, 86(3), 1131–1162.

CBC News. (2013, July 4). Babies: Born to be Good? *CBC News Player*. Retrieved from www.cbc.ca/player/Shows/ID/2296544019/.

(2012, October 19). 8 Ontario girls arrested in high school bullying case. *CBC News*. Retrieved from www.cbc.ca/news/.

CCRC. (2013). 10 Steps for Children in Canada—A Call to Action. Retrieved from http://rightsofchildren.ca/wp-content/uploads/10-Steps-for-Children-in-Canada1.pdf.

Chu, J. (2005). You Wanna Take This Online? Cyberspace is the 21st century bully's playground where girls play rougher than boys. *Time*, 6(6), 52.

Comacchio, C., Golden, J. & Weisz, G. (Eds.) (2008). *Healing the World's Children: Interdisciplinary Perspectives on Child Health in the Twentieth Century*. Montreal: McGill-Queens University Press.

Committee on the Rights of the Child. (2012, October 5). Consideration of reports submitted by States parties under article 44 of the Convention—Concluding Observations: Canada. Retrieved from http://rightsofchildren.ca/wp-content/uploads/Canada_CRC-Concluding-Observations_61.2012.pdf.

Culbert, L. & Hagar, M. (2014, April 23). Dutch man charged in Amanda Todd online blackmail case. *The Gazette*. Retrieved from www.montrealgazette.com/life/Amanda+Todd+case+Dutch+charged+online+blackmail+bullying/9749151/story.html.

Danay, R. (2010). The Medium is Not the Message: Reconciling Reputation and Free Expression in Cases of Internet Defamation. *McGill Law Journal*, 56(1), 1–37.

Eltis, K. (2011). The Judicial System in the Digital Age: Revisiting the Relationship between Privacy and Accessibility in the Cyber Context. *McGill Law Journal*, 56(2), 289–316.

Farmer, T. W., Petrin, R., Brooks, D. S., Hamm, J. V., Lambert, K. & Gravelle, M. (2010). Bullying Involvement and the School Adjustment of Rural Students With and Without Disabilities. *Journal of Emotional and Behavioral Disorders*, 20, 19–37.

Gould, M. S. (2001). Suicide and the media. *Annals of the New York Academy of Sciences*, 932(1), 200–224.

Gunn, J.T. (2006). The Religious Right and the Opposition to U.S. Ratification of the Convention on the Rights of the Child. *Emory International Law Review*, 111, 119–127.

Henderson, A. (2009). High-tech words do hurt: A modern makeover expands Missouri's harassment to include electronic communications. (Masters thesis, University of Missouri). Retrieved from http://law.missouri.edu/lawreview/docs/74-2/Henderson.pdf.

Hinduja, S. & Patchin, J. W. (2010). Bullying, cyberbullying, and suicide. *Archives of Suicide Research*, 14(3), 206–221.

Hinduja, S. & Patchin, J. W. (2014, April). A Brief Review of State Cyberbullying Laws and Policies. *Cyberbullying Research Center*. Retrieved from www.cyberbullying.us/Bullying_and_Cyberbullying_Laws.pdf.

Howe, R.B. & Covell, K. (2001). *The Challenge of Children's Rights for Canada*. Waterloo: Wilfrid Laurier University Press.

Howe, R.B. & Covell, K. (2007). *A Question of Commitment: Children's Rights in Canada*. Waterloo: Wilfrid Laurier University Press.

Juvonen, J. & Gross, E. F. (2008). Extending the school grounds?–Bullying experiences in cyberspace. *Journal of School Health*, 78(9), 496–505.

Kofoed, J. & Sondergaard, D. M. (2009). *Mobning: Sociale Processer Pa Afveje [Bullying: Social Processes Gone Awry]*. Copenhagen: Hans Reitzels Forlag.

Lankshear, C., Knobel, M. & Peters, M. (Eds.). (2008). *Digital literacies: Concepts, policies and practices* (Vol. 30). New York: Peter Lang.

Livingstone, S. & Brake, D. (2010). On the Rapid Rise of Social Networking Sites: New Findings and Policy Implications. *Children and Society*, 24(1), 75–83.

Lokeinsky, K. (2012, February 24) Post at your own risk: Teens need to be more concerned about Internet privacy. *The Lariat*. Retrieved from http://thelariatonline.com/?p=3608.

Lucock, C. & Yeo, M. (2006), Naming Names: The Pseudonym in the Name of the Law. *Ottawa Law and Technology Journal*, 3(1), 53–108.

MacKay, A.W. (2012). Respectful and Responsible Relationships: There's No App for That (Halifax, NS: Nova Scotia Task Force on Bullying and Cyberbullying). Retrieved from http://cyberbullying.novascotia.ca/media/documents/Respectful%20and%20Responsible%20Relationships,%20There's%20no%20App%20for%20That%20%20Report%20of%20the%20NS%20Task%20Force%20on%20Bullying%20and%20Cyberbullying.pdf.

McGuire, P. (2012, October 15). Amanda Todd's alleged tormentor named by hacker group. *CBC News*. Retrieved from www.cbc.ca.

McLachlin, B. (2003). Courts, Transparency and Public Confidence: To the Better Administration of Justice. *Deakin Law Review*, 8(1), 1–11.

Nies, Y., Donaldson, J. & Netter, S. (2010, January 28). Mean Girls: Cyberbullying Blamed for Teen Suicides. *ABC News*. Retrieved from http://abcnews.go.com.

Palfrey, J. (2009). Hearing on Cyberbullying and other Online Safety Issues for Children (United States House of Representatives, Committee on the Judiciary, Subcomittee on Crime, Terrorism and Homeland Security). Retrieved from http://judiciary.house.gov/_files/hearings/pdf/Palfrey090930.pdf.

Parker, I. (2012, February 6). The Story of a Suicide. *The New Yorker*. Retrieved from www.newyorker.com.

Prout, A. (2005). *Towards the Interdisciplinary Study of Children*. London: Falmer Press.

Reid, T. (2012, October 20). *The National*. Retrieved from www.cbc.ca/thenational/watch/.

Seidman, K. (2012, September 19). McGill law students in project that aims to curb cyberbullying. *The Gazette*. Retrieved from www.montrealgazette.com/.

Senoo, Y. (2007). Netto-ijime (cyber bullying): Bullying moves to cyberspace. Unpublished term paper for EDEM 609 Issues in Education Masters course, Prof. Shaheen Shariff, Department of Integrated Studies, Faculty of Education, McGill University.

Shariff, S. (In Progress). Defining the Lines on Cyberbullying Among University Students. In Helen Cowie & Carrie-Anne Myers (Eds.), *Bullying Amongst University Students*. (Prospectus submitted to Routledge (Taylor & Frances): UK).

Shariff, S. (Under Review). Defining the Lines on E-Girls and Intimate Images. In Jane Bailey & Valerie Steeves (Eds.), *E-Girls and E-Citizens*. (Publisher to be determined).

Shariff, S. (2008). *Cyberbullying: Issues and Solutions for the School, the Classroom, and the Home*. Ablington, Oxfordshire, UK: Routledge (Taylor & Frances Group).

Shariff, S. (2009). *Confronting Cyberbullying: What Schools Need to Know to Control Misconduct and Avoid Legal Consequences*. New York, NY: Cambridge University Press.

Shariff, S. (2012, April 30). Policy Brief to Canadian Standing Senate Committee on Human Rights. Brief delivered at the Canadian Standing Senate Committee on

Human Rights. Retrieved from www.parl.gc.ca/content/sen/committee/411/ridr/11ev-49495-e.htm.

Shariff, S. (2013). Courting Digital Citizenship: Keeping Schools Out of Court. In Hanewald, R. (Ed.), *From Cyber Bullying to Cyber Safety: Issues and Approaches in Educational Contexts* (pp.169–191). New South Wales: Nova Science Publishers.

Shariff, S. & Churchill, A. H. (2010). *Truths and Myths of Cyber-bullying: International perspectives on stakeholder responsibility and children's safety.* New York: Peter Lang.

Shariff, S., Wiseman, A., & Crestohl, L. (2012). Defining the Lines between Children's Vulnerability to Cyberbullying and the Open Court Principle: Implications of *A.B. v. Bragg Communications, Inc. Education and Law Journal,* 21(3), 231–262.

Shaw, G., Sinoski, K. & Quan, D. (17 October 2012). Online 'lynch mob' decried: Mother of man named by hacktivists pleads: 'Let police investigate'. *The Gazette,* A10.

Standing Senate Committee on Human Rights. (2012). Cyberbullying Hurts: Respect for Rights in the Digital Age. Retrieved from www.parl.gc.ca/Content/SEN/Committee/411/ridr/rep/rep09dec12-e.pdf.

Stoddart, J. (2012, November 9). Open Courts and Privacy Law in Canada. Remarks at the Supreme Court of British Columbia Education Seminar delivered at the Supreme Court of British Columbia. Retrieved from www.priv.gc.ca/media/sp-d/2011/spd_20111109_e.asp.

Suzuki, D. (2012, October 9). Babies: Born to be Good? *The Nature of Things.* Retrieved April 28, 2014, from www.cbc.ca/.../?page=2&sort=MostPopular-45k-2014-04-03.

UNICEF. (2008). UNICEF Innocenti Research Centre Report on Child Safety Online. Retrieved from www.unicef-irc.org/.

Van Praagh, S. (2005). Adolescence, Autonomy and Harry Potter: The Child as Decision Maker. *International Journal of Law in Context,* 1(4), 335–373.

Weber, S. & Mitchell, C. (2008). Imaging, keyboarding, and posting identities: Young people and new media technologies. In Buckingham, D. (Ed.), *Youth, identity, and digital media* (pp. 25–47). Cambridge: MIT Press.

Willard, N. (2010). Ensuring Student Cyber Safety. (Subcommittee on Healthy Families and Communities, Committee on Education and Labor). Retrieved from www.gpo.gov/fdsys/pkg/CHRG-111hhrg56926/pdf/CHRG-111hhrg56926.pdf.

Ybarra, M. & Mitchell, K. (2004). Online Aggressor/Targets, Aggressors, and Targets: A Comparison of Associated Youth Characteristics. *Journal of Child Psychology and Psychiatry,* 45(7), 1308–1316.

Young, H. (2011). But Names Won't Necessarily Hurt Me: Considering the Effect of Disparaging Statements on Reputation. *Queen's Law Journal,* 37(1), 1–38.

LEGISLATION

Accepting Schools Act (Bill 13), S.O. 2012 c.5.

Act Concerning the Strengthening of School Bullying Laws (2011) SB 1138.

Anti-Bullying Bill of Rights Act (2011) P.L. 2010, c. 122.

An Act to prevent and stop bullying and violence in schools (Bill 56), 2012.

Canadian Charter of Rights and Freedoms, Part I of the *Constitution Act, 1982,* being Schedule B to the *Canada Act 1982* (UK), 1982, c 11.
Convention of the Rights of the Child, Can T.S. 1992
Criminal Code, R.S.C.1985, c. C-46
Cyber-safety Act, SNS 2013 c.2.
Safe and Supportive Minnesota Schools Act, 2014.
Seth's Law, Assembly Bill 9, 2011.
U.S. Constitution, amend. I
Youth Criminal Justice Act, S.C. 2002, c. 1

CASE LAW

A.B. (Litigation Guardian of) v. Bragg Communications Inc., 2011 NSCA 26, 2011 CarswellNS 135 (N.S. C.A.); reversed in part 2012 SCC 46, 2012 CarswellNS 675, 2012 CarswellNS 676 (S.C.C.)
A.B. (Litigation Guardian of) v. Bragg Communications Inc., 2012 SCC 46, [2012] 2 S.C.R. 567.
A.B. v. State of Indiana, No. 67A01-0609-JV-372, 2007 Ind. App. LEXIS 694 (Ind. Ct. App. Apr. 9, 2007).
Canadian Newspapers Co. v. Canada (Attorney General), [1988] 2 S.C.R. 122, 1988 CarswellOnt 1023, 1988 CarswellOnt 1023F (S.C.C.).
D.C. v. R.R. 182 Cal. App.4th 1190 (Cal. App. 2 Dist, 2010).
Hazelwood School District v. Kuhlmeier (1988), 484 U.S. 260 (1988).
J.S. v. Bethlehem Area School District. (2000). 757 A.2d 412 (Pa. Cmwlth. 2000).
Miller, et al v. Skumanick. (2009) 605 F.Supp.2d 634 (M.D. Pa, Mar. 30, 2009).
R. v. Mentuck, [2001] 3 S.C.R. 442, 2001 CarswellMan 535, 2001 Carswell-Man 536 (S.C.C.).
R. v. D.R., [2008] 2 S.C.R. 3.
R. v. H. (D) 2002 BCPC 464, 2002 Carswell BC 2658 (B.C. Prov. Ct.).
R. v. Sharpe, [2001] 1 S.C.R. 45.
Tinker v. Des Moines Independent Community School District (1969), 393 U.S. 503 (1969).
United States v. Drew. (2009). 259 F.R.D. 449 (C.D. Cal. 2009).
Vancouver Sun (Re), [2004] 2 S.C.R. 332.

CHAPTER FIVE

From *Lord of the Flies* to *Harry Potter*: Freedom, Choices, and Guilt

> "*Where's the man with the megaphone? ...*" "*Aren't there any grownups at all?*" "*I don't think so.*" *The fair boy said this solemnly, but then the delight of a realized ambition came over him.*
>
> (Golding, 1954, p. 7)

> "*Harry, I owe you an explanation*" *said Dumbledore ...* "*Youth cannot know how age thinks and feels. But old men are guilty if they forget what it was to be young ...*"
>
> (Rowling, 2003, p. 728)

> "*It is our choices, Harry, that show what we truly are, far more than our abilities.*" – *Professor Dumbledore*
>
> (Rowling, 1998, p. 245)

INTRODUCTION

In this book, I have attempted to illustrate the generational rifts between adult perceptions of clear separations between the physical and virtual worlds and the fluid and integrated physical and virtual worlds of Digitally Empowered Kids (DE Kids) and Digitally Empowered Young Adults (DE Young Adults). As William Golding tried to show us many years ago, society's rules, if too inflexible or irrelevant, can crumble in situations where children are free to break them. It's all about how children and adults choose to apply the rules. This means appreciating that children will make thoughtless choices sometimes as they experiment with life and all that it has to offer. I quote the character of Professor Dumbledore from the *Harry Potter* books at the start of the chapter.

My thanks to Alyssa Wiseman, law student and MBA candidate at McGill University for her insight into the relationship between law and children's literature, and to my colleague, Professor Shauna Van Praagh, for sharing her papers on the value of using children's literature to inform legal analysis in private law.

He says: "...old men are guilty if they forget what it was to be young" (Rowling, 2003, p.728). In this regard, we are guilty if we choose to turn a blind eye to the conflicting tensions between young people's vulnerability and agency as they grapple with adolescence into adulthood. We are guilty if we forget to have "fun" and engage with DE Kids to redirect some of their confusion. We are guilty if, instead, we make the choice to incarcerate them for their vulnerability, confusion, and imitation of the models adults provide them with.

As the DTL Research and discussion on moral development in Chapter 2 established, children and adolescents want to have fun. They can act impulsively despite being fully aware of the potential consequences. In doing so, they may not always make anticipated ethical choices, even if their particular stage of moral development equips them with the necessary alerts.

So many other influences can impact what DE Kids say, do, or post online at any given time. Acting impulsively is a part of growing up because it is through such experimentation that children learn to test social boundaries. And when those boundaries are unclear and inconsistent, or too rigid, some youth fall through the cracks. To complicate the issue, young people are influenced by adult models that behave in a certain way. These models send conflicting messages regarding what types of behaviors are acceptable. Within young people's own peer groups there are unwritten boundaries of conformity and compliance. Anyone who crosses these boundaries might pay a heavy price. This is a double-edged sword. Youth can be judged by peer-developed codes of conduct as well as laws developed by adults who have long become disconnected from the lived realities of youth, especially those of DE Kids. Young people's actions and frank expressions of isolation, discomfort, or attempts to belong can be misunderstood by peers and adults who try to rein them in. Adults are often guilty, as Professor Dumbledore confesses to Harry Potter, of forgetting what it was like to be young.

THE ROLE OF LAW AND PARADOXES IN CHILDREN'S VULNERABILITY AND ACCOUNTABILITY

Legal academics (Van Praagh, 2005, 2007; Wiseman, 2012 [unpublished]; Manderson, 2003; Kasirer, 1992) suggest that children's literature, like the *Harry Potter* books, can illuminate our understanding of the nuanced complexities of adolescent vulnerability and autonomy and help us better understand how the law applies in cases involving youth. This especially applies to judgments related to culpability, accountability, and legal responsibility at various stages of adolescent development and under varying circumstances. According to Van Praagh (2005):

Adolescence is the process of childhood most obviously marked by the co-existence of the need for protection and the development of self-reliance and independence ... Harry

Potter books ... are a good place to look if we want to contemplate adolescence and its necessarily fluid character. The development of young people, or the way in which youth is linked to special vulnerability and to evolving autonomy, is central to J.K. Rowling's highly entertaining, thoughtful and well-cast prose. Private law, or, more specifically, the law of civil wrongs and liability, is also a good site for considering the texture and meaning of adolescence.

While not fiction of the same caliber or appeal as Harry Potter, stories in private law, can portray the particular complexities of adolescence and the paradoxical nature of youth. In particular, when law is confronted with children roughly aged 11 to 15 years, it must explicitly juggle needs and choices, protection and independence, strengths and weaknesses. (Van Praagh, 2005, p. 336)

Van Praagh (2007), in an article entitled *"Sois Sage" – Responsibility for Childishness in the Law of Civil Wrongs*, highlights numerous other children's stories, including the famous *Curious George* (H.A Ray), *Cat in the Hat* (Theodor Seuss Geisel [Dr. Seuss]) and the *Madeleine* series (Ludwig Bemelmans), and engages in a fascinating analysis of private law as it is applied in Quebec. I reiterate her explanation of "sois sage" (being wise) that I opened with at the beginning of this book because it resonates so strongly with the messages I want to convey:

The notion of being "sage" – good, wise, careful, in line with rules and expectations – is reflected in the picture of the reasonable person in the private law of civil wrongs. "Fun" is necessarily limited by "sagesse"; self-fulfillment is necessarily shaped by the obligation not to hurt others. As children explore themselves and their surroundings, gradually becoming aware of others in their lives, they begin to move beyond the realm of "carefree" and into that of "caring." The obligation to care for others is slowly added through childhood in one's sense of self. (Van Praagh, 2007, p. 63–65)

The clear challenge for educators, parents, policy makers, and others in the legal community is to recognize this transition and develop creative ways to facilitate and support the journey from being "carefree" to "caring" as youth develop their social relationships both on and offline. Van Praagh explains that private law and public policy confront a dual challenge when dealing with possible wrongdoing by children, for two reasons:

1) The rules of wrongdoing need to be adjusted based on the age of the child; and
2) The general emphasis on liability for one's own behavior shifts depending on our responsibility to protect others in our care.

Hence, she argues that when we focus on the "child as actor," we explore the standard of the "reasonable person" and analyze it within the context of childhood. When we focus on the "child of parents," we examine the responsibility of parents for the injury-producing acts of their children. Van Praagh's innovative application of children's literature also makes sense in the complex and nuanced online contexts discussed in this book. Although it is not within the scope of this final chapter to detail her analysis in great depth,

I highlight her work because it speaks strongly to some of the concerns, empirical evidence, and public policy challenges I have raised. This perspective supports my position that it is essential to rethink the role of the law and be flexible in its interpretation and application where DE Kids are concerned. It is particularly important to understand how the law applies to situations where DE Kids are testing boundaries; demeaning others to "have fun" and for peer acceptance; realizing the consequences; ignoring ethical monitors; and making conscious choices to challenge adult-made laws and rules. This is because they have already weighed the price of not participating in peer-led cyberbullying. The potential for ostracism from the peer group is too great for some DE Kids. Shunning, bullying, and isolation may be the result if they do not join the pack. This is evidenced in the statistics I presented earlier. It explains the reluctance of DE Kids to report being cyberbullied.

Van Praagh's approach, although it addresses private law rather than criminal justice responses, can be extended to support the argument in Chapter 4 that "big stick sanctions don't work" (Kift, Campbell & Butler, 2010). To apply criminal laws to DE Kids for what they perceive as "fun" is not a sensible public policy response. Such a response completely ignores the paradoxical and shifting vulnerabilities, as well as children's agency to make reasoned decisions about when to participate and when to refuse; of when to lie and when to tell the truth as they negotiate the boundaries of social behavior in an online world. As I have suggested before, this world resembles Golding's island in *Lord of the Flies* and even though adults participate in it as DE Generations, they are not bound by the same peer-applied boundaries that exist among DE Kids.

So where do we go from here? And how should we respond to the fact that not only are the behaviors of children complex at any given age and time, but that the law itself is not clear-cut and cannot simply be brought in to "control" the online behaviors of DE Kids. It is important to begin with a summary of the key issues, empirical findings, theoretical perspectives, and case law presented in preceding chapters. Together, these considerations and their implications inform my recommendations for substantive responses that conclude this book. I propose the responses recommended in this final chapter are promising because they take into account what DE Kids have told us. I am confident that the suggested initiatives will provide youth with enhanced opportunities to engage in policy making. This, in turn, will afford them agency toward informed and thoughtful decisions as they develop relationships in their own digital world and negotiate the boundaries of socially responsible digital citizenship that is acceptable to both DE Generations.

ROLE OF LAW: WE CANNOT CRIMINALIZE THOSE WE SHOULD PROTECT

As a fundamental premise, we need to appreciate that we do not have the right to criminalize those we ought to protect. As we consider the paradoxes that place children in positions of vulnerability, while expecting them to develop independence, agency, and the ability to make reasonable and thoughtful choices about what to put online, it is important to review the contradictions highlighted in this book. On the one hand, the very laws designed to protect children, such as child pornography laws, are being applied to arrest, charge, and punish them. On the other hand, human rights and constitutional principles that are supposed to protect children as vulnerable citizens – for instance, their privacy rights and protection from privacy harm – are less frequently considered or applied. In some cases, even some judges have denied children these protections (e.g., lower court decisions in *A.B. [Litigation Guardian of] v. Bragg Communications, Inc.*, 2011). I have expressed concerns over due process when the police make arrests under criminal laws. I have also complained about the general lack of public sensitivity regarding the lived realities, shifting norms, evolving decision-making capacities, and stages of moral development of DE Kids. I have talked about influences of popular culture and the devastating effects of rape culture as it filters through society to impact the choices that DE Kids make, and the blame they assign to their victimized peers. Reactive responses to sensationalized media reports that tend to blame the kids for their behavior without considering the context have resulted in the emergence of reactive state, provincial, and federal laws. Before I make my recommendations, let me undertake a quick review of the key issues raised in this book.

CONFORMING WITH THE PEER GROUP

Without going into the details in Chapter 2 and to some extent, Chapters 3–5, DE Kids have informed us that their first priority is to fit in with their peers and to have fun doing it. Moreover, DE Kids have confirmed that an individual's reputation among peers is crucially important. Some might argue that this is nothing new – we have known this for years. So what new information does the DTL Research provide? This empirical research provides clear evidence regarding the motivations of DE Kids when they engage in online abuse. It corroborates patterns we have seen in highly publicized media reports of offensive online abuse and non-consensual distribution of intimate images involving DE Kids. These patterns are also reflected in the case law that has emerged over the last five years, both in the United States and in Canada. Here is what the data confirm.

ROOT CAUSES

The research shows that traditional bullying and cyberbullying are rooted in notions of "difference" and intolerance toward others due to perceived or actual membership in a particular group. In addition to addressing any individual behavioral or relational issues connected to these phenomena, I have unpacked what it means to be "different" in the world of DE Kids.

Research on what makes a targeted individual different clearly indicates equality issues are at play. For example, I have highlighted scholarship that confirms gender conformity in an effort to decrease differentiation. This is the degree to which boys present themselves as sufficiently "masculine" and girls present themselves as sufficiently "feminine." Sexual orientation and racial differences, as well as physical and mental disabilities, are all factors that put some children and youth at greater risk of cyberbullying, sexual or homophobic harassment, ostracism, and threats than others. In effect, this bias-based and often sexualized cyberbullying constitutes a form of discrimination on grounds prohibited under human rights codes and in international covenants. It is further complicated by other influences such as popular and rape culture.

POPULAR AND RAPE CULTURE SENDS MIXED MESSAGES

As I have detailed in Chapters 1 and 2, girls receive conflicting messages from society. On the one hand, they see adult role models and powerful celebrities publicizing their sexuality. On the other, they are demeaned and "slut-shamed" if they dare to post images of their own sexuality or breach the unspoken boundaries of what is acceptable in certain peer groups. The slut-shaming is also a symptom of a misogynist rape culture where adult society perpetuates and sustains male role models, which pressures adolescent and young adult males to "prove" their maleness. To assert their maleness, as evidenced in the case law and empirical data presented in this book, male DE Kids and DE Generations slut-shame females through the posting and distribution of non-consensual images. They demean other males through homophobic harassment and bullying for the same reasons. Those targeted are dehumanized and blamed for either being too forward in their expressions of loneliness, or alternately, in expressing their physical features or exceptional talents that might set them apart from the crowd. This was the case with D.C.'s "golden brown eyes," the California libel case that I detailed in Chapter 4. These forms of harassment are often genuinely considered to be "jokes." And even when the consequences or harm to the victim is weighed against the risk of ostracism from the peer group, decisions are made, impulsive or thoughtfully, to post the offending material online anyway. This kind of decision making is evident in *State of New Jersey v. Dharun Ravi* (2012); the Maple Ridge rape case (Weisgarber, 2012); the case of Jane Doe in Nova Scotia (Global Montreal Staff, 2013); and the Steubenville High School case (Edwards, 2013).

ACCEPTED NORMS: I WAS "JUST JOKING"

So ingrained are discriminatory attitudes in society, especially sexism and homophobia, that in most cases the highly public and offensive comments are not considered outside of acceptable social norms. In this book, I have presented numerous examples from the DTL Research, case law, and publicized cases reported in the news media that confirm that DE Kids and DE Young Adults have difficulty defining the lines between what is a joke and what crosses legal boundaries to result in criminal threats or harassment, or libel or defamation resulting in psychological harm and harm to the reputation of individuals targeted.

PEER PUNISHMENT FOR CROSSING INVISIBLE PEER-GROUP LINES

What appears to be outside of acceptable norms is when those in the peer group stand out – either through expressing their sexuality, protecting others who are victimized, or expressing their deep sense of isolation. In fact, the DTL Research and the Amanda Todd case confirm that when those who are ostracized express their feelings in a highly public sphere, they are further demeaned, even after death in some cases, by "trolls" who continue to write offensive comments on victims' social media pages.

PUNISHMENT FOR CROSSING BLURRED LINES

Moreover, those who perpetrate online abuse, and who can, at various times, be either victim or perpetrator among DE Kids, are subject to increasingly harsher laws and penalties in society. I have argued that many of these are misapplied. I do not suggest that in cases where girls have been drugged, raped, and images of the attack have been posted online, that there should not be consequences. There is definitely a need for strong legal consequences when anyone is raped. Rape is a "physical assault" which should be dealt with on that basis. Those conducting the rape should be held criminally accountable for their actions. However, DE Kids or DE Young Adults who record video of the event without participating, and pass it on for posting online or post it themselves, need our guidance to rethink their choices and actions. They need practice in engaging in rational and logical thought processes that will ultimately help them take a step back and think about what they are about to post and its impact. The obligation is on older DE Generations to help youth see that not only will there be a negative long-term and life-altering impact on those who are targeted where sexually explicit images are posted non-consensually, but there will also be a potential negative impact on their own lives. Once they receive a criminal record, they will be legally bound to disclose it on every job and college application they fill out. If incarcerated, they will be taken away from their families and possibly spend time with hardened criminals. I am not simply making these statements – I have recommendations that show greater promise of guiding DE Kids to implement these thought processes *before* they make choices they will later regret.

Recently, I observed the experience of one DE Kid who made some very bad choices online. Although what she did was not related to online cyberbullying or sexting, her choices and actions did involve using the Internet to commit a serious crime. Here is what took place: A college close to my home has a four-month homestay program for international students who attend the college on an exchange from their private schools. Students come from various countries. This particular seventeen-year-old student was living with a couple who were extremely kind to her. They went out of their way to show her around, invited her friends to spend time with her on trips to Toronto and Quebec City, took her out to dinner and celebrated her birthday, and so on.

The girl somehow got hold of her homestay mother's credit card and spent over $2,000 on Apple iPhones, clothes from Nordstrom, and a range of other "goodies" for herself. What she failed to realize when making the choice to use the credit card was: 1) that her house mother did not use the card very often and would obviously be surprised when she received her billing statement; 2) that it would be evident that something was amiss when she all of a sudden began to receive a lot of packages at the house (she was not quite smart enough to have them delivered elsewhere); and 3) that her purchases could be tracked easily.

The unfortunate outcome was that the student was asked to pack her belongings, escorted from the house by college personnel, booked into a hotel and accompanied there for the night, and put on the first plane back to her home country. While I do not argue that this was clearly an appropriate way to deal with this, her choices and actions in some ways resembled those of kids who sext and cyberbully. The boundaries were blurred in an online realm because her homestay mother could not actually see her make the purchases online. She felt protected by a perceived sense of anonymity and perhaps the idea that she would be long gone by the time the family found out about the purchases. She ordered the items and they magically appeared at her door. What she did not realize, just like other DE Kids do not realize, is that because the Internet and all social and business transactions are in a highly public realm, these kinds of transgressions are much easier to track because there is a clear record.

The student was devastated and had not foreseen or even begun to consider the impact of her online actions – either on the family she victimized and took advantage of or on her status within the Canadian exchange program and possibly her education in her home country, if she were to be expelled for stealing. Thus, as we think about kids that make choices to post risqué images of themselves or others online, we need to find ways to remind them of the potential that their actions will come to light much faster online.

BIG STICK SANCTIONS AND CHILD PORNOGRAPHY LAWS

As I have highlighted, DE Kids are not child pornographers. The very laws that are supposed to protect kids are being applied to charge and convict children and adolescents with distributing child pornography. The case of the ten Laval adolescents who were having "flirty fun" with Snapchat is evidence of this. Having demonstrated the nuanced and paradoxical conflicts between children's vulnerability, immaturity, evolving independence, agency, risk taking, and impulsivity, as it emerged in the DTL Research and as it is addressed in the legal context (Van Praagh, 2005; 2007), it becomes very clear that criminalizing children is not the answer and that child pornography laws are not only misapplied, but they also breach the protections afforded to children under constitutional and human rights principles.

CONSTITUTIONAL AND HUMAN RIGHTS PROTECTIONS

I have demonstrated through an analysis of the protections of international human rights law, in particular the *International Convention on the Rights of the Child* (CRC), as well as analysis of court cases involving free expression rights, that "big stick sanctions" (Kift, Campbell & Butler, 2010) breach the rights of DE Kids entitled to protection under Article 19 of the CRC. I have also highlighted a Supreme Court of Canada decision (*A.B. [Litigation Guardian of] v. Drugg Communications Inc.,* 2012) that supports the privacy rights of young victims of online abuse to sue their perpetrators anonymously. These protections are important given the data presented regarding the reluctance of young people to report online abuse and cyberbullying for fear of being targeted further.

Nonetheless, one area that needs serious attention is the potential for law enforcement officers to abuse due process when they apply child pornography laws and other criminal charges when DE Kids are arrested. This is expected to increase, given the trend toward harsher and stricter laws against DE Kids for engaging in online threats, harassment, and other forms of cyberbullying. The irony of this, as I have pointed out, is that we blame the kids without considering the extent to which adults model not only online violence, but also physically horrendous forms of violence that children witness on the news and online (e.g. homicides, domestic violence, kidnappings, and acts of terrorism). We need only to tune into the daily news to see what havoc adults wreak against each other. We live in a world that is turning a blind eye to millions of displaced children and families resulting from the civil war and atrocities in Syria. We are also aware of the potential for similar situations in the Ukraine, to say nothing of the wars in Afghanistan and Iraq; random shootings in American and Canadian schools; and persistent gun lobbies. It makes me wonder how we can be so judgmental of our children. Nonetheless, the more children are made to look like criminals in the news, the harsher the response.

TOO MUCH MEDIA EXPOSURE RE-VICTIMIZES

I have also explained that too much media exposure can result in further victimizing and re-victimizing of targeted individuals and that every time the news media air or sensationalize a tragedy, the individual targeted, whether alive or dead, is publicly exposed, and in that regard, fulfills and supports the objectives of perpetrators. This is especially a victory for "cappers" – adult pedophiles or "trolls" who desecrate the social media pages of victims who commit suicide. I have also raised the point that DE Kids who might be on the verge of committing suicide, or contemplating it, may also see such news coverage as their last opportunity to draw attention to their plight. The last thing we want to do as a society is support the glorification of suicide.

CONCLUSION AND RECOMMENDATIONS

How do we move forward from here? I begin my conclusions and recommendations by reiterating some recommendations that my colleagues and I (Shariff *et al.*, unpublished) submitted in writing to the Canadian Minister of Justice, Peter MacKay, before he introduced Bill C-13. I conclude the book with what I believe is most important: engaging DE Kids in contributing to laws and codes of conduct; initiating legal literacy programs throughout North America; and adopting Van Praagh's (2005; 2007) concept of applying children's literature to better understand the law and turning it around to use children's literature to help DE Kids better understand legal concepts. Here are the recommendations that were included in our brief to the Canadian Justice Ministry:

A Holistic National Strategy
Responding to traditional and online forms of harassment, threats, discrimination, and cyberbullying in an effective way will require collaborative, multi-faceted initiatives as indicated in the Senate Human Rights Committee Report on Cyberbullying and related online offenses (Jaffer & Brazeau, 2012). The strategy should not rely solely on criminal law responses, but should also include educational initiatives designed to address root causes of traditional bullying and cyberbullying. With respect to the recommendations of the Senate report, I would still argue for the appointment of a children's commissioner. This would have to be someone who is knowledgeable and has researched the complexities of childhood and adolescence and is familiar with the lived experiences of DE Kids and DE Young Adults.

Sensitivity Education
The federal government should work with its provincial and territorial (and state) counterparts to support and encourage the following types of initiatives. It is imperative that law enforcement officers, prosecutors, defenders, and the judiciary who will apply and interpret these new laws are also sensitized to the shifting norms of online communication among youth, as well as the adult population. Professional development programs and courses for police, school teachers and administrators, and youth protection agencies are ways to ensure they understand their responsibilities to address cyberbullying in sensitive and informed ways that take into consideration age appropriate and

contextual factors. In order to do this, we must understand the assumptions and discretion they bring to their daily professional practices in arresting, prosecuting, judging, and sentencing digital natives, and applying new laws on cyberbullying as there is no turning back from such legislation.

In addition to the brief submitted to the Canadian Ministry of Justice, it is my hope that with respect to Bill C-13, the *Protecting Canadians from Online Crime Act*, if passed as is, Section 162.1(1) regarding the distribution of non-consensual images will be thoughtfully applied when DE Kids are involved. It is further hoped that the objectives of the *Youth Criminal Justice Act (YCJA)*, to reintegrate young offenders into society will be honored in relation to such legislation. Furthermore, the legal-academic community also awaits information as to whether the *Safe Streets and Communities Act* will be applied to subject DE Kids who are convicted to harsher and longer sentences. In light of the data presented in this book, this would make little sense, given that such a large percentage of DE Kids have less intent to harm than to fit into their peer groups. Consequently, there would be a need to consider discipline for DE Kids who are charged in such cases, that is *ex juris*, and that contains an educational component. It is important to impress on judges that an educational component does not include the option to write an essay about "the 'evils' of the Internet" or banning DE Kids from access to computers and smartphones. They can gain access to these anywhere. Again, it cannot be stressed enough that it is not the Internet that is "evil." It is the deeply embedded roots of discrimination and hegemonic symptoms of such attitudes that need to be addressed. In the United States, it is recommended that similar reactive state and federal legislation, as set out in Appendix A, be applied with similar educational and sensitivity training goals in mind.

Funding for Research on Assumptions Held by Law Enforcement Personnel

With regard to the need for sensitivity training, it is important for the government in both Canada and the United States to fund research that seeks to understand the biases and assumptions about DE Kids and DE Young Adults that inform police forces and law enforcement personnel. Joint funding initiatives between the two countries would also be beneficial because it would encourage partnerships and collaborations among academics, universities, schools, and the legal community in researching and developing shared curriculum programming initiatives and resources. Funding is also important to support the development of appropriate workshops that present members with scenarios similar to those used in the DTL Research to draw out answers from the DE Kids. It would be important to present members of the police department with similar hypothetical situations to assess how they might respond to calls from schools; how they would identify suspects; whose digital gadgets they would confiscate; and how they might use their discretionary powers to lay charges. There is a dearth of research in this area. If governments are really serious about preventing suicides and reducing cyberbullying among youth, it is important to assess the potential for breach of due process; police bias that might assume female victims "asked for it;" the potential for racial profiling; and so on. In Quebec, the police forces have been notorious for racial profiling, particularly in their handling of youth from visible racial minorities (Scott, 2011; CBC, 2011; Leclair, 2013).

Developing Non-Arbitrary and Informed Legal Responses

Federal, state, and provincial governments that are updating existing legislation and considering the use of a range of legal frameworks might be wise to consider the following:

- Human or civil rights models, such as those in Australia, which successfully engaged human rights commissions in addressing cyberbullying. In cases where criminal intent cannot be established but where discrimination is evident, this approach might serve to be both educational and effective.
- Develop best practices around the exercise of Crown and police discretion in cyberbullying cases in consultation with provincial, territorial, and state counterparts. This would ensure preservation of youth criminal justice goals while seeking to avoid non-prosecution of male perpetrators due to gender bias that holds young women especially accountable for their "bad reputations." This is particularly important in light of rape culture in contemporary society.

If a new *Criminal Code* provision is deemed necessary, it will be essential to pay attention to the following considerations, and inform them by undertaking a thorough review of existing empirical research on the way DE Kids engage online, like we did with our DTL Research:

- Include generalized and age-appropriate sanctions that extend to both youth and adults, given that adults are often the worst role models of malicious sexting and cyberbullying. Legislative committees will need to recognize that actions by children and youth may not necessarily be founded upon the same level of intent as those of adults. As such, it will be important to maintain youth criminal justice principles that focus on factors that could reduce the culpability of young people (such as diversionary or well-managed restorative justice measures), or indicate alternative mechanisms.
- Recognize that not all acts of cyberbullying are the same. For example, a specific offense for non-consensual distribution of sexual images holds some attraction for legislators because it would:
  - Apply to youth and to adults and websites specializing or profiting from non-consensual distribution of intimate images;
  - Send a significant message that such conduct is not acceptable in a Canadian society that does not tolerate sexual exploitation of any kind; and
  - Specifically address the forms of bullying and cyberbullying linked to a number of recent youth suicide tragedies.
- Ensure a clear *mens rea* requirement is included in any specific offense for non-consensual distribution of sexual images. This is important to

capture the deliberate use of words or images for the purpose of inflicting grave psychological, emotional, and/or reputational harm on the person targeted, but not so broad as to criminalize vast swaths of DE Kids who merely pass on such content (wrong as that may be from a social and moral standpoint).

- Ensure compliance with *First Amendment* and *Charter of Rights and Freedoms* protections, including equality, privacy and freedom of expression.
- Avoid officially sanctioned re-victimization of youthful targets. Research indicates that perpetrators of cyberbullying may also be targets of bullying who retaliate through cyberbullying. In this regard, best practices for police, Crown, and sentencing discretion should include attention to the larger relationship between individuals targeted by cyberbullying or sexting and the perpetrator(s) to ensure that perpetrators who have also been victimized are not subjected to harsher penalties than the original perpetrator.

Funding for Sustainable Policy and Program Initiatives

Governments can also fund and support sustainable policy and programming initiatives and North American networks for developing and implementing safe, accepting, and equitable school environments. Such initiatives would address online harassment, threats, libel, defamation, non-consensual distribution of intimate images, and other forms of cyberbullying in a range of ways.

University and School Programming, Legal and Digital Literacy

The gaps identified in previous chapters can be addressed through sustained financial and educational resources so that DE Kids are exposed to opportunities in every aspect of curriculum and school life to consider their legal and ethical responsibilities in an evolving social democracy. It is important to reinforce socially responsible citizenship and digital citizenship in every aspect of school and university life. As I have mentioned, this can be done effectively though the use of legal literacy approaches whereby children's literature is used to help DE Kids better understand legal concepts. It ought to be implemented with children from a very young age. Consider that there are approximately 260 international versions of Cinderella, a fairy tale that involved severe bullying by Cinderella's stepmother and sisters. Using versions of this story from a range of international countries would not only work to address bullying, but it would also address issues of duty of care by authority figures, in this case Cinderella's stepmother, as well as themes of negligence, hope, and resilience in the face of abuse, among others. The tale of Goldilocks and the Three Bears has been used to teach children about trespassing, negligence, and responsibility. Tolkien's *Lord of the Rings*, *Grimm's Fairy Tales*, *Harry Potter*, *Curious George*, *Dr. Seuss*, *The Hunger Games*, *Twilight*, and modern children's literature on bullying can incorporate legal concepts to help young people understand concepts of trust, risk, accountability, responsibility, and so on. Bruno Bettleheim (in Shariff, Case & Manley-Casimir, 2000), a child psychologist, maintained many years ago that children acquire their "moral underbelly" through learning notions of good and evil in children's literature. Jane Yolen, who has been called the Aesop of the twentieth century, agreed with this perspective. Consider what Andrew P. Morriss writes in analyzing J.K. Rowling's writing style and its potential effects on child moral development:

In the Harry Potter novels, I contend that we have a good example of...a calibration. That is, Rowling is not "play[ing] out the implications of...her underlying worldview... [which reflects her] understanding of society, psychology, and human behavior." Instead, Rowling asks the reader to judge the validity of her underlying model of human behavior when faced with the data provided by her characters' choices. (p. 51)

Importantly, many of the children and adolescents who read the *Harry Potter* series are at a stage in their life where they are beginning to determine their own values (Morriss, 2010). Throughout the novels, before and after learning the truth about his identity, Harry is conveyed as an awkward bespectacled teenager who is sometimes bullied by his peers. Because of Harry's relatable nature, children identify with his actions and behavior, whether or not they agree with them (Binnendyk & Schonert-Reichl, 2002). Witnessing the trials and tribulations of Harry and his peers allows readers to compare the moral frameworks displayed by the main characters to their own. Oftentimes, the child's values will resonate with those of the hero but perhaps more importantly, when there is dissonance, it forces the child to wonder why. In either case, the reader is forced to perform an introspective analysis and judge the main characters' reactions and choices, as well as their own, to determine their own notions of morality (Thomas, 2010). This is what should help drive and shape legal literacy at a younger age.

Better Prepare Teachers: University Programs in Legal, Digital, and Media Literacy

Teachers and school administrators are under increasing pressure, under state and provincial legislation, to provide safe school environments (e.g., Bill 56, *An Act to prevent and stop bullying and violence in schools*, 2012; Bill 13, *Accepting Schools Act*, 2013; *Cyber-safety Act*, 2013; *Anti-Bullying Bill of Rights Act*, 2011; *Safe and Supportive Minnesota Schools Act*, 2014; *Seth's Law*, 2011, and others).

As discussed in Chapter 2, Dalhousie Law Professor Wayne MacKay's report (MacKay, 2013), in response to the St. Mary's incident, is exemplary of the increasing responsibility of educational institutions in ensuring a secure and inviting learning environment. To reiterate, the report identified 6 Cs of desired culture change at universities: (1) commitment, (2) consent, (3) critical thinking, (4) communication, (5) collaboration, and (6) caring. Importantly, MacKay's recommendations further included (1) the development of a university-wide code of conduct, (2) a revision of the university's sexual assault policy, (3) efforts to increase the understanding of consent, and (4) encouraging and creating the infrastructure for teaching and research excellence in areas related to sexualized violence (MacKay, 2013).[1] These recommendations suggest a focus on legal literacy and awareness to diminish cyberbullying and rape culture.

University teacher education programs need to include courses on legal literacy, digital literacy, discrimination, and cyberbullying. Teachers need to understand human rights and constitutional protections. Educators need to learn how to better explain and illustrate notions of public versus private spaces. They need to be better aware of their legal obligations under tort law (as I explained in *Confronting Cyberbullying* (2009)) and our collective obligations for provision, protection, and participation of children under Articles 12, 13, and 19 of the CRC. If teachers are not themselves proficient in using digital media, they will not be able to help DE Kids think through the impact of online postings or help them resist the impulse and temptation to post harmful content online. In this regard, it is essential to prepare teachers – both in terms of digital and legal literacy. Governments would make a valuable investment if they provide funding for pre-service and professional development for teachers and school administrators, with a view to effectively address human rights, enhance legal and digital literacy, as well as digital citizenship and empathy-building curricula for students towards fostering learning environments (physical and virtual) free of discrimination and bullying; and encourage student-centered initiatives that support digital citizenship.

Sensitize the News Media

Although the news media have helped significantly in raising awareness of the devastating impact of cyberbullying, they too need to be sensitized to the harmful impact of over-sensationalizing news reports. This is especially true of repeated references to the social media pages of victims after their death. To that end, parents will also need to become more aware of their legal obligations and rights as legislation places increasing responsibility on their shoulders for the online actions of their children.

Engage DE Kids: Agency, Responsibility, and Benefit of the Doubt

I have saved the most important recommendation for last. Engaging DE Kids in the process of defining the lines for themselves is essential. This is the only way that they will be able to think through their impulsive actions. As part of my DTL Research, we engaged approximately twenty DE Kids in developing their own video vignettes, modeled after those that can be found on my DTL website at www.definethcline.ca. We wanted the DE Kids, still between the ages of

---

[1] In September 2014, California signed into law the Yes means Yes law, which seeks to improve how universities handle rape and sexual assault accusations and clarifies the standards, requiring an affirmative consent and stating that consent can't be given if someone is asleep or incapacitated by drugs or alcohol.

eight and eighteen, to develop scenarios involving either the distribution of non-consensual images or offensive or demeaning posts that contained a discriminatory, particularly homophobic or sexist, message and prepare a short video vignette to show us how they define the line between jokes and fun not meant to harm and harmful and intentional threats, harassment, demeaning comments and images, and so on.

While we ensured participants did not have access to demeaning images of anyone, especially their peers, while they worked we invited them to participate in a workshop presented by video-makers from the National Film Board of Canada (NFB). Despite the fact that they had such a short period of time to prepare and learn how to develop videos, and engage in the creative but serious process of where they might draw the line, we were pleased with the results. What was interesting to see was the collaborative work engaged in to work together on videos, the deeply focused attention, and most of all, the thrill of being asked to engage in creating their own work and giving us their own opinion.

Furthermore, there is research that confirms, beginning with bullying research guru Daniel Olweus (1994), that when children and youth contribute to developing their own rules and codes of conduct, they are likely to be more aware of their responsibility and accountability and violence and offensive communication is reduced by as much as 50 percent. Contributing to laws and rules will help DE Kids engage in leadership and as they become increasingly "legally" literate, foster an interest in contributing to the political process through votes, service, or running for public office. They will learn more about citizenship, digital citizenship, and constitutional and human rights principles through engaging in policy development. As I have mentioned in a number of keynote presentations to youths, they can apply to testify at parliamentary hearings for Bill C-13 because it will have significant impact on their lives. The politicians need to hear from DE Kids first-hand, with suggestions of what might work as sound and informed policy initiatives.

Moving from Reactive to Proactive Responses

In closing, I present an updated version of a concept map I have used in past publications, including *Confronting Cyberbullying* (Shariff, 2009). It is with some regret that I observe not much has changed in terms of the advice I have had to give in the past and continue to emphasize now. We really need to move away from reactive, Band-Aid solutions, to proactive, preventative, inclusive, and engaging initiatives.

I am convinced that preventative measures provide our best hope at reducing online abuse and moving toward human development and wellbeing (HDWB), as the arrow shows in **Concept Figure 5.1**.

Survival of the Fittest in a Digital World

The proactive approach highlighted on the concept map places the responsibility square in the hands of DE Kids who are society's future leaders. If we do not give them the responsibility to think through how they will improve their

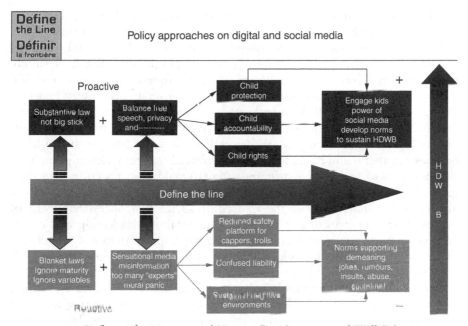

FIGURE 5.1: Defining the Line toward Human Development and Well Being

current and future social relationships and ultimately their own future society, how will they ever learn?

It is important to begin by giving them the benefit of the doubt. It is essential to expect them to deliver. With trust, youth take ownership because they do not want to let anyone down. If we do not give DE Kids the benefit of the doubt; always look for failings; and constantly them of being intolerant, violent, and offensive when, really, we as adults have provided them with these models and tacitly condone and mirror such behavior, how will they ever escape that vicious cycle and move toward a more inclusive, safe, and respectful society? As it is, we have created a living environment with rapidly depleting resources that will affect their future. We have created economies and infrastructures that are corrupt and crumbling. Many DE Kids may not have the career choices they want because of this. On the other hand, for the first time, DE Kids have at their disposal the fastest evolving technological capabilities. They have the platform from which to create innovative and unique initiatives that are already making traditional careers obsolete.

I strongly believe that the answer to reducing abusive forms of online communication lies in giving DE Kids ownership and responsibility. Invite them to collaborate with other DE Generations such as teachers and parents to facilitate digital literacy. Gain their trust and they will be more likely to openly share their concerns relating to online communications. Make them responsible for their own codes of online conduct and help them obtain a voice at the highest levels of policy development. Help DE Kids present as expert witnesses at the House of Commons and Parliamentary committees where they can voice the concerns they have about these issues. Help them contribute to the wording of legislation – because they understand the nuanced challenges and complexities of online communication among youth. All of this is possible if we simply make an effort to listen and actually "hear" them. Lip service will not be enough.

It is absolutely important that we move away from an accusatory focus on the bad "behavior" of DE Kids and recognize ways in which they can show us positive uses of online spaces. In many ways, DE Generations have brought people together. Facebook's Mark Zuckerberg may not have meant to bring families together – and he may not have perceived that only eleven years from the inception of Facebook that grandparents would be connecting with their grandchildren through this social medium. Moreover, DE Generations are not all doomed to fail. Look at the leadership advice that Sheryl Sandberg of Facebook (2013) gives young women about attaining leadership and career success. Some positive female role models young women can look up to include Queen Rania of Jordan, Hilary Clinton, Ellen Johnson Sirleaf, and J.K. Rowling.

Effective long-term responses will require proactive initiatives to ensure, among other things, that children, youth, and their teachers, caregivers, and parents are educated about equal rights and potential legal risks. They need to be offered anti-oppression education (though a funded curriculum delivered by those with expertise on these issues); and guaranteed equity affirming educational experiences in which respect for diversity is emphasized and modeled.

I hope that this book will make valuable contributions to the current public policy debate and be useful for educational purposes as a text for use in pre-service, graduate education, and professional development; and in "judge schools" (continuing legal education courses for judges to keep them apprised of social developments), continuing legal education courses, law schools, police academies, and public and private schools and universities.

Ultimately, it is crucial that legislators, the judiciary, and law enforcement personnel learn to question their own assumptions about children's culpability (and consequently their application of legal sanctions) in a society that consistently overwhelms children with violent and sexualized adult role models and images. The next phase in the DTL Research is to examine the assumptions that legislators, judges, and law enforcement bring to their legal decisions. The complexities and cases are too numerous to name in this book. This book is a stepping-stone to more in-depth analysis of the burgeoning litigation, statutes, and case law that are beginning to emerge globally.

I plan to report my findings in upcoming editions once the research is completed in 2016. In the meantime, I am confident that North American society can learn to promote equality, digital citizenship, and socially responsible uses of digital media among DE Kids. This can only be achieved through informed leadership, legal literacy, and well-crafted legal responses from all stakeholders, and especially, our policy makers.

REFERENCES

Binnendyk, L. & Schonert-Reichl, K.A. (2002). Harry Potter and Moral Development in Pre-adolescent Children. *Journal of Moral Education, 31,* 195–201.

CBC. (2011) Racial profiling 'real' problem in Quebec. *CBC News*. Retrieved on www.cbc.ca/news/canada/montreal/racial-profiling-real-problem-in-quebec-1.1034922.

Edwards, D. (2013, March 17), CNN grieves that guilty verdict ruined 'promising' lives of Steubenville rapists. *The Raw Story*. Retrieved March 18, 2013, from www.rawstory.com/rs/2013/03/17/cnn-grieves-that-guilty-verdict-ruined-promising-lives-of-steubenville-rapists/.

Global Montreal. (2013, December 5). Accused in [R.P.] case due back in court Jan. 9. *Global News*. Retrieved December 5, 2013, from http://globalnews.ca/news/1010915/case-of-teens-charged-with-child-porn-after-rehtaeh-parsons-death-due-in-court/.

Jaffer, M. (Senator) & Honourable Brazeau, P. (2012). Cyberbullying Hurts: Respect for Rights in the Digital Age Standing Senate Committee on Human Rights. *Parliament of Canada*. Retrieved from www.parl.gc.ca/Content/SEN/Committee/411/ridr/rep/rep09dec12-e.pdf.

Kasirer, N. (1992). The *infans* as *bon père de famille*: "Objectively Wrongful Conduct" in the Civil Law Tradition. *American Journal of Comparative Law, 40,* 343–377.

Kift, S., Campbell, M. & Butler, D. (2010). Cyberbullying in social networking sites and blogs: Legal issues for young people and schools. *Journal of Law, Information and Science,* 20(2), 60–97.

Leclair, A. (2013). Racial profiling complaints in Quebec up over 50 per cent. *Global News*. Retrieved on http://globalnews.ca/news/922013/racial-profiling-complaints-against-montreal-police-up-over-50-per-cent/.

Manderson, D. (2003). From Hunger to Love: Myths of the Source, Interpretation, and Constitution of Law in Children's Literature. *Law and Literature,* 15(1), 87–141.

Morriss, A.P. (2010). Moral Choice, Wizardry, Law and Liberty: A Classic Liberal Reading of the Role of Law in the Harry Potter Series. In Thomas, J.E. & Snyder, F.G. (Eds.), *The Law and Harry Potter* (pp. 49–66). Durham: Carolina Academic Press.

Olweus, D. (1994). Bullying at school: Basic Facts and Effects of a School Based Intervention Program. *Journal of Child Psychology and Psychiatry,* 35(7), 1171–1190. (pp. 97–130).

Sandberg, S. (2013). *Lean in: Women, Work, and the Will to Lead*. Alfred A. Knopf: New York, New York.

Scott, M. (2011). Outlaw racial profiling now: Quebec report. *The National Post*. Retrieved on http://news.nationalpost.com/2011/05/12/outlaw-racial-profiling-now-quebec-report/.

Shariff, S. (2009). *Confronting Cyber-Bullying: What Schools Need to Know to Control Misconduct and Avoid Legal Consequences*. New York: Cambridge University Press.

Shariff, S., Bailey, J., Steeves, V., MacKay, W.A., Mishna, F., Slane, A. & Roher, E. (2013, October). Policy Brief for Consideration by Federal Minister of Justice Peter MacKay prior to Bill C-13, *Protecting Canadians from Online Crime Act* [unpublished].

Shariff, S., Case, R. & Manley-Casimir, M. (2000). Balancing competing rights in education: Surrey school board's book ban. *Education and Law Journal,* 10(1), 47–105.

Thomas, J.E. (2010). Preface. In Thomas, J.E. & Snyder, F.G. (Eds.), *The Law and Harry Potter* (pp. vii–viii). Durham: Carolina Academic Press.

Van Praagh, S. (2005). Adolescence, Autonomy and Harry Potter: The Child as Decision Maker. *International Journal of Law in Context*, 1(4), 335–373.

Van Praagh, S. (2007). 'Sois Sage'- Responsibility for Childishness in the Law of Civil Wrongs. In Neyers, J.W., Chamberlain, E. and Pital, S.G.A. (Eds.), *Emerging Issues in Tort Law* (pp. 63–84). Oxford: Hart Publishing.

Weisgarber, M. (2012, February 10). Probation in rave rape case called a 'slap on the wrist.' *CTV News*. Retrieved from http://bc.ctvnews.ca/probation-in-rave-rape-case-called-a-slap-on-the-wrist-1.766872.

Wiseman, A. (2012). Harry Potter and the Chamber of Standards: What Child and Technological Exceptionality Means for the Functionality and Future of the Reasonable Child Standard. Unpublished term paper for WRIT 491 Term Essay 1 course, Prof. Shauna Van Praagh, Faculty of Law, McGill University.

LEGISLATION

Accepting Schools Act (Bill 13), S.O. 2012 c.5.

Anti-Bullying Bill of Rights Act (2011) P.L. 2010, c. 122.

An Act to prevent and stop bullying and violence in schools (Bill 56), 2012.

Cyber-safety Act, SNS 2013 c.2.

Safe and Supportive Minnesota Schools Act, 2014.

Seth's Law, Assembly Bill 9, 2011.

CASE LAW

A.B. (Litigation Guardian of) v. Bragg Communications Inc., 2012 SCC 46, [2012] 2 S.C.R. 567.

State of New Jersey v. Dharun Ravi (2012), N.J. Super. Unpub. LEXIS 1757.

Charting Out Canadian and U.S. Anti-Bullying Legislation (as it Applies or Can be Applied to Cyberbullying Incidents)

Canadian Legislation[1]

Jurisdiction	Legal Framework	Legislation/Policy	Status	Brief Description
Federal	Criminal	S. 140 of the Criminal Code: **Public mischief** (1) Every one commits public mischief who, with **intent** to mislead, causes a peace officer to enter on or continue an investigation by: (a) making a **false statement** that **accuses some other** person of having committed an offence; (b) **doing anything intended** to **cause some other person to be suspected of having committed an offence** that the other person has not committed, or to divert suspicion from himself; (c) **reporting** that an offence has been committed **when it has not** been committed; or (d) reporting or in any other way making it known or causing it to be made	Enacted	Prohibits public mischief. This includes: (a) falsely accusing someone of having committed an offence; (b) causing someone to be suspected of having committed an offence that the they did not commit; (c) reporting that an offence has been committed when it has not; or (d) reporting that he or some other person has died when he have not. *Jurisprudence:* *R v. R.B. (ONCJ, 2011)* – two fifteen-year-olds made a fake YouTube account with racist threats toward President Obama

Jurisdiction	Type	Statute	Status	Description
		known that he or some other person has died when he or that other person has not died.		
Federal	Criminal	S. 163.1 of the Criminal Code	Enacted	Prohibits making, possessing, and distributing child pornography
Federal	Criminal	S. 264 of the Criminal Code **Criminal harassment** (1) No person shall, without lawful authority and knowing that another person is harassed or recklessly as to whether the other person is harassed, engage in conduct referred to in subsection (2) that causes that other person reasonably, in all the circumstances, to fear for their safety or the safety of anyone known to them.	Enacted	Prohibits criminal harassment Eight girls in Ontario were arrested and charged with criminal harassment for a cyberbullying incident.
Federal	Criminal	S. 298–300 of the Criminal Code **Definition** 298. (1) A **defamatory libel** is matter published, without lawful justification or excuse, that is likely to injure the reputation of any person by exposing him to hatred, contempt or ridicule, or that is designed to insult the	Enacted	Prohibits defamatory libel

(cont.)

Canadian Legislation[1]

Jurisdiction	Legal Framework	Legislation/Policy	Status	Brief Description
		person of or concerning whom it is published.		
Federal	Criminal	S. 318–319 of the Criminal Code **Hate Propaganda** __Public incitement of hatred__ 319. (1) Every one who, by **communicating statements in any public place, incites hatred against any identifiable group** where such incitement is likely to lead to a breach of the peace is guilty of (a) an indictable offence and is liable to imprisonment for a term not exceeding two years; or (b) an offence punishable on summary conviction. __Willful promotion of hatred__ (2) Every one who, by **communicating statements, other than in private conversation, willfully**	Enacted	Prohibits hate propaganda and inciting hatred

		promotes hatred against any identifiable group is guilty of (a) an indictable offence and is liable to imprisonment for a term not exceeding two years; or (b) an offence punishable on summary conviction.		
Federal	Criminal	S. 13 of the Criminal Code **Child under twelve** 13. No person shall be convicted of an offence in respect of an act or omission on his part while that person was under the age of twelve years.	Enacted	
Federal	Criminal	*Youth Criminal Justice Act*	Enacted	Governs the procedure for prosecuting youth for criminal offences
Federal	Criminal	*Safer Streets and Communities Act*	Enacted	Amends the *Criminal Code* to increase or impose mandatory minimum penalties, and increase maximum penalties for certain offences. Also amends the sentencing and general principles of the *Youth Criminal Justice Act*, as well as its provisions relating to judicial interim release, adult and youth sentences,

Canadian Legislation[1]

Jurisdiction	Legal Framework	Legislation/Policy	Status	Brief Description
				publication bans, and placement in youth custody facilities.
Federal	Criminal/Evidence	Part VI of the Criminal Code: s. 118–149	Enacted	Governs when police can install a wiretap to intercept communications
Federal	Criminal	*Protecting Canadians from Online Crime Act* (Bill C-13)	Proposed	Makes it illegal to distribute "intimate images" without consent
				Grants broad discretion to judiciary and law enforcement re: search and seizure as well as surveillance
Federal	Constitutional	S. 2(b) of the *Canadian Charter of Rights and Freedoms* Everyone has the following fundamental freedoms: freedom of thought, belief, opinion and **expression**, including freedom of the press and other media of communication;	Enacted	Protects freedom of expression (as long as it is not violent in form)
Federal	Constitutional	S. 7 of the *Canadian Charter of Rights and Freedoms*	Enacted	Prohibits the deprivation of life, liberty, and security of the

Jurisdiction	Category	Law	Status	Details
Federal		Everyone has the right to life, liberty and security of the person and the right not to be deprived thereof except in accordance with the principles of fundamental justice.		person, except in accordance with the principles of fundamental justice The ONCA has found that the principles of fundamental justice include the principle that youth should be treated separately from adults in administering criminal justice (*R v. B (D)*, 2006)
Federal	Constitutional	S. 8 of the *Canadian Charter of Rights and Freedoms* Everyone has the right to be secure against unreasonable search or seizure.	Enacted	Protects against unreasonable search and seizure The BCSC found that users have no reasonable expectation of privacy in their IP addresses or Internet account information, which could let police identify them and, in a limited way, search files that they have uploaded (*R v. Caza*, 2012)
Federal	Privacy	*Privacy Act*	Enacted	Governs how agencies of the federal government can use, collect, and disclose personal information of individuals
Federal	Privacy	*Personal Information Protection and Electronic Documents Act (PIPEDA)*	Enacted	Governs how private sector organizations can collect, use, and disclose personal information

(cont.)

Canadian Legislation[1]

Jurisdiction	Legal Framework	Legislation/Policy	Status	Brief Description
Alberta		*Education Act* (2012)	Enacted	Defines "bullying" as repeated and hostile/demeaning behavior
				Students must report bullying behavior *whether or not it occurs within the school building, during the school day or by electronic means* (see section 31(e))
				Boards must provide a welcoming, caring, respectful and safe learning environment (see section 33(1)(d))
				Instigate *Bullying Awareness and Prevention Week*
				Students can be expelled for conduct injuring physical or mental well-being; whether or not it occurs on school ground (see section 37(1)(c))
British Columbia		*Safe and Caring Schools Communities (SCSCP)*	Last expanded in 2012	Guides boards of education and schools to:

				• Create safe and inclusive learning environments • Engage in school-wide efforts • Appoint District Safe School Coordinators and teams • Instill codes of conduct
British Columbia	Education	ERASE Bullying (*Expect Respect and a Safe Education*)	Anti-bullying strategy: 10 points of plan began in the 2012–2013 academic year	10-point strategy includes: • A five-year, multi-level training program for educators and community partners to help them proactively identify and address threats • New online tools, including a Smartphone app, for kids to report bullying anonymously • Dedicated safe school coordinators in every school district • Provincial guidelines for threat assessments • New online resources for parents • A provincial advisory committee with representatives from police, school, and social agency partners
Manitoba		*The Public Schools Amendment*	Enacted September 13, 2013	Defines "bullying" (Section 1.2)

(cont.)

Canadian Legislation[1]

Jurisdiction	Legal Framework	Legislation/Policy	Status	Brief Description
		Act (Safe and Inclusive Schools) (Bill 18)		School boards ensure establishment of: • Written policy incl. appropriate use of Internet – social media, text messages, IM, websites, emails, digital cameras, cell phones • Respect for human diversity
New Brunswick		Education Act	Enacted	Bullying and cyberbullying are included in the definitions of following terms: • Create a "positive learning and working environment" • Includes behavior or misconduct taking place outside school hours and off the school grounds • Pupils must contribute to a safe and positive learning environment
New Brunswick	Education	An Act to Amend the Education Act (Bill 45)	Enacted	S.1 Amends s.1, chapter E-1.12 of the Education Act to include a "positive learning and working environment"

Jurisdiction	Department	Policy/Motion	Date	Details	
Newfoundland and Labrador	Education	*Safe and Caring Schools Policy*	May 2006	which means a safe, productive, orderly, and respectable learning and working environment free from bullying and cyberbullying, including behavior or misconduct that occurs outside school hours and off school grounds to the extent that this behavior affects the school environment	Guiding principles include creating a positive learning environment, fair and consistently implemented school policies and codes of behavior to reduce bullying, racism, and other forms of harassment Bullying is only mentioned once in the document; cyberbullying is not mentioned at all.
Northwest Territories		*Motion 5–17(2): Anti-Bullying Measures*	Tabled on June 13, 2012		Legislative Assembly has to amend the *Education Act* accordingly within 18 months.

(*cont.*)

Canadian Legislation[1]

Jurisdiction	Legal Framework	Legislation/Policy	Status	Brief Description
				Recommends a territory-wide campaign to denounce bullying, including cyberbullying Recommends that the government review anti-bullying legislation measures in other jurisdictions and bring forward a bill for consideration within 18 months (December 2013)
Nova Scotia	Tort	*Cyber-safety Act (An Act to Address and Prevent Cyberbullying)* (Bill 61)	Enacted, 10 May, 2013	Purpose of the act is to "provide safer communities by creating administrative and court processes that can be used to address and prevent **cyberbullying**" **Cyberbullying** means any electronic communication through the use of technology including, without limiting the generality of the foregoing, computers, other electronic devices, social networks,

text messaging, instant messaging, websites and electronic mail, typically repeated or with continuing effect, that is intended or ought reasonably be expected to cause fear, intimidation, humiliation, distress or other damage or harm to another person's health, emotional well-being, self-esteem or reputation, and includes assisting or encouraging such communication in any way. Implication of parents where person is a minor (under 19 years of age)

Where the name of a respondent is unknown and cannot be easily ascertained, an application for a protection order may identify the respondent by an Internet Protocol address, website, username or account, electronic-mail address or other unique identifier, identified in the application as being used for cyberbullying

(cont.)

Canadian Legislation[1]

Jurisdiction	Legal Framework	Legislation/Policy	Status	Brief Description
				PROTECTION ORDERS s. 4 Applicant can apply for a protection order where a justice determines, on the balance of probabilities, that the respondent engaged in cyberbullying of the subject and are reasonable grounds to believe that they will engage in cyberbullying of the subject in the future Protection order generally involves discontinued contact, including confiscation of electronic devices capable of connecting to an IP address associated with the respondent, discontinuing access to Internet **LIABILITY FOR CYBERBULLYING s. 21** Cyberbullying as a tort Where defendant is a minor, parent is joint and severally liable for any damages awarded to the plaintiff, unless the parent can satisfy the Court

Jurisdiction	Act	Status	Details
			that they were exercising reasonable supervision over the defendant at the time the defendant engaged in the activity that caused the loss or damage and made reasonable efforts to discourage
Ontario	*Accepting Schools Act* (Bill 13)	Enacted	Defines "bullying" legally School boards must adopt policies promoting a positive school climate (inclusive) Required to establish a prevention and intervention plan Definition includes behaviors making use of electronic means (outlines a variety of online behaviors considered "cyber-bullying")
Ontario	*Anti-Bullying Act* (Bill 14)	Currently under consideration by the Standing Committee on Social Policy	Safe and inclusive environment free from harassment, violence, intolerance, and intimidation, all of which are forms of bullying Bullying Awareness and Prevention Week in schools: begins the third Sunday in November each year Amends section 1 of the *Education Act* by providing boundaries of bullying in

Canadian Legislation[1]

Jurisdiction	Legal Framework	Legislation/Policy	Status	Brief Description
				schools: (a) on a school site or public property within 50 meters of a school site; (b) activity, function or program that is conducted for a school purpose, whether or not on school site; (c) through the use of technology or an electronic device provided to pupils by a school; or (e) through the use of technology or an electronic device that is not provided to pupils by a school if the bullying has the effect or is reasonably intended to have the effect described in the definition of bullying Amends subsection 170 of the *Education Act* by adding instruction on bullying prevention Every board shall establish a bullying prevention plan, including descriptions of bullying, procedures to

			report bullying or retaliation to bullying, confidentiality of reporter, assessing needs, restoring a sense of safety, disciplinary action for falsely accusing another of bullying, notifying guardians, and notifying appropriate law enforcement agency if criminal charges may be laid against the perpetrator.
Québec	Civil Law	*An Act to prevent and stop bullying and violence in schools* (Bill 56)	Enacted	Schools must provide a healthy and secure learning environment • Adopt an anti-bullying and anti-violence plan (per school) • Rules of conduct include behaviors prohibited *at all times* (incl. social media) Defines legally "bullying" and "violence" School boards must enter into agreement with regional police force to deal with reported incidence of bullying or violence
Saskatchewan		*Caring and Respectful Schools – Bullying Prevention: A Model Policy* (2006)		• Prevention and Early Intervention • Caring, respecting, and safe school environments based on UNCRC

Canadian Legislation[1]

Jurisdiction	Legal Framework	Legislation/Policy	Status	Brief Description
				• Extensive definition of bullying based on literature
				Input and active participation from board of education, educators, students, parents, community members, and service providers
Saskatchewan	Education	*Saskatchewan's Action Plan to Address Bullying and Cyberbullying*	November 2013	Six key recommendations: update policies and procedures; anonymous online reporting tool; implications of federal legislation; **support students to develop appropriate and responsible online behavior;** provide a standalone website for anti-bullying tools; engage youth in building solutions to address bullying (p. 1) Four themes: build consistency; work across governments; develop appropriate online behavior; engage youth (p. 2) Focuses on maintaining a positive digital footprint, respecting intellectual property

Jurisdiction	Legal Framework	Legislation/Policy	Status	Brief Description
				boundaries, and protecting child and adolescent privacy online (p. 22)
Yukon	Education	*Safe and Caring Schools Policy*	Enacted January 31, 2008	Students and staff have the right to be treated in a fair, respectful, and equitable manner in a safe school environment free from all forms of bullying, harassment, and intimidation A 9-step process outlined for instances of bullying, including a final step of notifying the police and/or other "public agencies" when there is a risk to student or staff safety (p. 4)

U.S. Legislation

Jurisdiction	Legal Framework	Legislation/Policy	Status	Brief Description
U.S. Federal	Privacy	*Children's Online Privacy and Protection Act (COPPA)*	Enacted	Governs when and how websites can collect and use information on users under the age of 12 years. Includes what website operators should include in their privacy policies, how to get verifiable consent from a parent or guardian, and what responsibilities the operator must take on to

U.S. Legislation

Jurisdiction	Legal Framework	Legislation/Policy	Status	Brief Description
				protect children's safety and privacy online. Also includes restrictions on marketing to children under the age of 13 years.
U.S. Federal	Constitutional	First Amendment: Congress shall make no law respecting an establishment of religion, or prohibiting the free exercise thereof; or abridging the freedom of speech, or of the press; or the right of the people peaceably to assemble, and to petition the Government for a redress of grievances.	Enacted	Protects freedom of speech
Alabama	Education	*The Alabama Student Harassment Prevention Act (HB 0216)*	Enacted in 2009	Schools must develop policies to help with harassment, including electronic forms of bullying; "punishment shall conform with applicable federal and state disability, antidiscrimination, and education laws and school discipline policies."
Alaska	Criminal	SB 128, *An Act relating to the crime of harassment*	Introduced January 2014, first reading	Makes cyberbullying a crime of second-degree harassment

State	Category	Bill/Law	Date	Description
Arizona	Education	HB 2638	Enacted 2005	Requires school district governing boards to adopt and enforce procedures that prohibit harassment, bullying, and intimidation at school or during school trips
Arkansas	Criminal	Arkansas Code of 1987, Title 5, Chapter 71, § 217	Enacted July 2011	Cyberbullying is a Class B misdemeanor
California	Education	Yes means yes law	Signed into law in September 2014	Provides clear definition for when people agree to have sex (consent) Seeks to improve how universities handle rape and sexual assault accusations and clarifies the standards, requiring an affirmative consent and stating that consent can't be given if someone is asleep or incapacitated by drugs or alcohol
California	Education	AB 256, An act to amend Section 48900 of the Education Code, relating to pupils	Passed October 2013	Gives schools more power to intervene in bullying situations, discipline students who participate in cyberbullying. Before schools could only suspend or expel students if the act was related to a school activity or school attendance. Now they have the power to discipline students for activities originating off school grounds.

U.S. Legislation

Jurisdiction	Legal Framework	Legislation/Policy	Status	Brief Description
California	Education	Seth's Law, AB 9	Enacted	Requires school policy and investigation processes (named for thirteen-year-old who took his own life because of anti-gay bullying)
California	Education	*Bullying Prevention for School Safety and Crime Reduction Act* (2003) Chapter 828	Enacted	Requires the Department of Education to develop model policies on the prevention of bullying and on conflict resolution, makes the model policies available to school districts, and authorizes school districts to adopt one or both policies for incorporation into the school safety plan.
Colorado	Criminal	*House Bill 1131*	Voted down April 2014	Would have made it a misdemeanor to inflict "serious emotional distress on a minor" through cyberbullying.
Connecticut	Education	*An Act Concerning the Strengthening of Bullying Laws* (*SB 1138*)	Signed by Governor on July 13, 2011	School policies must "include provisions addressing bullying outside of the school setting if such bullying (a) creates a hostile environment at school for the victim, (b) infringes on

State	Type	Bill	Status	Description
Florida	Criminal	HB 451, Bullying	In committee (as of January 2014)	the rights of the victim at school, or (c) substantially disrupts the education process or the orderly operation of a school..." Creates an offense of "bullying" (misdemeanor in the first degree) with criminal penalties Creates an offense of "aggravated bullying" (bullies, while making a "credible threat"), a felony in the third degree, with criminal penalties
Georgia	Education	End of Cyberbullying Act	Proposed	Considers both on- and off-campus cyberbullying – charges schools with a responsibility towards both
Idaho	Education	Jared's Law (HB 750)	Enacted	Student who personally violates any provision of this section shall be guilty of a misdemeanor; possible suspension or denial of school attendance
Illinois	Criminal	House Bill 4583	Enacted in 2010	Renders sexting a misdemeanor
Illinois	Education	House Bill 3281	Effective January 1, 2012	"The board may suspend or by regulation authorize the superintendent of the district or the principal, assistant principal, or dean of students of any school to suspend a student for a period not to exceed

U.S. Legislation

Jurisdiction	Legal Framework	Legislation/Policy	Status	Brief Description
				10 school days or may expel a student for a definite period of time not to exceed 2 calendar years, as determined on a case by case basis, if (i) that student has been determined to have made an explicit threat on an Internet website against a school employee, a student, or any school-related personnel"
Maryland	Criminal	*Misuse of Interactive Computer Service (Grace's Law)*	In force as of May 2013	Prohibits electronic harassment of a minor based on sex, race, or sexual orientation Makes cyberbullying a misdemeanor; Violators would be fined $500 or face up to a year in jail
Massachusetts	Education	*An Act Relative to Bullying in Schools*	Approved by the governor May 3, 2010	Includes cyberbullying and addresses those behaviors that "materially and substantially [disrupt] the education process" Considers whether a hostile environment is being created at school

Minnesota	Education	*Safe and Supportive Minnesota Schools Act*	Will come into force July 1, 2014	Describes scope and application of the law: (1) on school premises, at school functions, or on school transportation, (2) by use of technology on school premises, during school functions, or on school transportation, (3) by electronic means to the extent that it **materially disrupts student learning or school environment**
New Jersey	Criminal	*An Act Concerning Diversionary Programs*	Enacted in 2011	Juvenile diversion program for first-time offenders; method of counteracting penalties that are overly harsh
New Jersey	Education	*Anti-Bullying Bill of Rights Act*	Enacted September 1, 2011	"Harassment, intimidation or bullying" means any gesture, any written, verbal or physical act, or any electronic communication, whether it be a single incident or a series of incidents . . . that takes place on school property, at any school-sponsored function [or] on a school bus, or off school grounds that **substantially disrupts or interferes with the orderly operation of the school or the rights of other students**"

U.S. Legislation

Jurisdiction	Legal Framework	Legislation/Policy	Status	Brief Description
New York	Education	*Dignity for All Students Act*	Scheduled to take effect July 1, 2012	All students in public schools deserve an environment free of harassment and discrimination
New York (Westchester County)	Human Rights	*LOCAL LAW amending the Laws of Westchester County to protect minors and students from cyber-bullying*	Recommitted in 2011 (going to committee), reintroduced 2014	Would make cyberbullying a misdemeanor with penalties of up to a year in jail and up to a $1,000 fine Would create a hotline run by the county Human Rights Commission Mandates a public education campaign
Nebraska	Criminal	*Legislative Bill 97*	Approved by the governor on June 4, 2013	Renders sexting a misdemeanor
North Carolina	Criminal	*School Violence Protection Act, 2012*	Came into force 2012	Criminalizes the cyberbullying of teachers (including making a fake Facebook profile and signing them up for spam or to pornographic sites), which means students could face fines up to $1,000 or jail time
Ohio	Criminal	*Senate Bill 103*	Proposed in 2009 but presently not in effect	Renders sexting a misdemeanor

State	Type	Law	Date	Description
Texas	Criminal	Texas Penal Code, § 43.261 (Acts 2011, 82nd Leg., R.S., Ch. 1322 (Senate Bill 407)).	Brought into force in 2011	Specifically addresses sexting Importantly, this section of Texas' Penal Code provides for increasingly harsh penalties depending on whether the defendant is a first-time offender
Utah	Criminal	House Bill 14	Signed by the governor in March 2014	Renders sexting a misdemeanor
Vermont	Criminal	An act relating to expanding the sex offender registry	Enacted in 2009	Special legislation decriminalizing sexting between two people if they are between the ages of 13 and 18 so long as they are first-time offenders Whether repeat offenders are tried under child pornography and exploitation laws is at the discretion of the prosecution
Wyoming	Education	Safe School Climate Act	Enacted in 2011	All school districts must have a policy in regard to bullying and cyberbullying and the punishments are at the discretion of the schools

[1] Please note that while this chart represents an extensive list of legislative responses, it is in no way exhaustive. Specifically, we have selected legislative responses that present unique qualities. This was compiled with the help of S. Hinduja and J.W. Patchin's *Brief Review of State Cyberbullying Laws and Policies* (2014). We will continue to update our resources on www.definetheline.ca.

Expanded DTL Research Data

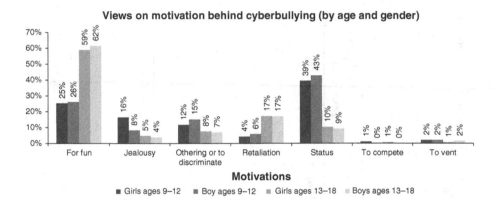

Views on motivation behind cyberbullying (by age and gender)

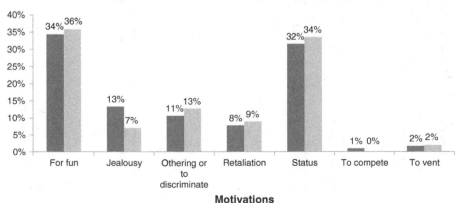

Views on motivation behind cyberbullying (by gender)

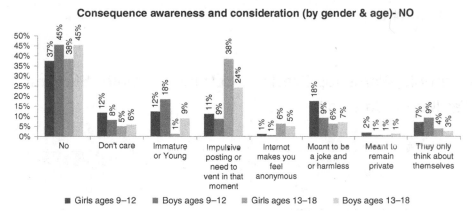

Consequence awareness and consideration (by gender & age)- NO

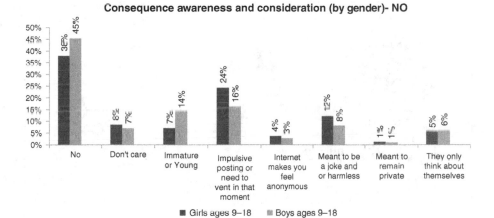

Consequence awareness and consideration (by gender)- NO

Sample Workshop Provided to Undergraduate Students at McGill University

Shaheen Shariff, Ph.D.
Associate Professor
McGill University, Faculty of Education
© Shaheen Shariff, Definetheline.ca - Projects on Cyber-bullying and Digital Citizenship, McGill University

Define
the Line
Définir
la frontière

Defining the Line: Jokes or Harm?

Workshops begin by engaging students in scenarios and activities to gauge their perspectives.

Activity 1: Define the Line (DTL) provides a chart composed of quadrants with various clipped scenarios. Participants are invited to post the scenarios along the lines or in the spaces that indicate whether they involve:

- joking; intentional threats; unintentional threats;
- gossip; fair comments; unfair comments; malicious comments; rumours; defamation; criminal threats; extortion; sexting; demeaning sexism, homophobia; racist, hate speech.

This is followed by facilitated discussion by DTL personnel or trained Student Resident Dons or Floor Fellows.

Define
the Line
Définir
la frontière

Defining the Line: Video Vignettes

Activity 2: Students will view and analyze video vignettes, media news segments, or YouTube clips involving scenarios of cyberbullying. These will be posted on www.definetheline.ca. We are in the process of developing vignettes at the postsecondary level.

Discussion will be facilitated by Define the Line personnel or Student Resident Dons or Fellows who will be trained.

Define the Line / Définir la frontière	Defining the Line: Rape Culture in Cyberbullying

Activity 3:

Definitions of rape culture will be presented together with links to references and scholarly articles on rape culture. Terms such as "slut-shaming"; "victim blaming"; "campus rape culture;" "date rape" and "normalized rape culture" and "homophobia" will be discussed in light of well-publicized cases, such as and including:

- Steubenville rape;
- St. Mary's University Frosh song, see
  http://www.youtube.com/watch?v=3IUQsrmWkrU
- Amanda Todd sexting online, cappers, cyberbullying, suicide and trolls
- Jane Doe filmed rape, distribution online, cyberbullying, and suicide resulting legislation in Nova Scotia
- Maple Ridge gang rape, filming and distribution, pornography charges and court decision
- Rutgers University Clementi filming of homosexual relationship, suicide, court decision
- Juicycampus.com – see Shariff & Churchill (2010), *Truths and Myths of Cyber-bullying*. Peter Lang. NY.

Define the Line / Définir la frontière	Information and Legal Literacy Session Begins

Once students have had an opportunity to discuss scenarios and think about how and where they would define the lines on what they post on social media such as Twitter, Facebook, and other popular online venues, Professor Shariff (or DTL personnel) would then explain the context and concerns about cyberbullying, with an introduction to the legal considerations.

Define the Line / Définir la frontière

Cyberbullying Definition for this Workshop

- Discriminatory: misogynist, sexist, homophobic, exclusionary
- Victims dehumanized and re-victimized with every access of posting
- Permanence: saved, stored on computers and resurfaces constantly
- Anti-authority cyberbullying undermines authority of professors, administrators, counselors, and employers in physical context
- Power imbalance and bystander support
- Impact: Psychological harm, drop in grades, school drop-out, stress, suicide, and long-term impact on employment (Li, Cross & Smith, 2012)

© Shaheen Shariff, Ph.D.

Define the Line / Définir la frontière

Influence of News Media

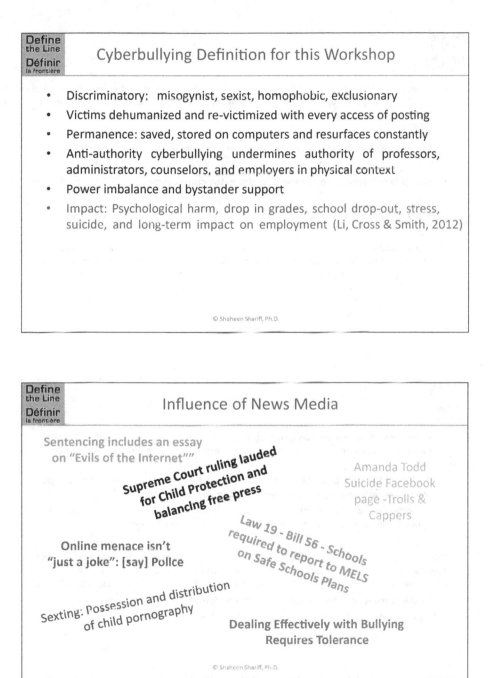

Sentencing includes an essay on "Evils of the Internet""

Supreme Court ruling lauded for Child Protection and balancing free press

Amanda Todd Suicide Facebook page - Trolls & Cappers

Online menace isn't "just a joke": [say] Police

Law 19 - Bill 56 - Schools required to report to MELS on Safe Schools Plans

Sexting: Possession and distribution of child pornography

Dealing Effectively with Bullying Requires Tolerance

© Shaheen Shariff, Ph.D.

Define the Line
Définir la frontière

Rape Culture, Homophobia, and Suicide

- News media has drawn attention to rape culture, which is playing out in most instances of cyberbullying (through misogynist language, slurs, jokes, or actual rape that is filmed and distributed online).

- Sensational news reports can glorify suicide and re-victimize those who commit suicide.

- Results in calls for harsher legislation and zero-tolerance policies.

- Many researchers and consultants continue to focus on "behavior" ignoring context.

- Digital media are not to blame - we need to harness digital natives' educational potential (Term "digital natives" coined by Prensky, 2001 for generations growing up immersed in technologies).

© Shaheen Shariff, Ph.D.

Define the Line
Définir la frontière

Rape Culture, Homophobia, and Suicide

- Postsecondary generation has grown up in a society that provides little guidance, often modelling and tacitly condoning offensive expression rooted in discrimination, sexism, and racism.
- Celebrities like Lady Gaga, Madonna, Miley Cyrus, Rihanna set standards for how girls and women are viewed (also consider sexist comedy, reality shows, and sitcoms).
- Corporate responsibility: intermediaries as "distributors" are not responsible for removing offensive content and in fact can exacerbate privacy breaches.

E.G. Photograph of Jane Doe surfaced in an ad for a dating website after her suicide from cyberbullying relating to a video-taped gang rape while she was unconscious: "Facebook apologizes for ad featuring [Jane Doe]." *The Gazette,* Wednesday, September 18, 2013, A14
- Canadian law is beginning to respond – information on emerging legislation to follow.
- Supreme Court of Canada has finally recognized "discernible harm."

© Shaheen Shariff, Ph.D.

Define the Line / Définir la frontière

Protect or Punish?

- Who is harmed? Perpetrators, victims, bystanders, families?

- How do we assess harm - especially when it is psychological through online abuse?

- Norms and perceptions of harm by "digital natives" (Prensky, 2001) have shifted:
  - Higher tolerance for insults, jokes, pranks;
  - Less consideration of impact on others;
  - Less recognition of boundaries between public and private spaces online;
  - Less awareness of legal risks (which are rapidly increasing as legal responses are evoked); and
  - Tacit condoning of intolerance by some policymakers and role models.

- An Austrian study found that anger and fun are at the top of youth motivations to cyberbully (Gradinger, Storhmeier & Spiel, 2012, In Smith et al, Wiley-Blackwell).

© Shaheen Shariff, Ph.D.

Define the Line / Définir la frontière

1. Rutgers University: Clementi Suicide

- Clementi's roommate Dharun Ravi filmed and posted videotapes of roommate Tyler Clementi in a homosexual relationship.
- Clementi committed suicide.
- Ravi convicted of fifteen counts including bias intimidation, invasion of privacy, and tampering with a witness and evidence. Faced up to ten years in prison.

SENTENCING JUDGE RULED: "Colossal Insensitivity" but no criminal intent to harm. Immature prank - thirty days in jail
- Digital natives impulsivity and Insensitivity - does this amount to criminal intent?
- An Austrian study found that anger and fun are at the top of youth motivations to cyberbully (Gradinger, Storhmeier & Spiel, 2012, in Smith et al., Wiley-Blackwell).
- Cyberbullying itself may not push someone over the edge but if there are existing mental health problems that might.

© Shaheen Shariff, Ph.D.

Define the Line Définir la frontière	2. Maple Ridge Rape: Joking or Breaking the Law?

- Sixteen year-old Canadian girl drugged, gang-raped at rave and videotape of the incident posted on Facebook– video spread virally.
- Police announced that anyone caught with the tape would be charged with possession and distribution of child pornography.
- Sixteen-year-old youth who video-taped the rape was charged under the *Youth Justice Criminal Act* and showed remorse at his hearing.
- Did not post it online but passed it on to an older friend to post on Facebook.
- More attention paid to the boy who took and shared the video than the actual rapists.

JUDGE SAID:

- Boy has "matured significantly."
- One year probation and ordered to write an essay on the "evils of the Internet" and a letter of apology.

© Shaheen Shariff, Ph.D.

Define the Line Définir la frontière	Maple Ridge: Just Joking or Breaking the Law?

VIDEOTAPE OF SEXUAL ASSUALT - DISTRIBUTION OF CHILD PORNOGRAPHY?

- Criminal intent or intent to embarrass?
- Will an essay about "evils of the Internet" teach him anything?
- Numerous cases like this involving sexting.
- Anger is another impulsive response when relations sour.
- Are child pornography laws appropriate?
- Intent of hard core child pornographers is very different - it involves the sexual abuse and exploitation of children for adult pleasure e.g. Cappers - a pedophile group that encourages teenage girls to undress online and then engages in extortion.

- Debate about intent to embarrass by immature youth and intent to harm.

© Shaheen Shariff, Ph.D.

3. Amanda Todd

Concerns:

- Sensational media reports
- Revictimized every time YouTube videos of Facebook page shown
- Platform for trolls - a captive public audience
- Misrepresentation of facts - false arrests
- Adult involved - extortion; distribution of child pornography; civil and criminal defamation - liable? YES
- Kids involved - cyberbullying - defamation; distribution of child pornography (?); criminal and civil defamation (?)

4. California Case:
Joking or Legal Liability?

JOKES AND SPREADING FALSE RUMOURS

- D.C. up-and-coming musician set up a website describing his appearance ("golden brown eyes") and his music, film contract, CD.
- His website had a guestbook inviting comments on his website.
- His guestbook received death threats and comments such as this one from R.R.:

"I will personally unleash my man-seed in those golden brown eyes." (*D.C. et al v. R.R. et al - Court of Appeal, State of California*, Reasons for Judgment, p. 5, March 15, 2010: p.5.)

- D.C. suffered psychological harm and the L.A. Police Department asked him to relocate to another school for safety. This came at a cost to family, his film contract was delayed, people began to believe he was gay, he underwent medical treatment, and his grades dropped along with his confidence.

Define the Line / Définir la frontière	California Case: *D.C. v. R.R. et al* (2010): Joking or Breaking the Law?

R.R defended his actions by testifying:
- He did not know D.C. or care if he was gay. A friend suggested he view the website.
- He was irritated by D.C.'s arrogance and description of his "golden brown eyes."
- It was a competition to see who could post the most outrageous comments.
- He described his own message as "[F]anciful, hyperbolic, jocular, and taunting" motivated by "[D.C.'] pompous, self aggrandizing, and narcissistic website - not his sexual orientation."(p.10-11).
- He explained his other motive as "pathological" (p.11) - to win the one-upmanship contest tacitly taking place between the message posters.
- **He argued that he assumed any rational person would understand his repulsion to D.C.'s self promotional style. (pp. 10-11, Reasons for Judgment). Reflects the shift in norms among digital natives.**
- Both he and his parents filed affidavits saying R.R. is non-violent, a vegetarian and a Buddhist.

© Shaheen Shariff, Ph.D.

Define the Line / Définir la frontière	California Case: *D.C. v. R.R. et al* (2010)

Court of Appeal Ruling:
Re: Free expression, public website and libelous content
- Although hyperbole and "mere jokes" (p.18) are protected by the First Amendment, the banning of "true threats" is not unconstitutional.
- Not necessary for speaker to intend the threat - fear of the threat disrupts lives. (p.17)
- Limiting online threats protects from the "possibility that the threatened violence will occur." (p.17)
- The further speech strays from the values of persuasion, dialogue, and free exchange of ideas and moves towards threats the less it is protected. (p. 18)
- Impact on victim, his family, and perceived threat to safety must be considered.
- False information on sexual orientation caused reasonable people to believe it as truth - therefore the expression was libellous.

© Shaheen Shariff, Ph.D.

Define the Line / Définir la frontière

Canadian Legal Responses: Provincial

- Quebec's Bill 56 – But this largely applies to schools being required to provide a safe environment – hasn't been applied to universities

- Quebec's Proposed Charter of Values – will contradict Bill 56 and create a chilled environment in all public institutions including universities with tacitly condoned intolerance and discrimination of religious minorities.

- *Accepting Schools Act*, Ontario – Similar to Bill 56 – Also largely applies to schools.

- Nova Scotia's *Cyber-safety Act*. Very comprehensive. Allows victims to sue under tort law for defamation, negligence. Holds parents responsible. Allows for criminal charges in certain instances.

- Other provinces have also put in policies to address cyberbullying

© Shaheen Shariff, Ph.D.

Define the Line / Définir la frontière

Canadian Legal Responses: Federal

Senate Standing Committee on Human Rights studied Canada's responsibility to protect youth under Article 19 of the *International Convention of the Rights of the Child*. Again, very little attention to postsecondary context even though cyberbullying is prevalent in universities.

Federal Parliament is going to table a bill in the Fall to amend the *Criminal Code* to include cyberbullying as a criminal offense. An earlier version under Bill-273 was defeated.

Canadian omnibus legislation – *Safe Streets and Communities Act*
- Harsher and longer sentences
- Raised to adult court at younger ages

Supreme Court of Canada decision in *A.B. v. Bragg Communications, Inc.* granted minimal rights to protection of privacy for plaintiffs in defamation suits – balanced free press and privacy.

IMPORTANT TO NOTE: Sexting now draws charges of distribution of child pornography or pornography depending on age of victim – whether it was intended as pornography or just as a joke.

© Shaheen Shariff, Ph.D.

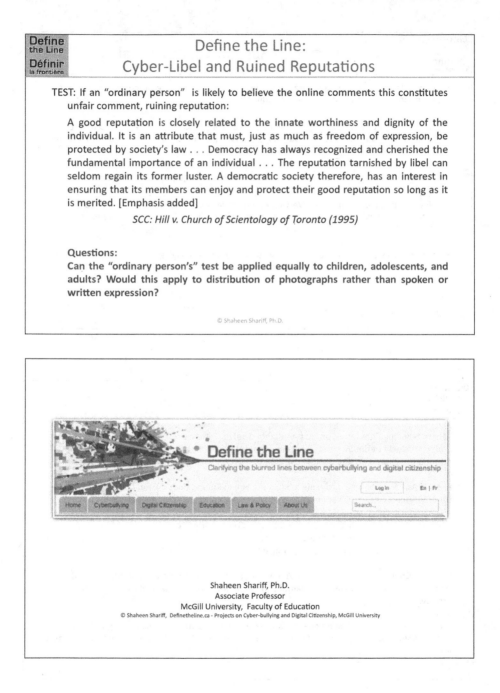

Define the Line:
Cyber-Libel and Ruined Reputations

TEST: If an "ordinary person" is likely to believe the online comments this constitutes unfair comment, ruining reputation:

A good reputation is closely related to the innate worthiness and dignity of the individual. It is an attribute that must, just as much as freedom of expression, be protected by society's law . . . Democracy has always recognized and cherished the fundamental importance of an individual . . . The reputation tarnished by libel can seldom regain its former luster. A democratic society therefore, has an interest in ensuring that its members can enjoy and protect their good reputation so long as it is merited. [Emphasis added]

SCC: Hill v. Church of Scientology of Toronto (1995)

Questions:
Can the "ordinary person's" test be applied equally to children, adolescents, and adults? Would this apply to distribution of photographs rather than spoken or written expression?

© Shaheen Shariff, Ph.D.

Define the Line

Clarifying the blurred lines between cyberbullying and digital citizenship

Log In   En | Fr

Home   Cyberbullying   Digital Citizenship   Education   Law & Policy   About Us   Search...

Shaheen Shariff, Ph.D.
Associate Professor
McGill University, Faculty of Education
© Shaheen Shariff, Definetheline.ca - Projects on Cyber-bullying and Digital Citizenship, McGill University

Public Policy, Law, and Digital Media
(Sample University-Level Course)

COURSE SUMMARY

This course is for undergraduate students in the Faculty of Law, but may also be of interest to Master of Law students who are interested in public policy as it relates to new technologies. It is also valuable for graduate education students (school principals, senior teachers).

CONTEXT, RATIONALE, AND OBJECTIVES

The goal of this course is to provide law students with an understanding of contemporary public policy challenges that have emerged with the rapid evolution of technologies and extensive adoption of digital forms of communication. Legal boundaries that were traditionally taken for granted have become increasingly blurred as policy makers in government, public institutions, and the corporate world attempt to balance free expression, privacy, protection, accountability, culpability, and regulation of online content. Students will consider questions about whether existing legal frameworks can adequately address and inform public policy, or whether public policy debates on uses of the Internet and digital media will inevitably re-shape the law.

Why is a course on public policy and technology important for law students? There is currently much debate in the news media and academic and public forums on how we might better manage, control, monitor, regulate, and legislate online communication, particularly as it relates to social media and smart phones. Of particular concern in these policy debates are cases involving online hate, cyber-threats; cyberbullying; sexting; child pornography; trolling; identity theft; online extortion; and similar offenses. An alarming number of teen suicides resulting from cyberbullying and online rape culture have brought urgency to public policy agendas that call for increased and focused legislative action at both the federal and provincial levels. Litigation involving abusive forms of online communication is on the rise in Canada, making it important that prospective lawyers and judges are aware of the nuanced and complex social contexts and public norms in which these cases occur. The Supreme Court of Canada recently addressed protection of privacy for teenaged victims in defamation cases. However, maintaining a balance between free press rights in an open-court system and plaintiff privacy can be challenging. Thus it is important for law students to consider concepts of privacy breach and privacy harm within a public policy context. This is especially true in an era of Wiki-leaks where citizens are increasingly worried about the capability of government security agencies to gather personal information about their own citizens, and trade secrets in other countries.

LEARNING OUTCOMES

By the end of this course, students should be able to synthesize and apply what they have learned through the following learning outcomes:

1) Students will engage in analysis of case studies, legal doctrines, and pertinent legislation, as well as debates and dialogue to assess whether traditional law is applicable in situations involving unprecedented online contexts. In other words, we will ask whether the law has kept up with the public policy needs of a digital society, and the extent to which we need to rethink existing legislative frameworks, legal tests, and doctrines. This is particularly important given public pressure on legislators to bring in harsher laws and penalties to deal with online behaviors that are difficult to monitor or manage. Calls for improved laws and demands for clear and effective policies increase when children and youth are involved.

2) Students will also be introduced to scholarly research and multidisciplinary academic discourse that argues against laws that target online abuse. A number of legal scholars and academics in education, psychology, sociology, and related fields of study, argue for public policies that focus on improved public education, critical legal literacy, critical media, and digital literacy. They suggest that new laws will not control or prevent negative online behaviors and may in fact censor online expression and limit access to valuable online resources.

3) Students will be equipped with contextual knowledge on how public policy relating to emerging technologies is developed and how it in turn shapes legal responses. For example, they will examine the historical trajectory and influence of public debates and dialogues that have resulted in contemporary laws or legislative amendments since the advent of new technologies and the Internet. They will consider how these new laws and landmark judicial decisions might in turn shape policy at public institutions.

4) A unit will also be dedicated to critical media literacy and the role of the news media in perpetrating moral panics that can, in turn, influence laws and resulting public policy.

This knowledge will be enhanced as students gain the ability to:

1) Research, interpret, and analyze case studies and the legal skills they are learning in their law programs to identify competing stakeholder rights and interests in diverse on-and offline public policy contexts.
2) Find the links and compatibilities between the scholarly literature and theories on the role of technology and law in public policy contexts to assess the relevance and applicability of both positivist (culpability, accountability) and substantive (human rights, constitutional) laws.
3) Consider the impact of law on children and teens who are growing immersed in digital media ("digital natives") who rarely differentiate between on- and offline boundaries and consider ways to enhance legal literacy among them.
4) Develop non-arbitrary public policies drawing on ethical, educational, and legally defensible standards and legal practices.

COURSE REQUIREMENTS AND EVALUATION

1) Case Study Analysis and Develop Public Policy Guidelines 30%

This will be presented in class individually.

- Students will identify a case study involving negative use of online communication
- Prepare a case brief
- Select applicable legal frameworks for the legal issues in question
- Identify key public policy concerns
- Identify relevant legislation, if any
- Examine public policy trajectory relating to the public policy concerns
- Identify key stakeholders impacted and those most active
- News media framing of issues, media influence on stakeholders, if applicable
- Evaluate competing rights and interests and weigh the pros and cons of new legislation or amending legislation
- Develop public policy guidelines that best address the issues and best benefit stakeholders in the case

Note: You can bring in a video or media report of the case if it is well known.

2) Moot Court Presentation: Legal and Public Policy Considerations 30%

Students will also take part in a Moot Court presentation (with 5–6 people depending on class enrolment) on a digital/social media topic that involves a legal and public policy challenge. The objective is to consider policy and legal practice approaches on a controversial public policy issue that might result in litigation.

- FACTS of the case: Highlight the social issue and/or political context/issue
- ISSUES: Why is the public policy controversial (e.g., considered unconstitutional)?
- STAKEHOLDER PERSPECTIVE: Group members can represent various stakeholder perspectives and argue for or against the public policy
- REASONS FOR JUDGMENT: Write up the reasons for judgment
- JUDGMENT: Write up the judgment and highlight key aspects that will shape and inform a new public policy (or retain the same one)

Make sure you take into account judicial assumptions about particular stake-holders' norms, needs, rights, and interests.

3) Final Research Paper 40%

Students will write a research paper on law, technology, and a public policy issue of their choice. The research paper should be a maximum of ten pages double-spaced. The paper should be properly referenced and include online resources, and be well-organized, cohesive, and coherent. The paper should connect issues covered in class and reference at least six online journal articles; six recent books or online scholarly blogs and/or media debates, policy briefs or reports, relevant case law, and statutes. Websites, videos, and other relevant material should also be referenced.

The research paper is due last day of classes.

NOTE: University values academic integrity. Therefore, all students must understand the meaning and consequences of cheating, plagiarism, and other academic offenses under the Code of Student Conduct and Discipline Procedures.

Students are allowed to submit papers in French. I will mark them for content and if you require marking for grammar I will have another faculty member review them.

READINGS AND RESOURCES

The reading and references that go with each lesson are listed below. Relevant articles/readings will be available on My Courses.

GUEST SPEAKERS

I will try to arrange for guest speakers during the term (policy makers, judges, school principals, and technology experts in the field, for example)

CLASS AND READING SCHEDULE

Week 1: Introduction to Public Policy

- Introductions
- Overview of course and evaluation
- Timelines for scheduling of assignments and group presentations
- What is "public policy"?
- Definitions of public policy
- Does law inform public policy or does public policy inform the law?

Class Activity

What kinds of public policies come to mind when you think about technologies, social media, and digital communication?

Week 2: Public Policy Debate on Cyberbullying

- What is cyberbullying and why is it so difficult to define?
- Defining cyberbullying in legal terms and applicable legal frameworks
- What are some current public policy debates relating to cyberbullying?
- What are the relevant legal frameworks involved?

Readings

- Prensky, M. (2001) Digital Natives, digital immigrants part 1. *On the Horizon,* 9 (5), 1–6.
- Tapscott, D. (2009). *Grown up digital: How the net generation is changing your world.* New York: McGraw Hill. chapter 2.
- Shariff, S. (in progress). Chapter 1 of new book with Cambridge University Press.

Class Activity

Students will be provided with hypothetical scenarios and presented with two Cartesian plains (moral and legal) depicting different stakeholders. Students will be asked to place the scenario in the quadrant belonging to the stakeholder they believe should be held responsible for the actions of the child in their hypothetical situation. Their placements will determine whether a law or policy has been breached.

Week 3: Institutional Obligations to Provide Safe Environments

- What are the legal obligations of public institutions to provide safe environments for learning and working?
- Which legal framework is most suited to this? Human rights, constitutional, criminal? How and why?
- What types of policies have resulted from case law regarding safe environments (physical and virtual)?

- Public policy guidelines to navigate a balance between free expression and safety in online environments

Readings
- *Tinker v. Des Moines Independent Community School District*, 393 U.S. 503 (1969).
- *Robichaud v. Canada (Treasury Board)*, 2 S.R.C. 84 (1987).
- *Davis v. Monroe County Board of Educ.*, 526 US 629.
- *Bill 56 – Quebec Ministry of Education – Law 12.*
- *Flanagan v. Canton Cent. Sch. Dist.*, 871 N.Y.S.2d 775 (App. Div. 2009).
- *Kara Kowalski v. Berkeley County Schools, et al.* (4th Cir. July 2011).

Class Activity
1) *Discussion of* **Tinker** *– why is it still relevant 40 years later?*
2) *Students will be presented with cases relating to institutional environments. Groups can develop a public policy based on the court decisions to ensure the policy does not breach legal provisions. Bring an existing institutional policy to class for this discussion to assess whether it complies with relevant laws.*
3) *Student presentations of Assignment 1 (*** number of presentations to be determined depending on enrolment).*

Week 4: Balancing Privacy Breach, Privacy Harm, and Freedom of the Press

- Ryan Calo's paper on subjective and objective privacy harm (as opposed to privacy breach)
- Do we need new definitions of privacy in an online context?
- How do we legislate privacy protections when governments have the ability to spy on its citizens and may, in fact, be doing so?
- To what extent should freedom of the press be limited? Can the limits be clearly defined? What kinds of public policies exist in Canada? How do they differ from those of the United States?

Readings
- Calo, R. (2011). "The Boundaries of Privacy Harm." *86 Ind L.J.* 1131.
- Electronic Frontier Foundation, *Jewel v. National Security Agency* (copy of complaint) (2008). www.eff.org/files/filenode/jewel/jewel.complaint.pdf.
- *Carolyn Jewel v. National Security Agency* (2011). Retrieved from cdn.ca9.uscourts.gov/datastore/opinions/2011/12/29/10-15616.pdf.
- *AB v. Bragg Communications Inc.*, 2010 NSSC 215 at paras 25, 28–34.
- *AB v. Bragg Communications Inc.*, 2011 NSCA 26 at paras 42–43, 90–100.
- *AB v. Bragg Communications Inc.*, 2012 SCC 46.
- Shariff, S., Wiseman, A., & Crestohl, L. (2012). Defining the Lines between Children's Vulnerability to Cyberbullying and the Open Court Principle: Implications of *A.B. v. Bragg Communications Inc. Education and Law Journal.* Vol. 21.3. Carswell.

Class Activity
Presentations of Assignment 1 and discussion

Week 5: Where is the Policy Line Between Free Expression and Censorship?

• Constitutional law as a balancing act – rights are not absolute

Readings
• Retter, C. (2013, Jan 8). *Are cyberposts protected speech under the first amendment?* Retrieved from http://definetheline.ca/dtl/are-cyberposts-protected-speech-under-the-first-amendment/.
• *Morse v. Frederick, 551 U.S. (2007).*
• *Hazelwood School District et al. v. Kuhlmeier et al.*, 484 U.S. 260 (1988).
• *R. v. Oakes* (1986) 1 S. C. R. 103.
• *PFLAG et al. v. Camdenton R-III School et al.* (2012). Retrieved from www.aclu.org/files/assets/camdenton_decision.pdf.
• Myers, J. J. "Untangling the Confusion involving Public School Censorship" in Responding to Cyberbullying (2011), Corwin. www.sagepub.com/upm-data/39416_Myers_Responding_to_Cyber_Bullying___Ch1.pdf.
• *Lovell by and through Lovell v. Poway Unified School District*, 90 F.3d 367 (9th Cir. 1996).

Class Activity
1) *Students will receive a hypothetical or actual case involving censorship. They will attempt to agree on the invisible line between free expression and censorship and draft the wording for a policy that meets that line.*
2) *Presentations of Assignment 1 by 2–3 students.*

Week 6: Rape Culture, High School and University Policy Related to Sexualized on- and offline Expression

• St. Mary's University rap video during frosh week and UBC's response to FROSH week sexism
• Miley Cyrus and online/offline vitriolic responses
• Amanda Todd and Jane Doe suicides
• Maple Ridge and Steubenville rape cases and their respective criminal responses (application of child pornography and assault laws)
• Emerging provincial laws (e.g., *Cyber-safety Act*, Nova Scotia)
• Do these postings come under criminal and child pornography laws? *Should* they?

Readings
• Albury, K. & Crawford, K. (2012). Sexting, consent and young people's ethics: Beyond Megan's Story. Continuum: Journal of Media and Cultural Studies.

- Toronto Star. (2013) "After [Jane Doe] death, Nova Scotia introduces legislation to fight cyberbullying." Retrieved from www.torontosun.com/2013/04/25/after-rehtaeh-parsons-death-nova-scotia-introduces-legislation-to-fight-cyberbullying.
- Graeme Hamilton (2012). "Amanda Todd and the greatly exaggerated cyberbullying plague: Web harassment not on the rise, researcher says." National Post. Retrieved from http://news.nationalpost.com/2012/10/26/amanda-todd-and-the-greatly-exaggerated-cyber-bullying-plague-web-harassment-isnt-rising-researcher-says/.
- CTV News (2012). "Probation in Rave Rape Case Called a Slap on the Wrist". Retrieved from http://bc.ctvnews.ca/probation-in-rave-rape-case-called-a-slap-on-the-wrist-1.766872.
- Almasy, S. (2013). "Two teens found guilty in Steubenville rape case." CNN. www.cnn.com/2013/03/17/justice/ohio-steubenville-case/.
- Richards, R. D. & Calvert, C. (2009). When Sex and Cell Phones Collide: Inside the Prosecution of a Teen Sexting Case. *Hastings Communication and Entertainment Law Journal*. HeinOnline.
- Bill 61 (Nova Scotia *Cyber-safety Act*), 2013.
- *Civil Code of Quebec*, Art 1459.

Class Activity
Are child pornography laws appropriate for defining sexting as a form of cyberbullying? How will these laws shape policies on teenagers who engage in this kind of online behavior? Does the Cyber-safety Act go too far in holding parents liable?

Week 7: Private (TORT) Law and Defamation

- Where is the line between gossip, rumors, and defamation on social media sites?
- If you were Facebook what kinds of policies would you put in place regarding the blurred legal boundaries relating to this type of speech?
- How can we address unfair comments, malicious comments that are untrue, and malicious comments that are true?
- What does the common law say about how educational institutions might address defamatory gossip and rumors?
- What is McGill's policy on this kind of speech?
- What protections does this policy afford those victimized?
- What remedies are available at the university level?

Readings
- *Civil Code of Quebec*, art. 1457, 1459, 1460.
- Wiseman, A. (2013). *The digital age and fault: Exploring the moral and generational gap.*
- Danay, R. (2010). The medium is not the message: Reconciling reputation and free expression in cases of Internet defamation. *McGill Law Journal*. Vo. 56, n.1, 1–37.

- Review *AB v. Bragg Communications Inc.*, 2012 SCC 46.
- *Newman et al. v. Halstead et al.*, 2006 BCSC 65.

Class Activity
Bring to class two different university policies that touch upon defamation. Compare them – what are their similarities and differences? Does one address the issue better? Why?

Develop a university policy that specifically addresses rumors and gossip on social media and consequences for defamatory online speech.

Week 8: Role of Media in Shaping Public Policy

- What is the role of media in shaping laws that ultimately result in changing public policy or vice versa?
- Discussions of moral panic, fear, lobbying, and pressure on government to develop reactive laws
- What are the legal limits on sensational news media reporting that mislead the public?
- What policies exist on the need for sensitive media reporting in cases of suicide linked to online abuse?

Readings
- Thom, K., Edwards, G., Nakarada-Kordic, I., McKenna, B., O'Brien, A., & Nairn, Raymond (2011). Suicide online: Portrayal of website-related suicide by the New Zealand media. *New Media & Society*, 13: 8, 1355–1372.
- Corbo, A. M. & Zweifel, K. L. (2013). Sensationalism or sensitivity: Reporting suicide cases in news media. *Studies in Communication Sciences*, 13: 1, 67–74.
- Pew Research Journalism Project. Principles of Journalism, www.journalism.org/resources/principles-of-journalism/.
- CBC Radio-Canada. Journalistic standards and practices. www.cbc.radio-canada.ca/en/reporting-to-canadians/acts-and-policies/programming/journalism/.
- World Health Organization (2012). Preventing Suicide: A Resource for Media Professionals. www.who.int/mental_health/prevention/suicide/resource_media.pdf.
- *Canadian Broadcasting Corp. v. New Brunswick (Attorney General)*, [1996] 3 S.C.R. 480.
- *AB v. Bragg Communications Inc.*, 2012 SCC 46.

Class Activity
1) *Analyze news media reports and discuss*
2) *Remaining student presentations for Assignment 1*

Week 9: Corporate Responsibility and Social Media

- Why don't corporate intermediaries take down offensive online expression right away?
- Discussion of social media policies – Facebook, Google, Tumblr, Twitter, etc.
- Discussion of case law relating to corporate responsibility

Readings

- *Zeran v. America Online, Inc.*, 129 F.3d 327 (4th Cir. 1997).
- Bernstein, A. & Ramchandani, R. (2002). Don't Shoot the Messenger! A Discussion of ISP Liability, *Canadian Journal of Law and Technology*, 2(1).

Class Activity

Bring ISP policies to class and discuss. Use your understanding of the issues (i.e., sexting, bullying, etc.) to determine whether these policies are doing enough. Were the policies easy to find? Are they written in plain language?

You are the lawyer for Facebook (or one of the other large corporate intermediaries). You have been asked to redraft their policies to provide a safe platform and avoid lawsuits because they are increasing in number. However, you are told not to compromise, under any circumstances, the company's ability to gather information about its users and publicly share it as they wish. How would you begin to develop this policy?

Week 10: Should Laws and Policies that Address Digital Communications be Different for Adults and for Kids?

- Adult modeling of on- and offline abuse, etc.
- How does the reasonable child standard complicate our understanding of cyberbullying and consequences for engaging in cyberbullying activity?
- Are our reasonableness standards changing? Should they be?
- Will the *Youth Criminal Justice Act* help to reduce the harsh impact of the *Safe Streets and Communities Act* on teenagers if they are convicted of cyberbullying under new laws?

Readings

- Praagh, S.V. (2007). Emerging Issues in Tort Law. In Neyers, J.W., Chamberlain, E., & Pitel, S. G. A. (Eds.) Chapter 3: 'Sois Sage'- Responsibility for Childishness in the Law of the Civil Wrongs. (p.63–84) Oxford and Portland, Oregon: Hart Publishing.
- Re-read: Wiseman, A. (2013). *The digital age and fault: Exploring the moral and generational gap.*
- *McHale v. Watson* (1966) HCA 13. (***used to understand reasonable child standard)

- Canadian Bar Association. Submission on Bill C-10 (*Safe Streets and Communities Act*). www.cba.org/cba/submissions/PDF/11-45-eng.pdf. (***pages to be determined)
- Perrin, B. (2011). "The government's omnibus crime bill is not draconian". National Post. http://fullcomment.nationalpost.com/2011/09/28/benjamin-perrin-the-governments-omnibus-crime-bill-is-not-draconian/.

Class Activity
Think of scenarios where the law might be unfair to children if applied in the same way as it is for adults.

Week 11–13: Group Presentations

- Group presentations (depending on enrollment these may start earlier in the semester)
- Guest speakers (or guests may be incorporated with relevant units)

Index